The Cantor

The Cantor

From the Mishnah to Modernity

WAYNE ALLEN

Foreword by Charles Heller

WIPF & STOCK · Eugene, Oregon

THE CANTOR
From Mishnah to Modernity

Wipf & Stock
An Imprint of Wipf and Stock Publishers
199 W. 8th Ave., Suite 3
Eugene, OR 97401

www.wipfandstock.com

PAPERBACK ISBN: 978-1-5326-5830-3
HARDCOVER ISBN: 978-1-5326-5831-0
EBOOK ISBN: 978-1-5326-5832-7

Manufactured in the U.S.A.   MAY 8, 2019

This book is dedicated to the cantors who have helped bring this book to publication—the Midwest Region of the Cantors Assembly (Matan Meital, Alberto Mizrahi, Rachel Rosenberg, Pavel Roytman, Jeremy Stein, Scott Simon, Steven Stoehr, Ben Tisser, and Roger Weisberg, all of who have sponsored this publication in honor of their membership), the leadership of the Cantor's Assembly, the Cantor's Assembly Foundation, the Toronto Council of Hazzanim and co-presidents Cantor Marshall Loomer and Cantor Eric Moses, and the Toronto Cantorial Trust Fund, Cantor A. Eliezer Kirshblum, Chairman, for their substantial support.

These distinguished cantors understand full well that the cantorate is not like any other occupation. It is, as Rabbenu Asher ben Yehiel called it, "a crown." I commend these cantors for wearing the crown well and for their commitment to bringing the story of the office of the cantor to a wide readership.

May all these cantors and their colleagues everywhere continue in their valued service to the Jewish community.

Contents

Foreword

OVER A PERIOD OF almost two thousand years, the role of the synagogue cantor developed into an art form unique in the world. While preserving traditional liturgy, the cantor expressed himself with the highest artistic standards of musical composition and vocal performance, and also with improvisation that grips the attention of worshippers. Yet now, at the beginning of the 21st century, this treasured position of synagogue cantor is on the edge of extinction due to neglect and ignorance on the part of the lay public, combined with willful opposition from synagogue leaders. It is against this background that Rabbi Allen reveals the remarkable history and nature of *hazzanut*, cantorial art, through the words and opinions of community leaders and rabbis over the millennia.

A key element revealed in Rabbi Allen's book is the creative tension between artistic innovations of the cantor and legal requirements of the rabbis, the guardians of tradition. Intriguingly, the innovations of cantors changed musical tastes which, in turn, allowed for rabbinic accommodations. This creative tension is indeed the key to understanding the unique nature of cantorial music, which musicologist Eric Werner called "stylized folk music"—a combination of traditional folk music and sophisticated artistic expression that has no parallel in other forms of folk music.

This book will be of great interest and value to all who cherish the cantor's art.

CHARLES HELLER is on the editorial board of *The Journal of Synagogue Music*, and is the award-winning author of *What To Listen For in Jewish Music* (www.ecanthuspress.com).

Preface

Two interests motivated the writing of this book: my lifelong appreciation for *hazzanut* (cantorial arts) and my curiosity regarding the evolution of Jewish custom. Growing up at a time and place when some of the great cantors were still in vogue—though not necessarily in their prime—I had the privilege of hearing in person Moshe Koussevitzky (1899–1965), his younger brother David Koussevitzky (d. 1985), and Shmuel Vigoda (1893–1990). I would soon as listen to recordings of Yossele Rosenblatt (1882–1933) and Leibele Waldman (1907–1969) as the Beatles. Later, I even had the merit of serving as the rabbi of the synagogue in which Leibele's son Harvey was the cantor: Congregation B'nai Jeshurun, Staten Island, New York. And later still, as the rabbi of Beth Tikvah Synagogue, Toronto, I had the privilege and the pleasure of working with Srul Irving Glick (1934–2002) of blessed memory, a master composer of Jewish music, and son of a cantor of considerable talent. More than anyone else, it was Srul Glick who opened my eyes to the manifold ways that music can affect prayer.

Hazzanut, to me, is soul music. It evokes within me some powerful feelings that no doubt contributed to my passion for the Jewish tradition and my decision to become a rabbi. It was through my rabbinical and philosophical studies that I became particularly interested in the development of custom. My master's degree in philosophy was a study in the origins of custom in secular sources. Previously, I had been both perturbed and surprised by the plasticity of custom in Jewish law and practice. As I came to more intensely study the latter, I saw consistent overlap with the former. To put it differently, I came to realize that many of the rules regarding cantors (or the exceptions to the rules) developed as concessions to custom. This book, therefore, is partly the result of my quest to understand why. And while a more comprehensive and specific study of custom, its origins, and development and connection with Jewish law must be reserved for a future study—please God—I believe that readers of this volume will gain some valuable insights into the topic.

To be clear, this book is not about cantors, but about the cantor: the position, not those who filled the position. As such, my approach is phenomenological, not biographical. There are many fine works available on the biographies of the great cantors, some of whom will be mentioned in passing. Those interested in learning more about the great cantors would do well to consult these works. This book, however, explores the origins of the office and ways in which the office evolved, sometimes under rabbinic constraint and sometimes beyond. The careful reader would further note that the office of cantor has grown organically, responding to the changes and challenges in synagogue life.

Furthermore, while much of this book focuses on Jewish law, it is not a book about Jewish law *per se*. My intention is not to offer a comprehensive disquisition on the laws of the cantor or to resolve halakhic disputes or to issue legal rulings. Rather, the selections included are intended to function as examples of the variety and range of issues related to the office of cantor as it developed historically in order to trace its evolution.

The value of this book, I contend, lies in two areas. It may provide a better understanding of the history of an important communal position. Hence, it can serve as a tool for accessing the past. It also helps to lay the groundwork for assessing the future. It is to these tasks that I turn.

Acknowledgments

I WISH TO ACKNOWLEDGE a select group of people who have helped bring this book to publication. My colleague, David Golinkin, who shares my interest in the development of the office of the cantor, suggested how best to proceed when I was first considering the idea for this book. As always, his insights were particularly useful. And his book recommendations were instrumental in allowing me to discover earlier treatments of the subject. I also acknowledge another colleague, Elliot Gertel, who provided me with valuable comments that improved this work. He also brought to my attention sources I had not previously known were available. There are few rabbis like him who have both breadth of traditional Jewish learning and a thorough grasp of popular culture and history.

Joe Levine was enthusiastic about this project from the first time I shared my interest with him. He was determined to find ways to bring this book to publication and I am happy that his determination has been rewarded. I always appreciated his encouragement.

I must give special thanks to my colleague, Michael Brown, who, when asked only to review an early version of the manuscript for suggestions, voluntarily took on the task of combing the manuscript for inconsistencies, correcting grammar and spelling, and pointing out passages that needed clarification or explanation. His guidance, scholarship, and expertise were invaluable in bringing this book to completion. I am indebted to him for the time and effort he generously gave to my project. I may not have followed all his advice, but I certainly took everything he said into serious consideration. If there are any remaining errors or if any passages seem unclear, it is certainly not due to Michael's careful scrutiny.

I also acknowledge one of my most ardent supporters and my most careful reader, Marcus Bornfreund. His keen eye and attention to detail keep me sharp. I am blessed to call him my son-in-law. Marcus has passed on that same attentiveness to his son and my grandson, Solomon Bornfreund, who takes words and their meaning seriously. At the age of seven he is an old soul. He delights in finding Sabba's errors and I delight that he has the ability to find them.

Lastly, I acknowledge my wife, Patti, for her forbearance, understanding, and grace. Writing this book while teaching full-time required taking time that could have been given to other activities. More often than not, she was the one who had to deal with my absence, mostly without complaint. I appreciate her more and more every day.

Abbreviations of Scripture and Other Ancient Sources

SCRIPTURE ABBREVIATIONS

Hebrew Bible

Gen	Genesis
Exod	Exodus
Lev	Leviticus
Num	Numbers
Deut	Deuteronomy
1–2 Sam	First/Second Samuel
1–2 Kgs	First/Second Kings
Isa	Isaiah
Jer	Jeremiah
Ezek	Ezekiel
Hos	Hosea
Zeph	Zephaniah
Mal	Malachi
Pss	Psalms
Prov	Proverbs
Song	Song of Songs
Lam	Lamentations
Eccl	Ecclesiastes
Dan	Daniel
Neh	Nehemiah
1–2 Chr	First/Second Chronicles

New Testament

Matt	Matthew

OTHER ANCIENT SOURCES

Tractates of Mishnah and Talmud

Ber.	Berakhot
Ter.	Terumot
Bik.	Bikkurim
Shev.	Shevi'it
Sab.	Sabbath
Eruv.	Eruvin
Pes.	Pesahim
Suk.	Sukkah
R.H.	Rosh Hashanah
Ta'an.	Ta'anit
Meg.	Megillah
M.K.	Mo'ed Katan
Hag.	Hagigah
Yev.	Yevamot
Ket.	Ketubot
Sot.	Sotah
Git	Gittin
Kid.	Kiddushin
B. Kam.	Bava Kamma
B. Metz.	Bava Metzia
San.	Sanhedrin
Mak.	Makkot
A. Z.	Avodah Zarah
Men.	Menahot
Hul.	Hullin
Bekh.	Bekhorot
Arkh.	Arakhin
Tam.	Tamid
Sof.	Soferim

b. preceding a tractate indicates Babylonian Talmud
y. preceding a tractate indicates Jerusalem Talmud

Tosef.	Tosefta

Midrashim

Mid. Tan.	Midrash Tanhuma
ARN	Avot D'Rabbi Natan
Pesiq.	Pesiqta Rabbati
PDK	Pesikta D'Rav Kahana
Yalk	Yalkut Shimoni

Later Rabbinic Sources

Tos.	Tosafot
Tos. Y.	Tosafot Yashanim
MT	Mishneh Torah
OH	Orah Hayyim

Introduction

IT SHOULD NOT BE surprising that the cantor—as a professional or as a skilled amateur charged with leading communal prayer services among other duties—is a relatively late development in Jewish history.[1] The position of cantor itself, let alone the qualities of any person who might occupy the position, has also remained controversial since its inception. Prior to considering the controversial nature of the cantor as an official religious functionary, some explanation for the relatively late emergence of the position of cantor is in order.

Jewish communal prayer itself is a relatively late development. Biblical prayer consisted of either individualized prayer (that is, spontaneous prayer recited by a solitary worshiper in response to a specific circumstance and limited to that circumstance), or institutionalized prayer, (that is, prayer recited as part of a ceremony or pageant). Examples of individualized prayer include Abraham's prayer for the restored fertility of Avimelekh and his household (Gen 20:17); Moses' prayer for the recovery of his sister, Miriam (Num 12:13); David's confessional prayer (2 Sam 24:10); and Daniel's supplication (Dan 9:4–5, 17–18). Examples of institutionalized prayer include the Song at the Sea (Exod 15:1–21);[2]

1. There have been attempts, however, to date the institution of the cantor to the prophetic period or shortly thereafter, cf. Finkelstein, "Origin of the Synagogue," 59; Max Kadushin also writes: "Nonsacrificial worship, in its various forms, was developed after the period of the prophets" (*Worship and Ethics*, 287n7) meaning, following the conclusion of the period of the prophets, i.e., in the sixth-century BCE. However, evidence for both views is lacking.

2. Irene Heskes, in "Miriam's Sisters," argues that in leading the refrain of the Song of the Sea, Miriam performed a "significant communal ritual function" (1193). Accordingly, she may be the biblical precedent for the role of the cantor (as well as the precedent for women as cantors). However, unlike another Jewish woman—Hannah—whose attentiveness in prayer was applauded by the rabbis (*b. Ber.* 31a) and seen as a precedent for the intentionality and inwardness required of all Jews in prayer—neither

the Priestly Blessing (Num 6:22–27); the covenantal ceremony at Mount Gerizim (Deut 27:11–26); the septennial reading of the Torah to the assembled nation (Deut 31:10–12); and the public affirmation of the Torah for returning exiles (Neh 8:5–8). Of all institutionalized prayer, only the septennial Torah reading recurs. Neither form of prayer was communal in the sense that Jews understand the term today (i.e., a standardized liturgy cyclically recited within a defined community and regulated by set rules).

While the Mishnah[3] attests to an early example of communal prayer, there is no evidence that any Jews other than the *kohanim* (priests) in temple service followed a pattern of communal prayer. For the ordinary Jew, worship was participating in the sacrificial ritual while listening to the Levitical choir and orchestration of the Psalms. Communal prayer in its fullest sense only emerged after the destruction of Solomon's Temple, when the sacrificial cult could not be observed and synagogues[4] came to replace the Temple and prayer came to replace sacrifices.

The precise origins of the synagogue are obscure. Abraham Millgram postulates a "plausible conjecture."[5] The aftermath of the destruction of Solomon's Temple left a "religious void." A new type of religious experience was needed to fill the void. But any new form of worship that the exiles could devise would imply the "abolition of the divinely ordained sacrificial ritual of the Temple."[6] Accordingly, Jews gathered informally and periodically for mutual encouragement. Ultimately, these gatherings developed into a permanent religious institution. Some prophetic texts offer evidence for this conjecture. Writing to the Babylonian exiles, Jeremiah (29:12) advises them to gather together and "pray" unto God who will hear them even outside the temple precincts. And the elders approach Ezekiel in Babylonia "to inquire of God" (Ezek 20:1–3, 27, 30).

Miriam nor Deborah served as a similar precedent. To the rabbis, who were not averse to citing a woman as a precedent in matters of prayer, it would seem that Miriam led a spontaneous exultation, not standardized, communal prayer.

3. *m. Tam.* 5:1.

4. To be precise, the proper terms for a building set aside for Jewish prayer is *proseuche* or *eucheion.* "Synagogue," from the Greek for "collection," refers to a group of Jews who are empowered to make communal decisions and, later, to the gathered Jewish community. A papyrus from the first century BCE neatly makes the distinction: "At the session [*synagoges*] held in the *proseuche*." Cf. Feldman, "Diaspora Synagogues," 50.

5. Millgram, *Jewish Worship*, 64.

6. Millgram, *Jewish Worship*, 64.

Diaspora synagogues, it seems, initially[7] became places for the faithful to gather and pray. It is reasonable to assume that priests—those once authorized to conduct sacrificial rituals—led prayer at this time.[8]

While the number of synagogues proliferated,[9] the content of the service in the synagogue remained amorphous and fluid. While it is possible that the first-century-CE Theodotus inscription omitting any reference to prayer in the synagogue he built may be ascribed to its proximity to the temple (his synagogue was located in Jerusalem), it is just as likely to reflect the fact that communal prayer had not yet been standardized.[10] What is clear, however, is that the public reading of the Torah was essential to early synagogue ritual.[11] And it is in this context that the title *hazzan* first appears.[12]

The talmudic tradition credits the body of scholars assembled by Ezra with the first attempts to compose communal prayer. But while

7. But synagogues were not exclusively places for prayer. Cf. Levine, "Second Temple Synagogue," 14–15 for a list of other activities.

8. Ezekiel himself was a priest (Ezek 1:3). Cf. also Levi, *Yesodot Tefilah*, 86, who writes: "During the days of the Second Commonwealth, as new congregations were founded throughout Israel, education and guidance, particularly prayer, was in the hands of the priests."

9. Cf. *b. Ket.* 105a: "Rabbi Pinhas in the name of Rabbi Hoshaya stated that there were 394 courts of law . . . in Jerusalem and an equal number of synagogues . . ." The Jerusalem Talmud disagrees, putting the number at 460 synagogues (*y. Ket.* 8:1) or 480 (*y. Meg.* 3:1). In any case, by the third century, the number of synagogues in Jerusalem alone had mushroomed.

10. Cf. Shinan, "Synagogues in the Land," 143, where prayer in the early synagogues is described as "variegated, flexible, and changing." It is also noteworthy that there is no text of any synagogue prayer datable to the Second Temple (Levine, "Second Temple Synagogue," 19). And there is no reference to crystallized prayer in any of the Qumran material. While absence of evidence is not evidence of absence, it is a fact that cannot be discounted.

11. Cf., for example, Josephus, "Against Apion," 803. Cf. also Levine, "Second Temple Synagogue," 17. Also, Shinan, "Synagogues in the Land," 131.

12. See *m. Yoma* 7:1; *m. Sot* 7:7; *Tosef. Meg.* 3:21, Lieberman, *Tosefta Kifshuta*, 359; Emanuel, *Teshuvot Ha-Ge'onim Ha-Hadashot*, No. 34. The *hazzan* was also charged with other functions: teaching small children (*m. Sot.* 9:15; *y. Sab.* 1:3), preparing the guilty for corporal punishment (*m. Mak.* 3:12), blowing trumpets (*Tosef. Suk.* 4:11, 12), and making public service announcements (*ARN* 35). The use of the title *hazzan* to describe a prayer leader cannot be dated earlier than the third century CE (Cf. *y. Ber.* 9:1, 12d). Later, authorities assumed that the early *hazzan* was assigned general custodial duties as well (Cf. Rabbi Ovadiah MiBertinoro, Commentary on *m. Sot.* 7:7; ben Yehiel, *She'lot U'Teshuvot Rabbenu Asher* 5:17; Karelitz, *Hazon Ish*, Hashmatot, No. 217:7).

a third-century authority asserts that: "The Men of the Great Assembly . . . instituted for Israel blessings and prayers, sanctifications and separations,"[13] the precise wording of those prayers goes unstated. And Rabbi Yohanan's pronouncement that "a hundred and twenty elders, among whom were many prophets, drew up eighteen blessings in a fixed order,"[14] only adds a modest clarification. It is highly likely that the impetus for standardizing communal prayer grew out of a response to the destruction of the Second Temple and the reorganization of Judaism under the leadership of Rabban Yohanan ben Zakkai and the scholars at Yavneh.[15] This is not to say that some form of communal prayer did not predate the destruction of the Second Temple. Gedalyahu Alon[16] points to the dispute between the disciples of first-century-BCE scholars Hillel and Shammai recorded in Tosefta *Rosh Hashanah* (4:11) that shows that while the precise number of blessings to be recited on the Sabbath that coincides with holidays is in question, the first three and last three blessings of the *Amidah* were not. But the destruction of the Second Temple accelerated the process of formalization and standardization. To compensate for the absence of the sacrificial cult, the rabbis emphasized the study of Torah, the performance of meritorious acts, and especially prayer.[17] By the end of the first century CE, the synagogue liturgy had, for the most part, taken solid shape. The final consolidation of communal prayer is credited to the authoritarian leadership and deliberate effort of Rabban Gamliel II.[18] Thus, in the second century, Rabbi Nathan imagines God saying: "If a man occupies himself with the study of Torah and with good works and prays with the congregation, I account it to him as if he had redeemed Me and My children from among the nations of the

---

13. *b. Ber.* 33a.

14. *b. Meg.* 17b.

15. Cf. I. Weiss, *Dor Dor v'Dorshav*, 67.

16. Alon, *Jews in Their Land*, 1:167–68.

17. Cf. *m. Avot* 1:2; *b. Ta'an.* 2a; *b. Ber.* 32b; *Mid. Tan.*, Ki Tavo 1.

18. Rabban Gamliel II makes three daily prayer services incumbent on every Jew, commissions the last blessing to the *Amidah*, and insists on the uniform calendrical calculation of the holidays to ensure conformity in prayer. Cf. *m. Ber.* 4:3; *m. R.H.* 2:8–9; *b. Ber.* 26b, 28b. Thrice-daily prayer had substantially earlier roots. Daniel (6:11) customarily prayed three times daily. He was probably not alone. Cf. Melamed, *Pirke Minhag v'Halakhah*, 130–31.

world."[19] Communal prayer was invested with supreme value. It was also ruled mandatory.

Initially, rabbis alone were entrusted with leading communal prayer. The Talmud recounts how second-century authorities like Rabbi Akiva,[20] Rabbi Ilfa,[21] and Rabbi Abba Arekha[22] would lead prayer services. That rabbis would lead communal prayer is not surprising for two related reasons. First, the common folk were generally illiterate.[23] Until the establishment of the first school system by Rabbi Joshua ben Gamla in the first century CE, Hebrew literacy was entirely contingent on paternal fluency.[24] And even after local schools were founded and staffed, it would take several generations before the number of literate Jews would reach a threshold whereby general competency could be expected. Moreover, handwritten scrolls upon which the literate might rely were costly and rare. Besides, the very writing of blessings—the basic component of Jewish prayer—was prohibited.[25] Second, unlike common folk who were unreliable because their grasp of the Hebrew language was suspect and their familiarity with a recently finalized liturgy was uneven, rabbis had the expertise to be able to fulfill the obligation of communal prayer for others. In isolated communities not often served by resident rabbis, alternatives were necessary. Here again, it is likely[26] that the liturgical duties would by default fall to the *hazzan ha-kenesset*,[27] the synagogue caretaker, who was capable enough to teach children and read Torah, although others would be sought out in special circumstances. Mishnah *Ta'anit* (2:2), for example, recommends finding an elder to lead communal prayers convened to pray for rain during a drought.

19. *b. Ber.* 8a. The seventy daily sacrifices were previously considered to be redemptive.

20. *b. Ber.* 31a. The "inconvenience to the congregation" would result when he would prolong the service he was leading.

21. *b. Ta'an.* 24a.

22. *b. Ta'an.* 24a.

23. Harris, *Ancient Literacy,* 281–82 exposes what he calls "the mirage of mass literacy" in first-century Judaea. Rather than point to extensive literacy, the gospel accounts (Matt 12:3; 19:4; 21:42) only evidence textual expertise among the elite. Further, the implication of John 7:14–15 is that a person of Jesus' (low) social standing would not be expected to know how to read.

24. Cf. *b. B. Bat.* 21a.

25. *Tosef. Sab.,* 13:4; Lieberman, *Tosefta Kifshuta,* 58; *Mid. Tan.* Re'eh 12, Zundel, *Midrash Tanhuma,* 108.

26. Melamed, *Pirke Minhag v'Halakhah,* 138.

27. Cf., *m. Yoma* 7:1.

In time, a variety of common folk assumed the responsibility of leading prayer services[28] with mixed results.[29] So rules were established to ensure the quality of prayer leaders.[30] While the intent was to ensure the highest degree of worthiness, the consequence was to limit the role to the select few.[31] That few could match the stated requirements necessitated the acceptance of the best available man.[32] The tension between appointing the ideal prayer leader as required by law and conceding the position to the best available man has persisted since the fourth-century. Of course, the easiest resolution was to institutionalize the position of prayer leader, ensuring that the most qualified individual assumes the role permanently. Evidence shows that the position of a permanent cantor was in place by the second century.[33]

This brief historical account differs from previous accounts that date the emergence of the cantor to sometime between the sixth and eighth

28. Such as mule drivers and farmers (Cf. *y. Ta'an.* 1:4) and teachers of small children (*b. Ta'an.* 24a).

29. Cf. *b. Ber.* 34a; *b. Meg.* 24b; *y. Ber.* 9:1.

30. Cf., *b. Ta'an.* 16a.

31. *b. Ta'an.* 16a.

32. *y. Ta'an.* 2:2.

33. Cf. *b. Ta'an.* 24a; *y. Ber.* 9:1, 12d. (Both sources are cited below.) Idelsohn, *Jewish Music*; Landman, *Cantor*; and Sky, "Development of the Office," do not share my conclusion. Idelsohn concedes that while the qualifications of the cantor were fixed in the second century, the professionalization of the office cannot be dated earlier than the sixth or seventh-century (106, 107). But if by "professionalization" Idelsohn means "salaried," the earliest source that confirms the hiring of a paid cantor dates to the Geonic period, at least two hundred years later. And if "professionalization" implies a permanent position, then both the Babylonian and Jerusalem Talmud confirm such a circumstance at least four hundred years earlier. Landman asserts that the office of the *hazzan* ought to be dated to the sixth-century. But all his supportive sources (126n18) are adduced from the Tractate *Soferim* that cannot be dated that early (see below, Geonic Literature), making his dating of the emergence of the office far later than he intends and in striking contrast to the Talmudic sources. In his introduction, Sky writes that the office of the *hazzan* ought to be dated to the seventh or eighth-century, but later (172) massages the date to "before the beginning of the seventh-century." Even so, he does not take into account the sources I have cited. My conclusion is consistent with the view of Alon, who writes: "public congregational prayer already became part of life in the synagogue many generations before the Destruction [of the Second Temple in the year 70 CE]" (*Jews in Their Land*, 1:266). It is reasonable to believe that the office of *hazzan* would emerge in the next generations thereafter. The view of Burkholder et al. (*History of Western Music*, 238) that the appointment of a specific person to perform the chants of the Jewish liturgy as a cantor dates only to the sixteenth-century is preposterous.

centuries, linking it with a rise in persecution and with the development of *piyyut*[34] as a musical form and its integration into Jewish prayer. Leo Landman, following Abraham Zevi Idelsohn, maintains that in the period of anti-Jewish fervor of the sixth and seventh centuries, in Byzantine Christian, Persian, and Muslim territory, when centers of Jewish learning were under threat and sages were killed or suppressed, the resultant descent into ignorance required that a knowledgeable professional lead illiterate communities in prayer. They further maintain that the inclusion of the new and complex musical form of *piyyut* necessitated the skill of a professional, namely the cantor.[35]

But I believe they are mistaken on both points. While there was serious anti-Jewish sentiment in this time period—J. F. Haldon cites at least three major polemical treatises against Jews[36] written in this span—and Jews endured persecution under King Kavadh I (who reigned until 531 CE) and Hormizd IV (579–590 CE), this does not necessarily imply diminished Jewish literacy. Besides, schools of Jewish learning reopened in 589 CE. The persecutions were erratic and short-lived: unlikely to have caused the reversal in Jewish literacy that Idelsohn and Landman claim. They also seem to have dated the emergence of *piyyut* too early. The first to react to this new and controversial musical form were the Babylonian Geonim, whose responsa on the appropriateness of their inclusion in prayer dates to the ninth-century.[37] Idelsohn and Landman construe the emergence of the cantor as a reaction to crisis. However, the rabbinic sources tell a different story. It seems that the office of the cantor naturally evolved as standardized prayer grew increasingly complex and rabbinic requirements for reciting those prayers grew more exacting.

Controversy necessarily followed the emergence of the office of cantor. Initially, views diverged on questions regarding the proper qualifications of the cantor, with age being the chief among them. Rabbinic law considered a boy over thirteen an adult in all matters.[38] But the Mishnah insisted on a degree of maturity well beyond the minimum age.[39] The Geonim promoted the age of seventeen or eighteen (or perhaps even

.

34. See below.

35. Idelsohn, *Jewish Music*, 106; Landman, *Cantor*, 5.

36. Haldon, *Byzantium in the Seventh-century*, 347n72.

37. Cf. Levi, *Otzar Ha-Geonim*, 178–80.

38. *m. Avot.* 1:24.

39. *m. Meg*, 4:6; *m. Ta'an.* 4:6. See also *Tosef. Hag.* 1:3.

twenty[40]) as the minimum age of a cantor with the absolute lowest age of thirteen. Maimonides concurred with the minimum age of thirteen even though the youngster may not have grown a beard—a physical sign of maturity. Yet in fourteenth-century Spain, younger cantors were allowed to assume the office on occasion, with dissent from German and North African authorities of the same period. One thirteenth-century Italian authority attempted to reapply the Geonic standard of an older age for cantors thus leaving the entire matter unresolved.

While the question of the age of the cantor was the earliest controversy, it was not the only controversy, or even the most intense or persistent. In its interpretation of the Mishnah, the Talmud[41] asserts that two qualities of a suitable cantor are *beito reikam* (literally, that "his house is empty") and *pirko na'eh* (literally, that "his limb is becoming"). The latter expression seems to imply that the cantor must have no physical defect. Yet the Mishnah[42] rules that a blind man may lead the recital of *Shema*. The Geonim go further, allowing a blind man to lead all prayers and thus implying that blindness is no defect at all. However, thirteenth-century Spanish authority Rabbi Yom Tov ben Abraham[43] excludes a blind man from serving as a cantor, implying that blindness is indeed a defect. But in seventeenth-century Germany, a one-eyed cantor was deemed acceptable, thus suggesting that it is the absence of sight that concerned the Mishnah and not the absence of an eye. The one-eyed cantor has a physical defect, but not one that renders him excludable. Similarly, thirteenth-century German authority Rabbi Meir of Rothenberg rules that an armless cantor is acceptable. A missing limb is not a defect that renders the cantor excludable. And most remarkably—even counterintuitively—seventeenth-century rabbi Yair Bachrach rules that a deaf cantor is permitted to lead prayers, as hard as it may be to imagine how. And as late as the twentieth-century, scholars debated whether the infirmities of old age are a physical defect that would exclude a cantor from service.

The former expression—*beito reikam*—comes to be understood as "free of fault,"[44] that is, enjoying a good reputation, though RaShI ascribes

40. See *b. Sof.* 14:17.

41. *b. Ta'an.* 16a–b.

42. *m. Meg.* 4:6.

43. See below in full.

44. Following the interpretation of Sa'adiah Gaon, who understood the term to mean no past indiscretions. See below.

this quality to *pirko naeh*.[45] What kind of "fault" was intended (and thus disqualified a cantor from service or a candidate from appointment) has been subject to persistent dispute during the last eleven hundred years. The earliest fault was that of lateness. By the time of the Geonim, the number of cantors who suffered a lack of punctuality (thus diminishing the professionalization of the office) made a legal ruling necessary. The Geonim generously held that lateness was not a disqualifying fault even though it was surely a cause of communal dissatisfaction and frustration. The Geonim did not seem to consider lateness to be a severe infraction. This was the first—but certainly not the last—rabbinic defense of questionable cantorial conduct. Rabbi Hai Gaon was prepared to forgive cantors who were adulterers, robbers, or liars, provided they were repentant. Rabbi Isaac al-Fasi permitted a repentant cantor to continue to serve even though he had sworn falsely. Like the Geonim, twelfth-century rabbi Joseph ibn Migash set aside a cantor's bad reputation so long as he was repentant. Maimonides ruled that a penitent cantor would be forgiven his drunkenness. Thirteenth-century German rabbi Meir of Rothenberg ruled in favor of a spiteful cantor. His Austrian contemporary, Rabbi Isaac ben Moses, permitted a cantor who had committed manslaughter to continue to serve in his appointed office. Turkish rabbi Elijah ben Abraham Mizrahi allowed an apostate to serve in a cantorial capacity. Though Rabbi Isaac Bruna understood the Talmud to mean that a cantor should not serve even when a member of his household was tarnished by a bad reputation, he nonetheless permitted a cantor whose daughter's reputation was impugned to lead the congregation in prayer when there was no one else capable to do so. It also seems that Rabbi Nahman of Breslov was prepared to accept a cantor suspected of adultery.[46] Polish authorities of the nineteenth-century refused to bar a cantor who had committed ritual infractions unless there was a broad consensus to do so among the members of the entire community. Even repentant mercy-killers were allowed to lead prayers. And in the twentieth-century, Sabbath-violating cantors were also allowed to lead prayers.

What led rabbinic authorities to tolerate, defend, and protect cantors[47] more than the local rabbis and congregants who were too often dis-

---

45. *b. Ta'an.* 16b, *s.v. pirko*. Knowing that the Mishnah allows for a blind man to lead *Shema*, RaShi may have concluded that *pirko naeh* cannot thus refer to a physical defect and thus assigns to the term the meaning of a moral defect.

46. See Kaplan, *Until the Mashiach, Bi'ur Halikutim*, 73.

47. This view is not shared by Gila Flam who, in her otherwise impressive article,

satisfied with them was the value they invested in the office more than the worthiness of the individual cantor. Rabbi Isaac ben Moses of Vienna,[48] for instance, wrote that the cantor is essential to sustaining the Jewish community through his prayer, teaching, and guidance. Rabbi Menahem Ha-Meiri went further. He claimed that the cantor alone had the power to "save" the Jewish community. Rabbenu Asher ruled that if the Jewish community could afford to pay the salary of only one professional and the community had to choose between hiring a rabbi or hiring a cantor, the community should hire a cantor—unless the rabbi was an exceptional scholar. The office of the cantor was preeminent because, as Rabbi Moses Alshikh explains, the cantor had the ability to "refresh the soul."[49]

Given the important role assigned to the cantor by many eminent rabbinic authorities, it should come as no surprise that other rabbinic authorities would support cantors in their financial disputes with their respective communities. Since the thirteenth-century, when cantors began to be paid a salary,[50] communities debated whether the salary should be paid by the wealthy few or by the community as a whole. Rabbi Solomon ben Abraham, Rabbi Isaac bar Sheshet, and Rabbi Jacob Moellin ruled that the cantor should be paid from communal funds, thus elevating the cantor to the same stature as the rabbi, who was paid similarly, and thus assuring that the cantor's salary was guaranteed. And, like the rabbi, the cantor was exempted from paying communal taxes.[51]

The requirement of unanimity for the appointment of a cantor instituted in fifteenth-century Germany, and the concurrence of Rabbi Leon di Modena in seventeenth-century Italy, would certainly be an exception to the general support of rabbis for cantors in their dealings with the community. Unanimity was always more difficult to secure, thus making cantors vulnerable to dismissal. But compensating for this loss of security for the cantor was both the ruling of seventeenth-century rabbi Yair Bachrach, which allowed for a cantor to sign a contract longer than

---

"Music," 14:659, writes that the rabbis very often rejected *hazzanim* or resigned themselves to the demands of the public. The evidence, however, seems quite the contrary.

48. See *Or Zaru'a*.

49. See Rav Peninim Alshikh, on Proverbs 25:13.

50. See Adret, *She'elot U'Teshuvot Ha-RaShBa*, Part I, No. 450. This is the earliest mention of cantors being paid. In fact, in an earlier responsum (No. 300), there is no mention of cantors being paid. So it would seem that salaried cantors can be dated to Spain, sometime during the life of Rabbi Solomon ben Abraham.

51. See *Resp. MaHaRITZ*, No. 104.

the three-year term set for rabbis, and the ruling of seventeenth-century Ukranian rabbi Jacob Reischer, which allowed for any cantor to renege on any contract he signed. These rabbis assured both security and freedom for cantors.

Moreover, rabbinical authorities made the dismissal of cantors increasingly difficult. Sa'adiah Gaon allowed for the dismissal of a cantor on the basis of congregational complaints. But three hundred years later, the power of the congregation to dismiss a cantor diminished when Rabbi Meir of Rothenberg ruled that a minority could not effect the dismissal of the cantor except for the Days of Awe. Around the same time, Rabbi Solomon Adret ruled that a cantor could not be dismissed for reasons of advanced age or declining vocal ability. Shortly thereafter, Rabbi Simon ben Zemah Duran ruled that a cantor could not be dismissed for growing deaf. In sixteenth-century Italy, Rabbi Meir Katznellenbogen ruled that a cantor could not be dismissed on the complaints of an enemy. In Poland, at the same time, Rabbi Mordekhai Yaffe, in an attempt to avoid "baseless disputes,"[52] ruled that a cantor could only be dismissed on the will of the majority. Nineteenth-century rabbi Moses Schreiber ruled that a cantor could not even be dismissed on the grounds of moral turpitude. Rabbi Isaac bar Sheshet ruled that the community had the power to hire and fire its religious professionals. As one seventeenth-century Italian authority put it, "prayer is the domain of the congregation." And it is the congregation that has the ultimate power to decide who its professionals will be. Even so, rabbis worked assiduously to champion the tenure of cantors even at the risk of alienating congregations and some individual members who objected to the cantor's performance.[53]

It is only in the modern era that rabbinic support for cantors in contractual disputes has waned. For instance, Israeli authority Rabbi Zalman Druck, reversing seven hundred years of rabbinic support for cantors, ruled that a cantor could be dismissed provided that the congregation pays the cantor severance. Ironically, over time, rabbinic support for cantors resulted in exposing rabbis to financial difficulty and creating potential friction between the two. The change in the Jewish community's perception of its own power exacerbated the tension. Irving Howe, for one, identified a dramatic change in community attitudes toward both rabbis and cantors following the mass immigration movement to the United

52. Yaffe, *Levush Ha-Tekhelet*, 53:20.
53. Modena, *Ziknei Yehudah*, No. 107.

States in the first decades of the twentieth century. "Rabbis imported from Europe," writes Howe, "found it hard to adapt to the styles of American congregations and quickly had to confront a crisis in authority."[54] With the economic success of the new immigrants came a newfound confidence. And with that confidence came a greater assertiveness, sometimes bordering on the vulgar. Rather than defer to the authority of the rabbi, congregations arrogated to themselves the power to make decisions, even religious ones—much to the grief and humiliation of the rabbis. Filling the role of rabbis who were increasingly reluctant to serve under such conditions were nonordained "so-called reverends"[55] who gladly officiated in rabbinic capacity for a quick dollar. The easy availability of such rabbinic substitutes, and the low standards associated with them, made them less valued, while the premium attached to great musical talent made cantors more greatly valued.[56] Thus, "it was not the rabbi but the *hazan* who was considered the important functionary . . . The rabbi, unless he was a popular preacher, was considered a somewhat superfluous burden; he received only a small salary, or none at all, having to rely for a living on the emoluments of the rabbinical office."[57]

The financial disparity between cantors and rabbis is not a recent phenomenon. Communal records of Renaissance Italian Jews reveal that in 1572 Verona, the cantor was paid sixteen ducats along with certain exemptions from taxes, and in 1584 Padua, the cantor was paid twenty-six ducats along with free housing. In contrast, in 1579, the rabbi of Verona earned fourteen ducats aside from fees he received from writing Torah scrolls, *tefillin*, and *mezuzot*.[58] Part of the disparity is attributable to the fact that cantors also filled the role of communal recorder and scribe "preparing Hebrew documents according to custom."[59] But it is also at-

54. Howe, *World of Our Fathers*, 194.

55. Howe, *World of Our Fathers*, 194.

56. At his arrival in America in 1909, Yossele Rosenblatt was paid the astonishing annual salary of $2,400. A decade later, Josef (Yossele) Shlisky was rumored to have earned $15,000 for the High Holidays alone.

57. Wiernik, *History of the Jews*, 284. Kimmy Caplan explored meager rabbinical salaries between the years of 1881 to 1924, in Caplan, "In God We Trust."

58. Bonfil, *Rabbinate in Renaissance Italy*, 105. On average, between the years of 1543–1599, cantors were remunerated at a rate 55 percent higher than that of rabbis. The disparity would be even greater were it not for the remarkable salary of thirty ducats and a housing allowance of twenty-two ducats paid to Rabbi Mordekhai Bashan in 1593.

59. Bonfil, *Rabbinate in Renaissance Italy*, 95.

tributable to the vital role the cantor played in the spiritual life of Italian Jewry.

Even so, the economic and spiritual disparity was not necessarily a source of conflict. In assessing rabbinic salaries during this period, Robert Bonfil concludes that rabbinic salaries were insufficient to support them: earning less yearly than what a construction supervisor would earn in a month.[60] Cantor salaries, while higher, did not make them significantly better off. Both cantors and rabbis faced similar financial challenges. They suffered the same economic disadvantages. Hence, they were more likely to be allies than rivals.

Twentieth-century life, however, proved to be different. The status of the cantor continued to grow, and with that status came a sense of entitlement. Some cantors began to assume rabbinic functions that cantors had not performed for centuries. By the 1940s, cantors were teaching, preaching, and leading congregations. In reaction, Rabbi Boaz Cohen reported to the 1947 (Conservative) Rabbinical Assembly convention in the name of the Law and Standards Committee that:

> The committee deemed it improper for the cantor to read the Ketubah in the presence of the officiating rabbi: neither may a cantor arrogate to himself the designation of spiritual leader or a minister of religion. With regard to the cantor's prerogative to lecture on the Shulhan Aruk (sic) in the Chapel of the synagogue, it cherishes the view that it is the duty and privilege of every Jew to impart Torah if he is competent to do so. However, it would not be proper nor (sic) permissable (sic) for a cantor to teach Torah in the synagogue without the rabbi first passing upon his qualifications, or without his approval.[61]

In contentious tones, Conservative rabbis declared that the cantor was henceforth to subordinate himself to the rabbi who determines what role, if any, the cantor may assume outside of his liturgical duties.

The Conservative movement was not alone in circumscribing the role of the cantor in the synagogue. While in a 2005 document, entitled "A Sacred Partnership,"[62] the Reform movement pays homage to clergy teamwork and concedes that a hierarchical model is not ideal, its leadership also affirms "that each synagogue needs to have a captain, and that

60. Bonfil, *Rabbinate in Renaissance Italy*, 106n288.

61. Golinkin, *Proceedings of the Committee*, 1:195.

62. Approved by the CCAR Board of Trustees, March 27, 2005, and by the CCAR Convention, March 29, 2005.

it is the rabbi's responsibility to fill that role." Perhaps anticipating the change in attitude toward cantors, cantors themselves began to organize at the beginning of the twentieth century. Cantor Pinchas Minkowsky advocated establishing a centralized cantor's union with an associated placement service. He also propounded a series of rules he hoped would rein in certain cantors who might jeopardize the office.

The area in which rabbinic solidarity with cantors historically softened was with regard to musical innovations and fidelity to the liturgy. Music was an important component of early Israelite history and subsequent temple service. The salvation of the Israelites at the Red Sea was celebrated in song and musical accompaniment (Exod 15:1–21). As much for being a military hero, David was renowned as a singer/musician (2 Sam 23:1) who soothes King Saul's depression with his harp and voice (1 Sam 16:17–23). Though the origins of the poetic prayers that make up the book of Psalms are obscure,[63] in temple times the psalms[64] made up the Levitical choir's repertoire.[65] The prophet Amos (5:23; 6:5) references music and song as part of the First Temple service. And Ezra and Nehemiah (e.g., Ezra 2:41, 70; Neh 7:1, 44) list the "singers" among returning exiles as a separate category from the Levites as a testament to their special standing. The memory of the temple music even after the year 70 CE remained strong. Mishnah *Tamid* (3:8), somewhat exaggeratedly, reports that the music and song from the temple in Jerusalem could be heard as far away as Jericho—more a recollection of their importance to the temple service than a statement about the volume. And Rabbi Joshua ben Hananiah—the elder sage of the first century—recalls with relish his personal role in the Levitical choir[66] prior to the destruction of the temple, especially on the day of the Water Libation Festival.[67]

Hence, it is entirely consistent with this musical tradition to expect that any cantor should have a good voice.[68] This is particularly the case

---

63. Cf. Adele Berlin and Marc Zvi Brettler's introduction to Psalms in *Jewish Study Bible*, 1281–82, for a synopsis of the research on the problems with assigning Davidic authorship.

64. The word "psalm" itself derives from the Greek *psalmos*, meaning "a song with the accompaniment of a stringed instrument."

65. *m. Tam.* 7:4.

66. *b. Arkh.* 11b.

67. *b. Suk.* 53a.

68. *b. Ta'an.* 16a.

with the *hazzan* who, as Torah reader, was required to read melodious-
ly.[69] In fact, a system of manual signs and visual cues (chironomy) was
developed to ensure that the Torah reader sang the designated notes
correctly.[70] By the time of the Talmud, a pleasant voice became a requirement for the office of cantor:[71] a talent the Geonim considered a virtue.[72]
Yet, how to balance the desirable vocal ability against the other essential
traits such as modesty, gentility, fluency, and virtue became an ongoing
dilemma as well as a point of controversy. What emerges is a progression
from consideration of the cantor's voice as being an asset to being an
essential,[73] and later, to being a distraction.

This progression parallels how the function of the prayer leader was
perceived. When the function of the prayer leader was supposed to fulfill
the incapable worshipers' obligation for prayer, the quality of voice was
of little consequence. Thus Rabbenu Simhah, a student of RaShI, states:

> It is customary among all Jews in Spain, that is, España (Is-
> famia) that in order to fulfill the obligation for those who are
> not learned, the *hazzan* begins with the blessings for washing
> hands [in the morning] and [followed by] the order of all the
> blessings.[74]

The role of the cantor (*hazzan*) is to fulfill the obligation of prayer
for the congregation. The musical way in which the obligation is fulfilled
is not mentioned because it is not relevant. On the other hand, Sa'adiah
Gaon[75] makes no mention of fulfilling the congregation's obligation for
prayer. Instead, he conceptualizes the role of the cantor as mediating between Israel and God:[76] a function where a good voice would be useful.
Accordingly, Sa'adiah acted to ensure that those with demonstrated musical talent could not easily be removed.

The defense of cantors, though less ardent, continued with twelfth-
century rabbi Joseph ibn Migash, who tolerated the cantor's vocal

69. *b. Meg.* 32a.

70. *b. Ber.* 62a.

71. *b. Ta'an.* 16a.

72. Ben Hayim, *Teshuvot Ha-Geonim, Sha'are Zedek,* No. 178 mentions that a cantor with a good voice honors God with his talent.

73. Cf. *b. Sof.* 3:10.

74. Hurwitz, *Mahzor Vitry,* 1.

75. See below.

76. As does the author of *Or Zaru'a.* See below.

flourishes though it prolongs the prayer service. German authorities of the same period were also inclined to forgive the cantor's excesses provided that they were performed with the proper attitude. Cantors who sang only for the acclaim they would receive for their performance were sanctioned but those who sang to inspire were to be applauded. The authorities, however, offer no clue on how the listeners could judge the difference. Perhaps the introduction of *Mahzor Hadrat Kodesh*, published in Venice in 1512 with instructions on how a *hazzan* should sing certain passages, was an attempt to solve this problem.

After the passing of the twelfth century, however, the vocal gymnastics of the cantor were openly disdained. Polish authorities were particularly incensed. Rabbi Benjamin Aaron Solnik (1550–1620) censured Jewish communities that engaged cantors who prolonged the prayer service using their mellifluous voices to sing melodies borrowed from the gentiles and the theater.[77] And Rabbi Abraham Gumbiner cites earlier authorities in condemning cantors who prolong the service by "separating one letter from another and one word from another."[78] Rabbis were further annoyed by the introduction of foreign melodies into the prayer service. Rabbi Isaac al-Fasi forbade applying popular Arabic tunes to traditional prayers as early as the eleventh century, with his opinion endorsed by thirteenth-century rabbi Solomon Adret and sixteenth-century rabbi David ben Zimra. Maimonides considered the study of any music book "a waste of time and vanity."[79]

The introduction of extraneous and often extemporaneous interpolations into the prayer service laid the grounds for further controversy. The ancient aesthetic value of musical and artistic innovation was served by *piyyut*. Joseph Yahalom construes *piyyut* as "a rebellion against standardized fixed prayer."[80] This construction, however, may be somewhat overstated: it is unlikely that the "creators"[81] of prayer would rebel against the Creator for whom the very prayer was intended. Nevertheless, *piyyut* did represent liturgical creativity, enhancing the fixed liturgy with new and interesting ways of building on set themes. *Piyyut* allowed for the liturgical freedom that was suppressed once communal prayer was

77. Solnik, *Mas'at Binyamin*, No. 6.

78. Gumbiner, *Magen Avraham* on *Shulhan Arukh*, OH 281, subparagraph 4.

79. Cf. Commentary on *m. San.* 10:1.

80. Yahalom "Piyyut as Poetry," 111.

81. *Paytanim* (plural of *paytan*) from the Greek, meaning "creators;" *piyyut* being the "creation."

standardized. Third-century cantors embraced the opportunity to be creative, and yet were met with rabbinic displeasure.[82] The Geonim reiterated that same displeasure more emphatically. They are reputed to have ruled: "A *hazzan* who knows *piyyut* (*i.e.* who employs it in the liturgy) shall not be admitted to the synagogue."[83] Maimonides totally opposed the inclusion of *piyyut* in any part of the prayer service.[84] The elasticity of the fixed liturgy remained at issue. In the nineteenth century, Rabbi Moses Schick expressed rabbinic concern for retaining the integrity of standardized prayer by forbidding cantors to repeat words in their attempt to fit the liturgy to the melody or to intensify the emotional connotation of the words of prayer.

The pattern of cantorial innovation and rabbinic limitation repeated over centuries. A number of rabbinic authorities were willing to accept what cantors introduced into the prayer service—within certain parameters—under the principle of the power of custom to modulate tradition. It was also the sway of custom that accommodated the limitation of a cantor's contract to three years and the allowance for the cantor to break a contract (usually) without penalty. Likewise, custom allowed for bequeathing the office to an heir and granting a dismissed cantor severance. Even the use of a pitch pipe or tuning fork was accepted, albeit begrudgingly, on account of a long-standing practice among cantors.[85] But when it came to massaging the liturgy or introducing what the rabbis perceived to be alien melodies, the battle lines were drawn.

With the position of cantor established and the qualifications for office circumscribed, the decisors of Jewish law were left the task of further defining the nature of the qualifications and determining how—or whether—said qualifications applied in new circumstances. In some instances—certainly in the modern period, and particularly after the introduction of printing when prayer books were relatively cheap and accessible[86]—there is some discussion about whether cantors are needed at all! This discussion intensified and persists to this day as the number

82. *y. Ber.* 9:1.

83. Levin, *Otzar Ha'Geonim* I:70.

84. Maimon, *Teshuvot Ha-RaMBaM*, No. 207.

85. Hoffman, *Sefer Melamed L'ho-il*, No. 63.

86. The first *siddur* (prayer book) was printed in Italy in 1485/6, Spain in 1490, and Germany and Poland in 1508. Cf. Posner and Ta-Shema, *Hebrew Book*, 209. Most early editions were 400 copies or fewer (Posner and Ta-Shema, *Hebrew Book*, 87) owing to the scarcity of paper and the intensity of labor.

of congregations hiring cantors continues to shrink and the number of cantors being graduated from (surviving) cantorial schools remains low.

To be sure, there are those who agree with the observation of the grandfather of Rabbi Hanokh ben Judah Leib:

> The *hazzanim* in these areas are generally not learned men and do not understand the prayers. They pay no attention to the sense of the text and thus render the prayers meaningless . . . When it comes to the *piyyutim* they recite them with such rapidity that even a horseman could not overtake them . . . The *hazzan's* intentions are primarily to show off his voice . . . he chants one word at length . . . and then he recites many blessings in one breath. And in the middle of one blessing he suddenly lets out a loud and bitter cry that frightens everyone who hears it . . . And all this is only to entertain people. Actually, it is only a mockery and a travesty, so that anyone who hears it laughs.[87]

There are those, just as surely, who sympathize with "S.R.," a letter-writer to the editor of New York's *Jewish Daily Forward* two hundred years later:

> I decided to go to the synagogue [on the Days of Awe]. I went not in order to pray to God but to heal and refresh my aching soul with the cantor's sweet melodies . . . Sitting in the synagogue among *landsleit*[88] and listening to the good cantor, I forgot my unhappy weekday life, the dirty shop, my boss, the bloodsucker, and my pale sick wife and my children. All of my America with its hurry-up life was forgotten.[89]

As the legal and folk literature will attest, cantors have been—and can be—buffoons, reprobates, egotistical performers, self-promoters, frauds, and ignoramuses. Cantors have been—and can be—moody, fickle, unreliable, tardy, meddling, and disrespectful. On the other hand, cantors are gifted with the unique and potent ability to delight and transfigure. There are moments when the cantor's skill can arouse a worshiper to ecstasy, transport a worshiper to another and higher plane of reality, and vocally escort the congregation to an encounter with the divine. To

---

87. Leib, *Reshit Bikkurim*, 29a–b. Cf. Millgram, *Jewish Worship*, 529, whose translation I largely follow.

88. Yiddish for "fellow Jews," usually from the same town in Eastern Europe.

89. This 1909 letter is cited in Chazan and Raphael, *Modern Jewish History*, 183. This, and other Yiddish letters to the *Forward*, were collected and published under the title *Bintel Brief*. It is also cited in part by Heller, *What to Listen for*, 166.

be sure, cantors remain a source of frustration and exasperation moderated by the prospects of inspiration. Cantors have been and will continue to be controversial. The chapters that follow will explore the ambivalence toward the cantor in all of its complexity.

NOTES ON TRANSLATIONS, TRANSLITERATIONS, AND ACRONYMS

I have translated into English for the first time most of the texts in chapter 1 from the Geonic period and thereafter. In some noted instances I have modified earlier translations. My approach is to remain as loyal to the original Hebrew or Aramaic text as possible, while allowing some license for rendering foreign idioms into a more comprehensible and fluent English. In all the English passages in chapters 1 and 2, whether in the original or in translation, I present them with the spelling and transliterations of the author or translator though they may not be consistent with those I would otherwise use. Well-known Hebrew words (e.g., Shabbat, Rosh Hashanah—when referring to the holiday—and Yom Kippur) appear in the common, transliterated form without translation and capitalized. Names of specific prayers, tractates of Talmud, or technical terms are always italicized. Genres of rabbinic literature (e.g., Mishnah, Tosefta, Responsa) are always capitalized and in plain text. When necessary, explanations of those terms will appear in a footnote. Transliterations follow the *Encyclopedia Judaica* (2nd edition) general transliteration key. Likewise, I follow the *Encyclopedia Judaica* transliteration of terms. For example: *sheli'ah zibbur*, even though this transliteration does not reflect the proper Hebrew pronunciation of the term.[90] I have intentionally chosen to use capital letters for each of the initials used to identify rabbinical scholars in order to more closely represent the way the acronym appears in Hebrew. Thus, for example, I use RaMBaN for Rabbi Moses ben Nahman or Nahmanides. In cases where the initial for the acronym must be rendered in two English letters, the second appears in lower case, like RaShI.

---

90. Correct Hebrew would require transliterating the phrase as: *shli'ah zibbur*.

CLASSIFIED TERMINOLOGY

The common term for a prayer leader in the rabbinic tradition is *sheli'ah zibbur*. There are few technical terms that have elicited as much difference in translation as this one. Some translators take a more literal approach. Thus, Herbert Danby[91] translates the term as "agent of the congregation" in Mishnah *Berakhot* 5:5 and *Rosh Hashanah* 4:9 *inter alia*. A considerable measure of support for this translation comes by way of Professor Saul Lieberman, who translates the term as "agent of the congregation."[92] And while Jacob Neusner translates the term as "reader of the congregation,"[93] in an earlier volume he translates the term as "agent of the congregation."[94] It would seem to some that the word "agent" is more suited to the realm of business than to prayer. Accordingly, Abraham Millgram[95] and Hayim Halevi Donin[96] prefer "emissary of the congregation," particularly "in divine worship."[97] A variant of this modification is "messenger of the congregation" preferred by Professor Blu Greenberg[98] and Jonathan L. Friedmann.[99] Similarly, Rabbi Karen Medwed[100] translates *sheli'ah zibbur* as "representative of the congregation" even though she also translates the term as "prayer leader," certainly a sound description of the role performed by the *sheli'ah zibbur*. A looser translation appears as an alternative definition in Marcus Jastrow's work[101] ("public reader of prayers"), as well as in the Soncino edition of the Talmud[102] that renders *sheli'ah zibbur* as "congregational reader," a more palatable alternative to the arcane "precentor" that was favored by the 1909 edition of the *Jewish Encyclopedia*[103] which also found its way

---

91. Danby, *Mishnah*, 6.

92. Lieberman, *Hellenism and Jewish Palestine*, 82n272.

93. Neusner, *Talmud of the Land*, 16:99.

94. Neusner, *Talmud of the Land*, 1:218.

95. Millgram, *Jewish Worship*, 518, 519.

96. Donin, *To Pray as a Jew*, 16, 63.

97. Millgram, *Jewish Worship*, 535.

98. Greenberg, "Woman as Messenger."

99. Friedman, "Know Before Whom You Stand."

100. Medwed, "Walk Humbly with God," 19.

101. Jastrow, *Dictionary of the Targumim*, 1274, s.v. *zibbur*.

102. *b. R.H.* 34b.

103. Singer, *Jewish Encyclopedia*, 6:285.

into a footnote in Danby.[104] Idelsohn[105] translates *shel'iah zibbur* as "messenger of the community" but also uses the arcane "precentor."[106]

Given all these alternatives, it is not surprising that Hyman E. Goldin[107] and Hyman Sky,[108] among others, chose not to translate the term at all. This is neat and simple. Nevertheless, I have opted to translate the term *shel'iah zibbur* in two different ways. In talmudic sources and passages that cite talmudic sources, I translate *shel'iah zibbur* as "lector" for two reasons. First, it corresponds in time and in purpose to the same functionary in early church history where an expert fulfilled the requirements of prayer for the congregation. Justin Martyr (d. *ca.* 165 CE), for instance, writes of the *anaginoskon*—the public reader—best translated as "lector." (In this regard, Rabbi Isaac Klein[109] has it right when he translates *sheli'ah zibbur* as "reader.") And second, it connects well with the term for the place in the synagogue from which prayers are led, namely, the lectern. For post-talmudic times, I translate *shel'iah zibbur* as "prayer leader," fitting the primary function that person serves.

The literature includes two other terms synonymous with *shel'iah zibbur*: *over lifnei ha-tevah* and *yored lifnei ha-tevah*. The *tevah* to which both terms refer is likely the portable chest in which the Torah scrolls were stored,[110] and, in ordinary circumstances, would be positioned near the front of the synagogue.[111] E. Z. Melamed[112] explains that both terms were coined when the synagogue floors were sloped downward from the rear-like amphitheaters so that when prayer leaders came forward to recite the *Amidah* aloud they would "go down before the chest"[113] or "pass before the chest." Archaeologists, however, have discovered no sloped floors in synagogues in late antiquity. And by the third and fourth centuries, the portable chest had been replaced by a permanent niche (*aedicula*) in the wall facing toward Israel or, inside Israel, toward Jerusalem.[114] Of

104. Danby, *Mishnah*, 6n10.

105. Idelsohn, *Jewish Music*, 102.

106. Idelsohn, *Jewish Music*, 104.

107. Goldin, *Code of Jewish Law*.

108. Sky, "Development of the Office."

109. Klein, *Guide to Jewish Religious Practice*, 197, 200, 219.

110. Cf. *m. Ta'an.* 2:1, *m. Meg.* 3:1

111. Cf. *b. Sot.* 38b, bottom.

112. Melamed, *Pirke Minhag v'Halakhah*, 138.

113. Cf. *b. Ber.* 34a.

114. Cf. Meyers, "Current Galilean Synagogue Studies," 130.

course, if this chest were portable, there would be no expectation that any trace of it would be found today.[115] Hence, there is no confirmation for Melamed's derivation of the term. So rather than literally translate these two terms, which would be historically dubious, I have rendered them either "lead the service" or "go to the lectern," depending on which better fits the context.

The term "cantor" is the Greek for "singer." Historically, it is a term that could not have been applicable to a synagogue prayer leader until after such time that singing was considered an essential function of the prayer leader. Hence, when the term *hazzan* or its Aramaic cognate appears in a text where it clearly refers to that function, I translate the term as "cantor." Likewise, I also use the term "cantor" when it is clearly the author's intention to refer to the person charged with leading the prayer service musically even though the author uses a different term—such as *yored lifnei ha-tevah.*

ORGANIZING PRINCIPLES
AND GENERAL OBSERVATIONS

I have chosen to be selective and representative in my treatment of the sources and not comprehensive. Listing every text, responsum, story, or anecdote related to the cantor was never my goal. I have included a sampling of sources that reflect the range of issues regarding the cantor as they have evolved historically with the objective in mind of trying to understand the phenomenon better. No doubt there will be readers who might challenge some of my choices or contend that other sources have been erroneously or carelessly omitted. I believe, however, that citing representative sources enables us to draw legitimate conclusions. Among them are the following:

Concerns over the qualifications of a prayer leader are ubiquitous and persistent. Rabbinic scholars have debated the prerequisites of prayer leaders since the time of the Mishnah—when specific qualifications are first mentioned—and the Talmud—when such qualifications are enumerated. Sources from the Babylonian Geonim to those of contemporary Israeli authorities—including those in every major Jewish community— reveal an ongoing interest in formalizing and standardizing qualifications for prayer leaders. Particular concerns, however, have varied. For

115. Meyers, "Current Galilean Synagogue Studies," 129.

instance, the earlier sources concern themselves with the minimum age for prayer leaders. But thirteenth-century Spanish authorities shifted their concern to the upper age limit—if any—for prayer leaders. Twentieth-century American authorities show a renewed interest in considering the minimum age,[116] perhaps reflecting the modern attitude that involvement of youth in public prayer is essential for Jewish continuity.

Similarly, since the time of the Talmud, concerns over the moral rectitude of the cantor have been ubiquitous and persistent. The literature includes some damning stories of cantors who have violated virtually every category of Jewish law, from the theological to the matrimonial. Determining whether such gross misconduct disqualifies a cantor from service or whether the communal need for a proficient cantor trumps personal failings was a topic for the Geonim and the rabbis of eleventh-century North Africa, twelfth-century Spain, twelfth-century North Africa, twelfth-century Germany, thirteenth-century Austria, fifteenth-century Turkey, fifteenth-century Germany, sixteenth-century Bohemia, nineteenth-century Poland, twentieth-century Poland, and twentieth-century Israel.[117]

Important to note is that since the Geonic period, the single most frequently recurring issue is that of the terms of employment and grounds for dismissal of the cantor. Such considerations surface in every century and in virtually every Jewish community. Thus it should not surprise the reader to note that I have included a significant number of texts on this subject. The number of texts I have included, however, is a fair representation of the weight rabbinic authorities give to the subject.

Interesting to note is that the issue of proficiency in textual learning for prayer leaders—emphasized in the early sources[118]—is all but ignored in the later sources. This may reflect an implicit rabbinic judgment that, given a general decline in textual literacy, expectations of scholarship are unrealistic or, alternatively, other considerations—like musical ability—are more important. Sources that support both of these views are included in the ensuing chapter.

Of particular interest to contemporary advocates of the rights of the disabled, the sources show that physical disabilities were never a bar to holding a cantorial position. Old, infirm, unsteady, blind, and even

---

116. See these sources below.

117. These sources appear below.

118. *b. Ta'an.* 16a; *y. Ta'an.* 2:2, 65b. These are cited below.

deaf cantors served with distinction and were supported by rabbinical rulings. I include a representative selection of sources that confirm this observation.

My exclusive focus is on the cantor within the Jewish community and from the Jewish perspective. However, it is interesting to note that that the Catholic musical tradition, which also included a position of cantor, has addressed some strikingly similar controversies. In the Catholic rites, the cantor was leader of the choir tasked with singing the opening words of the antiphon (psalms or canticles) that elicited a congregational response,[119] exactly as directed by the Talmud for synagogue practice.[120] This role was particularly important with the founding in the seventh century of the *Schola Cantorum*, the choir that sang when the pope officiated at observances.[121] But even earlier, the cantor had achieved certain official standing. Canon 15 of the Council of Laodicea, a city on the Turkish-Syrian border (ca. 344–360) states: "No other shall sing in the assembly except the cantor who has been canonically chosen to ascend the ambo[122] and chant from the parchment."[123] It was roughly the same time the office of *hazzan* is established in the Jewish communities of Israel. Canon 24 parallels the same concerns the Talmud expresses for the good character of the prayer leader: "No one of the clergy, from presbyters to deacons, and so on in ecclesiastical rank from subdeacons, readers, singers, exorcists, doorkeepers, or any of the order of ascetics, ought to enter a tavern."[124]

The church was similarly conflicted regarding cantorial qualifications, wavering between emphasizing good character or musical skill. One of the first acts of Pope Gregory I (590–604) was to abolish the tradition of making any good singer a deacon. He writes: "It has long been a custom in the Roman Church to ordain cantors as deacons and to use them for singing instead of preaching and caring for the poor. This has the consequence that at divine service, more is thought of a good voice than of a good life. Consequently, no deacon may sing in the chant."[125]

119. Cf. Burkholder et al., *History of Western Music*, 56.

120. *b. Sot.* 30b.

121. Burkholder et *al.*, *History of Western Music*, 29.

122. In Hebrew, *bimah.*

123. *New Catholic Encyclopedia*, s.v. "Cantor in Christian Liturgy."

124. *ibid.*

125. Patterson, "Cantor," 25.

The Benedictine Rules of sixth-century Italy parallel the concern of the Mishnah[126] when it includes (Rule 19) such "mindfulness" that would allow "our mind and voice [to be] in harmony."[127] Just as the rabbis guarded the liturgical text from innovations, so did the church. Pope Gregory I is reputed to have regulated and standardized liturgical chants, essentially codifying the liturgy, which remained essentially untouched until the sixteenth century.[128] And sometime around 820 CE, Helisachar, chancellor to Louis the Pious of France, was given the task of standardizing and unifying the liturgy using only the "authoritative" versions. Writing to archbishop Nidibrius of Narbonne, Helisachar complains that some antiphons had been "corrupted in various places by the negligence of scribes or the arrogance of cantors." After his consultations, research, and review, Helisachar states that: "there will be no straying in any way from the authority of the melodic art."[129]

The same virtues of the cantorial arts trumpeted by Rabbi Menahem Ha-Meiri, and articulated even more powerfully by Rabbi Moses Alshikh, are also reflected in the book *Ars Musica,* written by Aegidius of Zamora in Spain around 1240 CE. In chapter two he writes: "Music gladdens the sorrowful . . . and braces those who languish; it calms agitated souls, banishes care and anxiety."[130] One final parallel: Catholics share the Jewish desire for congregational involvement in prayer but try to achieve it differently. Jewish congregations seem to think that engaging a cantor stifles congregational participation. Catholics see the opposite. With the promulgation of the Constitution of the Sacred Liturgy adopted by Vatican II in December 1963, Catholics recommitted themselves to active musical participation (Section 30) which restored the office of cantor to a position of importance, both in terms of his musical expertise and also in terms of managing the pace of the service and "injecting emotion" into the liturgy (Section 36). For Catholics today, the cantor is a needed professional who can revitalize congregational participation. For Jews, the cantor is much less so.

While all these parallels between the cantor in Judaism and the cantor in Catholicism are intriguing, any conclusions that might be drawn

---

126. *m. Ta'an.* 2:2 states that the leader's prayer should be whole-hearted.

127. Strunk, et al., *Source Readings in Music History,* 164.

128. See Burkholder et al., *History of Western Music,* 33.

129. Strunk, et al., *Source Readings in Music History,* 176–77.

130. Strunk, et al., *Source Readings in Music History,* 248.

must only be tentative pending further research. That research is outside the scope of this study.

The historically positive attitude of rabbis toward the cantor—not the relationship between rabbis and cantors—has remained steady until recently. No doubt there was an initial sympathy toward cantors as well since rabbis themselves served as the earliest prayer leaders.[131] Respect for the office of the cantor and the recognition of the important function the cantor performs characterized the rabbinic attitude toward the cantor in twelfth-century Germany, thirteenth-century Spain and Provence, fourteenth-century Germany and Spain, and sixteenth-century Israel.[132] In fact, there is ample evidence that rabbis valued the position highly and esteemed those who served as cantors. Some rabbis were effusive in their praise for the inspiration that cantors might provide. Other rabbis were so protective of the office, they were willing to overlook the indiscretions of individual cantors and consistently favor the cantor's side in contractual disputes, notwithstanding the ongoing criticism of cantorial excesses during public prayer.

At times, rabbis were ambivalent. For instance, Polish *hasidim* cite in the name of Rabbi Hanokh Henikh of Alexandropol, that when he heard Rabbi Cantor Zvi Hirsch intone the words "Do no manner of work on the Sabbath day," Rabbi Hanokh Henikh was so moved that "he lost all desire to do any work on the Sabbath for more than six months."[133] This remains a testament to the inspiration the cantorial arts can provide. Yet the Kotzker Rebbe is reputed to have told the same cantor that the reason his house had burnt to the ground was because he prolonged his recital of the words "Who by fire,"[134] a repudiation of cantorial showmanship. However, the enthusiastic endorsement of the office of the cantor remained substantially intact.

In more recent times, however, rabbis have been less enthusiastic, partly because of the democratization of the prayer service that emphasizes participation by as many individuals as possible rather than reliance on a single professional, and partly because of the economic hardships faced by many congregations who cannot afford a full staff of clergy. In

131. *b. Ta'an.* 16a; 24a; *b. Ber.* 31a.

132. All these sources are included below.

133. Alfasi, *HaRav Mi-Kotzk*, 263.

134. Alfasi, *HaRav Mi-Kotzk*, 62. Rabbi Cantor Zvi Hirsch of Parzow served as a cantor for seventy years, including in the chapels of the Seer of Lublin and the Kotzker Rebbe.

this socioeconomic climate, rabbis and cantors have been compelled to compete for the affections (and limited resources) of their congregational benefactors, resulting in a climate of competition rather than cooperation, jealousy and suspicion rather than respect. Since the turn of the fourteenth century, Jewish law has given preference to the cantor.[135] But this is no longer the rule. As an example, of the three affiliated conservative congregations in Alabama in 2015, none had a cantor while two full-time rabbis serve one, a visiting rabbi serves another, and a rabbi serves the third. Even though there is no comprehensive data on all American congregations, the anecdotal evidence points to the fact that small or shrinking congregations are more likely to be served by student rabbis, visiting rabbis, circuit rabbis, and even laymen, rather than by a cantor.[136]

In part, this development is the unsurprising outcome of the denigration of cantors in popular culture over the last century—or even longer.[137] The chapter on "The Cantor in Jewish Lore" cites a considerable number of sources that cast the cantor in a less than flattering light in order to better understand this dramatic shift. The observation that emerges is that while rabbis remained committed to the preservation of the office of cantor, the general public was less sanguine. I explore what caused the public change of attitude in the same chapter.

Needless to say, there have been and will continue to be rabbis and laymen alike who treasure the function and contribution of cantors. Whether or not these champions of the cantor can or will save the institution of the cantorate is the subject of the final chapter.

Toronto, Canada
January 2019

135. Unless, according to Rabbenu Asher, the rabbi is a notable scholar. See below.

136. Cf. Fishkoff, "As Rural Congregations Get Smaller."

137. In fact, as early as the twelfth-century. See Segal, *Book of Tahkemoni* cited below.

1

The Cantor in Jewish Law

THE PERIOD OF THE MISHNAH

ACCORDING TO ABRAHAM GOLDBERG, the Mishnah is "the carefully worded literary formulation of Pharisaic-rabbinic law as it developed in the late Second Temple period and some generations afterwards."[1] Stated more simply and in consonance with how later rabbis understood it, the Mishnah represents the thematic collection of oral traditions passed down in Hebrew since the time of Moses, and filtered through the pioneering effort of Rabbi Meir and Rabbi Akiva. These traditions were anthologized by Rabbi Judah the Patriarch and finalized around the end of the second century of the Common Era.

Although there is no designated section that describes or defines the office of cantor, there are several passages related to leading communal prayers that are applicable here. They are the starting point from which subsequent rules develop.

The first two passages describe the procedure followed on public fast days. The third passage articulates a rule for public prayer ascribed to Rabban Gamliel of the first half of the first century of the Common Era. This rule helps explain why, in the fourth and the fifth passage, mistakes are intolerable: the cantor acts not merely for himself, but for all those who rely on his expertise. The fourth passage also implies that in

1. Goldberg, in Safrai, *Literature of the Sages*, 1:211.

ordinary circumstances, protocol requires anyone asked to lead prayer services to refuse initially. It is a formalization of the humility that later authorities expect from a cantor. The sixth passage shows the limitations placed on a minor, the improperly dressed, and the blind. It suggests that the term "elder" of the first two passages was intended to exclude a minor.

Mishnah Ta'anit, Chapter 2, Mishnah 1:
An Elder Prayer Leader

At the time of the dedication of the temple, King Solomon addressed God in the presence of the people of Israel gathered together for the occasion: "Should the heavens be shut up and there be no rain because they have sinned against You, and then they pray toward this place and acknowledge Your name and repent of their sins" God would consequently "send down rain upon the land" (1 Kgs 8:35–36). Famine was linked to sin and sin is redressed through prayer and repentance. The Mishnah outlines what steps should be taken to induce repentance. The use of ashes was a sign of mourning. While both passages assign the task of impelling the community to repent to an elder, the second passage adds that old age alone is insufficient: the prayer leader must have fluency in the words that are part of the procedure.

> What is the procedure on fast days? They bring the Ark [housing the Torah scrolls] into the city thoroughfare and put ashes on the Ark, on the head of the patriarch, and the head of the court. The eldest of them exhorts them to repent, saying: "My brothers, regarding the inhabitants of Nineveh the text does not say 'And God saw their sackcloth and their fasting' but, rather, 'God saw their deeds since they had repented of their evil ways.'" (Jonah 3:6)

Mishnah Ta'anit, Chapter 2, Mishnah 2:
Requirements of a Prayer Leader

The Mishnah presumes that a prayer leader's devotion can vary according to his personal circumstances. The most competent person with the deepest conviction is the best choice for prayer leader.

> They stood in prayer. They bring before the Ark an elder who is well versed in the words and who has children he cannot support so that his prayer will be wholehearted.

Mishnah Rosh Hashanah, Chapter 4, Mishnah 9:
Function of the Lector

The Mishnah implies that the institution of an official prayer leader was already in place before the destruction of the Second Temple. The only question to resolve was his function.

In context, this next Mishnah relates to prayer recited on the New Year and specifically—according to all authorities—to the prayer recited silently and while standing at attention (*Amidah*). By extrapolation, however, later authorities applied the same principle to all prayer services of the year. The first, anonymous opinion held that all those who are capable of praying must do so on their own. The prayer leader functioned only to represent those unable to pray. Rabban Gamliel held that the prayer leader fulfills the obligation of the entire congregation at all times and for those of every grade of competence. It is Rabban Gamliel's opinion that was adopted as law.

> Just as the lector is obligated, so is every individual obligated. Rabban Gamliel says: the lector fulfills the obligation to pray for others.

Mishnah Berakhot, Chapter 5, Mishnah 3:
Competency of the Lector

> If someone went to the lectern and erred, let another take his place and at that moment, let him not refuse. From where does he begin? From the beginning of the blessing in which the other erred.

Mishnah Berakhot, Chapter 5, Mishnah 5:
Further on the Same

> It is a bad omen for him who prays and errs. If he were a lector, it is a bad omen for the congregation that appointed him, for a man's agent is like himself.

Mishnah Megillah, Chapter 4,[2] Mishnah 6:
A Minor and a Blind Man as a Lector

A minor may read the Torah and translate [into Aramaic] but may not lead the *Shema*[3] with its blessings or go to the lectern or raise his hands [for the Priestly Benediction]. He whose clothes are torn may lead the *Shema* with its blessings and translate, but may not read the Torah, nor go to the lectern, nor raise his hands. A blind man may lead the *Shema* with its blessings and translate. Rabbi Judah says: He who has never seen the light of day from birth may not lead the *Shema* with its blessings.

From the Tosefta, Israel, Second Century:
Determining Who Is an Adult Lector

Dated by Abraham Goldberg to one generation after the completion of the Mishnah (220–230 CE), the Tosefta is more than a mere "addition," the meaning of this collection's Aramaic name. The Tosefta is a complement and supplement to the Mishnah—including opinions of the last Tanaitic generation that lived after the completion of the Mishnah. The Tosefta is also a commentary on the Mishnah. Given its multifaceted purpose, it is no wonder that the Tosefta is three times as large as the Mishnah. The arrangement of its content parallels the Mishnah (without the tractates of *Tamid, Middot*, and *Kinnim*). The most important scholarly edition of the Tosefta is that of professor Saul Lieberman: *Tosefta Kifshuta*.

Tosefta Hagigah 1:3[4]

This passage considers when a boy comes of age. The unattributed statement identifies two separate stages in adulthood. Reaching puberty,

---

2. Following Rabbi Isaac al-Fasi and Maimonides, and not as in the printed editions of the Talmud that number this chapter 3.

3. Hebrew: *pores al shema*. RaShI (*b. Meg.* 23b) explains that *pores* derives from the root meaning "part." Latecomers to the synagogue would have one of their number stands and recite *Kaddish, Barkhu*, and the blessing preceding *Shema*. Maimonides (MT, Laws of Prayer 8:5), following the *Arukh*, explains that *pores* is synonymous with "blessing," whereby one recites the blessings for *Shema* and others respond "Amen." This is somewhat close to the conclusion drawn by Professor Ezra Fleischer in "Towards a Clarification," 133–44, who, after surveying all the explanations for the term, concluded that it meant reading aloud responsively with the congregation. Accordingly, the term will henceforth be translated as "leading the *Shema*."

4. Cf. y. *Suk.* 3:13, 54a (end) and *b. Hul.* 24b.

presumed to be the appearance of secondary sexual characteristics, is the threshold for becoming responsible for performing all the command- ments and becoming liable for punishment if they are violated. An ex- ample of such liability is the law of the rebellious son. The penalty for the rebellious son applies only to a son who has reached puberty. An older age, however, is necessary for a boy to serve in the capacity of prayer leader or, if the fellow is a *kohen*, offering the Priestly Blessing. The older age required is not enumerated. Rather, it is linked with full beardedness that current medical authorities associate with the middle of the third decade of life:

> . . . and similarly, a youngster who developed two pubic hairs is obligated to perform all the commandments in the Torah and may be considered a rebellious son. When his beard fills out, he may be appointed lector to go to the lectern and to raise his hands.

THE PERIOD OF THE TALMUD—BABYLONIA AND ISRAEL—SECOND, THIRD, AND FOURTH CENTURIES

The Aramaic Gemara followed after the Hebrew Mishnah. Rabbinic scholars in several centers of learning adduced anecdotal, legendary and legal materials to interpret the Mishnah. The scholars emended the Mish- nah, adjusted its phrasing, limited its application, expanded its purview, resolved differing opinions, found patterns, and derived abstract prin- ciples from it. The Gemara added to the Mishnah and was called Talmud. Two parallel processes began after the publication of the Mishnah—one in Babylonia and one in the land of Israel—with the former extending ap- proximately a century longer than the latter. The final editing or redaction of the Babylonian Talmud began in the fifth century, but seems to have continued to the last quarter of the seventh century. Recent scholarship has concluded that the Gemara was orally transmitted until the middle of the eighth century. The preference of the Babylonian Talmud over the Jerusalem Talmud by the Babylonian authorities of the ninth to eleventh centuries made the Babylonian Talmud preeminent.

In the first passage cited here, the Talmud, noting that in two places the Mishnah requires that someone who is older and more mature exhort the community or lead prayers on fast days, considers whether this is absolutely required. The Talmud concludes that old age is preferable, but not absolute. In the hierarchy of preference, learning trumps age. Then, citing the Mishnah, the Talmud adds that expertise is more important than age. Other qualities of a prayer leader are listed in a tradition ascribed to the second-century rabbi, Judah bar Ilai. These qualities were to be found in the person of the fourth-century Rav Isaac ben Ami. Rav Hisda, who headed the Academy in Sura during the last years of his life in the early fourth century, explains that "an empty home" must mean something different from one absent of people. Otherwise, it would contradict the qualification that a prayer leader must have young children he cannot support. Rav Hisda concludes that "empty" must mean devoid of sin. Abaye, who died near the middle of the fourth century, explains that one's reputation is earned early on. Thus, anyone who committed a youthful indiscretion that is recalled by others would not be suitable to serve as a prayer leader. Finally, while the chain of transmission is in doubt, the application of a disparaging verse in the book of Jeremiah to an unworthy cantor implies that a cantor must be worthy of his position.

Babylonian Talmud, Ta'anit 16a: Qualifications of a Lector

The rabbis taught: If there is someone who is older [present], let him speak. If not, let the most learned speak. And if there is no one learned [present], let a man of stature speak. Does the word 'old' mean even if he is not learned? Abaye said: "This is what it means: If an elder scholar is present, he exhorts them, and if not, then a younger scholar exhorts. And if [there is] no [younger scholar], then a man of stature [exhorts][5] . . ."

'They stood in prayer.' Even though a wise, old man [is present], the only one they bring in [to lead prayers] is one who is well versed [in the words]. Rabbi Judah says: "One who has young children he cannot support,[6] toils in the field yet his home is empty; enjoys a good reputation, [is] humble, is agreeable to the people, possesses a sweet and pleasant voice, and is expert in reading [the words of the] Torah, prophets, and writings, Mishnah, Midrash, laws, lore, and expert in all the blessings." So they cast their eyes on Rabbi Isaac ben Ami.

---

5. Following RaShI and Tosafot. His imposing height would be intimidating. Rabbenu Asher, however, defines "adam shel tzurah" as either an advanced student not yet at the level of a sage, or one suitable to hold public office.

6. Following Rabbenu Hananel and RaShI.

Is 'one with young children' the same as 'one whose house is empty?' Rav Hisda said: "This one [*i.e.* the latter] means one whose house is free from sin."

'And enjoys a good reputation:' Abaye said: "One free from any youthful aspersions."

"My own people acted toward Me like a lion in the forest; she raised her voice against Me" (Jeremiah 12:8). What does 'she raised her voice against Me' mean? Mar Zutra bar Tuviah said in the name of Rav, or, some say, Rabbi Hama [said] in the name of Rabbi Elazar: "This [verse] applies to an unworthy lector who goes to the lectern [to lead the prayer service]."

By way of comparison, the Jerusalem Talmud interprets the same Mishnah. Since the interpretation is anonymous, it is impossible to date accurately, but it is most likely around the same period. The list is less extensive than that of the Babylonian Talmud, though agreeing that the prayer leader must be modest, well versed, and pressed to support his family. The Jerusalem Talmud adds two pieces not found in the Babylonian Talmud. First, the prayer leader must be gentle to the young—perhaps a reference to earlier times when the *hazzan* was a teacher of young children. And second, the congregation is entitled to appoint anyone they see fit to serve as a prayer leader if there is no one who fulfills the stipulated qualifications.

Jerusalem Talmud, Ta'anit 2:2, 65b: Qualifications of Lector

'An elder who is well versed.' It has been taught: [He should be] modest, gentle to the young,[7] well versed in wisdom, well versed in lore, and own a house and a field. We have learned [in the Mishnah]: 'Whose house is empty,' yet you say this (i.e. that he owns a house and field)! [It means] he should have sons and daughters. If they do not have [someone with all these qualities], they appoint whomever they wish.

---

7. See Avot 3:12, where the same term appears. Cf. Frankel, *Korban Ha-Edah on Jerusalem Talmud, ad loc.*

Israel, Third Century:
A Worthy Lector's Prayers are Answered

While the Babylonian Talmud—as cited above—condemns an unworthy cantor, the Jerusalem Talmud cites a series of cases that demonstrate that the prayers of a worthy cantor are answered. First, a man who would rather go begging than try to recover his own property he suspects to have been illegally gained is considered to be a man worthy of leading prayers and having them answered. Second, during a drought, a particular mule driver was determined to be the proper person to lead communal prayers by virtue of a concurrent dream experienced by the local rabbis. His credentials were confirmed when the rabbis learned that he compromised his own livelihood to save a woman from choosing prostitution. Third, a similar story is told regarding a dream of a woman saved from a life of sin, and a worthy cantor. In this case, Rabbi Abbahu dreams that a man with an odd name should be appointed as prayer leader to avert a drought. His appointment proved successful and that aroused Rabbi Abbahu's curiosity. Upon questioning him, Rabbi Abbahu learns that this man leads an ignoble life with only one redeeming feature: he prevented a woman from becoming a prostitute. For that one virtuous deed, he merits having his prayers answered. The fourth and longest story also involves a concurrent, precognitive dream that requires the rabbis to seek out the subject of the dream whose prayers for rain would be answered on account of his piety. As a literary construct, the story engages the reader with a pattern of bizarre behavior that seems to contradict the presumption of merit. As a warrant for appointing a worthy cantor, this last story suggests that worthiness is a function of mindfulness and good character.

Jerusalem Talmud, Ta'anit 1:4, 64b–c: A Worthy Lector

A man came to one of Rabbi Yannai's relatives and said to him: "Master, gain [the] merit [of giving alms] through me." He said to him: "Didn't your father leave you money?" He said to him: "No." He said to him: "Collect what your father left as deposits." He said to him: "I heard they were stolen property." He said to him: "You are worthy to pray and to have your prayer answered."

A certain muleteer appeared in a dream to the rabbis. He prayed and the rain fell. They sent for him and brought him to appear before them. They said to him: "What is your worthiness?" He said to them: "Once, I rented out my mule to a certain woman. Along the way she began to cry. I said to her, 'What troubles you?' She said to me: 'My husband is in [debtors'] prison and I wanted to see what I could do to free him.' So I sold my mule and I said to her: 'Here is your money. Free your husband and do not sin.' They said to him: 'You are worthy to pray and to have your prayer answered.

Rabbi Abbahu had a dream. A certain fellow named Pentakaka prayed that rain would come, and rain fell. Rabbi Abbahu sent for [him] and [they—the messengers] brought him [to Rabbi Abahu]. He said to him: "What is your occupation?"[8] He said to him: "I commit five sins[9] every day: pimping, cleaning the brothel, bringing home the garments to wash them, dancing, and accompanying them with cymbals." He said to him: "But what good have you done?" He said to him: "Once I was cleaning out the brothel and a woman came and stood behind a pillar and cried, and I said to her: 'What troubles you?' and she said to me: 'My husband is in prison and I wanted to see what I could do for him.' So I sold my bed and covers and I gave her the money and said: 'Here is your money. Free your husband and do not sin.'" He said to him: "You are worthy to pray and have your prayer answered."

A pious man from Kefar Imi appeared to the rabbis in a dream as one who would pray and the rains would fall. The rabbis went to him. His wife told them that he was sitting atop a hill [in the fields]. They went out to see him. They said to him: "May you succeed in your work," but he did not respond. He sat down to eat but he did not say to them 'Join me in breaking bread.' When he returned home he put his cloak on top of a bundle of twigs. He came inside and said to his wife: "These rabbis are here to ask me to pray for rain. If I should pray and it rains, it would be a disgrace for them. If [I do] not [pray], it would be a desecration of God's name. Let you and me go up to the roof and pray. If it rains, we will tell them 'Heaven performed a miracle.' If it does not [rain], we shall tell them that we are not worthy to pray and have our prayers answered." They went up and prayed, and the rain fell. [When] they came down they said to them: "Why have the rabbis bothered to come here this day?" They said to him: "We need you to pray so that the rains will fall." He said to them: "You need my prayers? Heaven has already performed a miracle!" They said to him: "When we were on the hill, why did you not reply when we wished you success?" He said to them:

8. Following the emendation of Rabbi David ben Naftali Frankel.

9. Thus his name: penta-kaka.

"I was doing my job. Should I distract myself from my work?" They said to him: "And why, when you sat down to eat, did you not say to us 'You break bread too?'" He said to them: "Because I had only a meager piece. Had I invited you to join me I would appear to be a flatterer." They said to him: "When you got up to go, why did you put your garment atop the bundle?" He said to them: "Because the garment was not mine. It was borrowed so I could pray in it. Should I have ruined it?" They said to him: "And when you were atop the hill, why did your wife wear dirty clothes but when you came down from the hill she wore clean clothes?" He said to them: "When I was atop the hill she wore dirty clothes so that no man would leer at her. When I came down she wore clean clothes so that I would not leer at any other woman." They said to him: "You are worthy to pray and have your prayer answered."

Place Uncertain, Date Uncertain:
The Lector's Humility

Since there are no names or places mentioned in this passage, it is next to impossible to state with certainty when and where this tradition arose. Nevertheless, it advances the understanding of the virtue of humility included in the *Ta'anit* 16b list of the cantor's qualifications, and further develops the process mentioned in the Mishnah. Refusing the appointment suggests the cantor-designate feels unworthy of the honor. Of course, excessive refusal borders on arrogance. Hence, this anonymous tradition settles on a choreographed response to the invitation to serve as a prayer leader.

Babylonian Talmud, Berakhot 34a: A Lector's Humility

Our rabbis taught: Someone going to the lectern must first refuse, and if he does not refuse he is like an unsalted dish. Yet if he refuses overly much he is like an over salted dish. How should he behave? The first time [he is asked] he refuses. The second time [he is asked] he waivers. The third time [he is asked] he picks up his feet and goes.

Israel, Third Century: The Lector's Merits

The rabbis were curious about why some prayers were answered and others not. Knowing the reason for a prayer's acceptance would be most useful. Two talmudic anecdotes show that the character of the cantor can account for a prayer's acceptance. The second anecdote confirms that there were permanent cantors in place in certain communities before the third century and their duties included teaching children.

Babylonian Talmud, Ta'anit 24a

Rabbi [Judah the Patriarch] once ordained a fast [to end a drought] but no rain fell. Ilfa—some say: Rabbi Ilfi—went down [to the lectern to lead in prayer] and said: 'He makes the wind blow' and the wind blew; 'He makes the rain fall' and the rain fell. So Rabbi [Judah the Patriarch] asked him, 'What is your special merit?' He said: 'I live in a poor, remote place where wine for *Kiddush* and *Havdalah* is hard to come by yet I make a special effort to get wine for me and to assist others to fulfill their obligations.' Rav [Abba Arekha] happened to be in a certain place where he ordained a fast [to end a drought] but no rain fell. The lector went down to the lectern and said: 'He makes the wind blow' and the wind blew; 'He makes the rain fall' and the rain fell. So Rav [Abba Arekha] asked him: 'What is your special merit?' He said: 'I am a teacher of small children who teaches the poor and rich alike. I take nothing from those who cannot afford to pay. And I have a fishpond. To anyone who is reluctant to learn I offer fish as a bribe to get them to want to read.'

Israel, Second Century: The Pace of Prayer

The noted *tanna* (teacher) of the late first and early second century, Rabbi Eliezer, is the focus of two successive anecdotes. The first emphasizes that a slow pace in prayer is not a vice. The second implies that the cantor should not cut prayers short. In the Mishnaic period, it seems, the prayer leader had license to vary the length of certain prayers, and the liturgy was still fluid. Later authorities assumed that what worried Rabbi Eliezer was not that the content could be shortened, but the pace could be quickened to the point of being unintelligible.

Babylonian Talmud, Berakhot 34a

The rabbis taught: It once happened that a certain student went to the lectern in the presence of Rabbi Eliezer and went on longer than necessary. His students said to him: "Our rabbi, what a slow-poke he is!" He said to them: "He is not any slower than Moses our teacher about whom it is written: 'I fell down before the Lord . . . forty days and forty nights . . .' (Deut 9:18)." Again it once happened that a certain student went to the lectern in the presence of Rabbi Eliezer and shortened more than necessary. His students said to him: "What a short-cutter he is!" He said to them: "He is not shorter than Moses our teacher about whom it is written: 'Heal her now, O Lord, I beg you.' (Num 12:13)."

Israel, Third Century: Proper Enunciation

Not only must the cantor have a pleasant voice and be well versed in the liturgy, he must also be able to enunciate the words clearly. Like many languages, Hebrew was spoken in accordance with local dialects, some of which were problematic. The inability to clearly distinguish between similar—though different—letters would compromise intelligibility and consequently disqualify the inarticulate from serving as a cantor, at least according to the opinion of the late-third-century *amora* (post-Mishnaic teacher), Rav Assi.

Babylonian Talmud, Megillah 24b

Rav Assi said: A *kohen* from Bet Haifa or Bet She'an should not lift up his hands [to recite the Priestly Blessing]. It has likewise been taught: We do not bring down to the lectern men from Bet She'an or from Haifa or from Tiv'onim,[10] because they pronounce "alefs" as "ayins"[11] and "ayins" as "alefs."

10. The exact reference is unclear. Tiv'on, perhaps Tubun, a Galilean town west of Sepphoris is intended.

11. The letter "ayin" was a guttural, unlike the unaspirated "alef." Yemenite Jews preserve the difference to this day.

Israel, Third Century: Limiting the Lector's Creativity

The precise words of prayer seem to be fluid early on. And it was the prayer leader who might choose to embellish the language of prayer coined by the sages. It would seem that this phenomenon was particularly the case in the remote south of the land of Israel. The absence of standardization caused friction within the community. The Jerusalem Talmud reports of a small delegation sent to the south to bring order to the liturgy and put to rest the existent controversy. Hearing the prayer leader add two additional descriptive adjectives expressing God's power ("*abir*" or powerful, and "*amitz*" or valiant) in the opening blessing of the *Amidah*, they intervened. Whether the silencing of the cantor occurred during the actual prayer service or afterward is subject to debate. But the effect was the same. The rule that words of prayer composed by the rabbis are fixed and inviolate was asserted and enforced. It is of special interest that the text uses the word "*hazzana*" to describe the prayer leader.

Jerusalem Talmud, Berakhot 9:1, 12d

The text actually uses the Aramaic "*hazzan*" to refer to the prayer leader, making it the earliest instance of the use of the term for a prayer leader.

> Rabbi Yohanan and Rabbi Yonatan went to make peace in those villages of the south. They came to one place and found the cantor saying: 'God, the great, mighty, awesome, powerful, and valiant.' So they silenced him. They said to him: "You do not have the right to add to the formula that the sages established for the blessings."

GEONIC LITERATURE

By the middle of the eighth century, over 90 percent of world Jewry was located within the Islamic world. With the rise of the Abbasid dynasty, whose capital was in Baghdad, the Jewish community in Babylonia emerged as the preeminent moral and intellectual force in Jewry, surpassing the authority of the Jewish community in Israel. Babylonian Jewry was organized around two central institutions. The exilarch and his bureaucracy served primarily as the temporal and political leaders. The gaon served as the religious leader, presiding over the great academies of learning in Sura and Pumbedita. During this time, the first prayer book and the earliest legal codes in Judaism were generated, complementing a significant body of responsa—written answers to questions of law and interpretation. Yet few of the responsa of this period have reached us in their original form. Geonic traditions remain difficult to attribute. Even so, any tradition ascribed to the Geonim demanded due consideration by the medieval rabbis.[12]

Born in Upper Egypt, Sa'adiah ben Joseph al-Fayyumi (882–942) reached the climax of his career as the head of the academy in Sura, where he served as gaon. His commentary on the Torah has survived piecemeal, but his book on philosophy, *Beliefs and Opinions*, written in 933 CE, remains a classic in Jewish philosophy. He was a key figure in a series of disputes—with the Karaites, with the exilarch, and with the scholars of the land of Israel—that established the parameters and the primacy of the Geonate. Sa'adiah is also attributed with ordering one of the first Jewish prayer books. Notable as well is that the last paragraph near the end of *Beliefs and Opinions* on the eight rhythmic modes is the oldest known Jewish text on music. Sa'adiah writes that music may influence ethics.

Teshuvot Ha-Geonim Ha-Hadashot, No. 24: Dismissing a Cantor[13]

They asked him: Is it possible to dismiss a prayer leader and replace him with another when the congregation complains against him? And he responded that this requires resolution. Of course, the law allows for replacing him with another. Someone who mediates between Israel and their Father in heaven[14] must be righteous, upright, bodily clean, and free of any fault. If this is not the case, the sages have already said (*Ta'anit* 16b): "'She raised her voice against Me therefore I have despised her (Jer 12:8)' this applies to an unworthy lector who goes down to the lectern."

Without qualification, this applies to weekdays—even those which are not fast days—and certainly to the New Year

---

12. Cf. Brody, *Geonim and the Shaping*.

13. The following responsum also appears in the *Siddur of Rav Amram*, 94, sec 55.

14. It is noteworthy that Sa'adiah sees the role of the cantor as a mediator of prayer—a spiritual role, rather than a functionary who fulfills congregants' obligation to pray—a legal role. Later authorities will dispute this.

and the Day of Atonement, fast days, and any day when there is a need to add prayers for mercy where the cantor must be—as Rabbi Judah said—a father of young children whom he cannot support, etc. until "free from aspersions from youth" [—in his youth, from which we deduce that is he must be removed for past indiscretions, how much the moreso for current complaints].

Teshuvot Ha-Geonim, Sha'arei Teshuvah, No. 51: Dismissing a Cantor

And further on this matter: Should a prayer leader about whom terrible things are being said be removed and another put in place?

And he answered: This matter need not be asked at all. Yet if there is no one there comparable to him, he must be scolded and rebuked [but left in place]. And if they scolded him and he does not listen to them, he is removed on account of ". . . she has uttered her voice against Me, therefore I have despised her." (Jer 12:8)

Teshuvot Ha-Geonim, Sha'arei Teshuvah, No. 50: Grounds for Dismissal

Rabbenu or Rav Hai was the last of the Babylonian Geonim based in Pumbeditha. He ascended to office in 1004 and died in 1038. His response, despite its brevity, can be divided into two parts. In the first part, Rav Hai ruled that a cantor whose current behavior was respectable retained his appointment despite a reputation for prior bad acts. Interestingly, Rav Hai seemed to say that repentance was necessary for suspicion of wrongdoing separate from actual wrongdoing. In the second part, Rav Hai ruled on who was suitable to lead prayer services on a fast day. After declaring that suspicion of past sins was insufficient to disqualify a cantor from leading prayers generally, he likewise ruled that a cantor of dubious reputation was not to be dismissed even on a fast day, presumably because of the complexity of the liturgy and the congregation's need for a skilled prayer leader to mediate the words. However, on a fast day a cantor who did not fast could was to be dismissed since his leading the service would be an exercise in hypocrisy: reciting a text that assumed he was fasting when he was not. A current lack of piety was grounds for dismissal, while past suspicions were not.

Rabbenu Hai:

With regard to what you[15] asked: May a person whose reputation is impugned and is suspected of committing adultery or rob(bery) or oppress(ion) serve as a prayer leader?

If he repented, we accept him and follow his leading. In any case, on a fast day, we do not dismiss him if his reputation was sullied in the past. Similarly, a prayer leader who does not fast on a fast day is dismissed since only one who is fasting can really say 'Answer us [. . . on this day of our fasting].' Someone who is not fasting cannot say 'Answer us.'

Teshuvot Ha-Geonim, Sha'arei Tzedek, No. 50: A Cantor With an Impugned Reputation

The question posed is the same as the previous one answered by Rav Hai. But the unnamed responder gave a different answer. Even if he repented, a prayer leader who was suspected of past sins could not lead prayers on fast days since he had violated the requirement of being of good stature as understood by Abaye in Ta'anit 16a. Both this responsum and the previous one reveal that the institution of a permanent cantor was well established in the Geonic period and once appointed to the position, only the most serious and uncorrected behavior could remove a cantor from office.

> You asked about a prayer leader who was rumored or suspected of adultery or theft or extortion.
>
> If he repented, he may be appointed and followed in prayer, except on fast days, when he may not go down to the lectern because he fails [to comply with the requirement of] 'good stature' since his reputation has been previously sullied. Similarly, someone who has fasted, so that he may say 'Answer us' in earnest, should replace a cantor who did not fast along with the congregation. Anyone who has not fasted cannot possibly say 'Answer us.'

Teshuvot Ha-Geonim, Ge'onei Mizrah u-Ma'arav, No. 171: A Cantor With an Impugned Reputation

To Rav Yosef, May his soul rest in paradise:

15. The unidentified questioner.

"Reuven," a *kohen*, has been among us for many years as a guest in our community, and he has been appointed a prayer leader. In time, a rumor spread that he regularly did business with deviants who visit prostitutes. Though this rumor persisted, the members of the community did not feel a need to check or investigate the reports about him since he was the permanent prayer leader and led prayers morning and evening in the synagogue. But the rumors grew more and more intense, so much so that people in the community came forward and testified that they saw him frequently leaving brothels. They further testified about this "Reuven" that gentiles accosted him in the alleyway where he resided until he paid them off to leave him alone. And another testified that he saw him speaking with a woman on the road. He solicited her and she evaded him and then turned to him and revealed this to him saying, "Reuven, don't you know that I am Jewish. I am so-and-so daughter of so-and-so and you are pressing me so much." When he heard this he recoiled. And others testified, saying they heard from gentiles who were disparaging Jews saying 'This is your ethical code? A man so perverted serves as your cantor?' And another testified that he had corrupt relations with a certain boy. With this cumulative testimony, the community dismissed him. And now, may our rabbi rule for us: May this "Reuven" be restored to his position and apply to him [the principle] 'He repented' without any equivocation? And may he eat *hallah* and bless first—or not?

Answer:

. . . even though there were no eyewitnesses to his conduct in the brothels, there is suspicion. And he should not have put his reputation at risk. He should have distanced himself from all things foul and even remotely foul. Since he did not do so and did not circumscribe his behavior, he became blemished, whether for prayer or priesthood. And the prayers that you mention he led morning and evening were reminders of sin before our Father in Heaven, as it says (Jer 7:9–10): "Will you steal, murder, and commit adultery . . . and come stand before me in this house [where my Name is called." And then it says there "has this house become a den of violators" (v. 11) and in the end it says: "I will cast you out of My sight" (v. 15).

And the elders of the community did not act properly when they did not take the rumors seriously and they did not act rightly. A prayer leader must be excellent in his ways and circumspect in his actions since he is the mediator between Israel and their Father in Heaven. And thus we have learned (*b. Ta'an.* 16a).

With regard to restoring him: how is that possible after all the testimony against him that would require punishment in court? (Have we not learned explicitly: "Rav said: We administer lashes over evil rumors, as it says [1 Sam 2:24]: 'Don't, my sons! It is no favorable report I hear the people of the Lord spreading about'?") He has abased himself and thus rendered himself unfit.

Therefore, this "Reuven" is presumed to be like any other Jews with regard to [being allowed to read Torah] but not to aggrandize him in any other way.

And peace to you.

Babylonia, Tenth Century

This responsum is attributed to Rav Yehudai Gaon and appears in *Halakhot Ketzuvot*, No. 9. It is also cited by Rabbi Mordekhai ben Hillel, a student of thirteenth-century rabbi Meir of Rothenberg, and found in manuscript form.

Teshuvot Ha-Geʾonim Ha-Hadashot, page 40, n. 65: Leading Prayers By Heart

And [regarding] what you asked: may a prayer leader recite the penitential[16] prayers and hymns by heart? This is the custom in Pumbedita. But in Sura, a cantor may only recite the penitential prayers and hymns for the Day of Atonement from a text so that he makes no mistakes and [better] directs his heart. However, on other holidays, if he wants to recite the prayers by heart, he may choose to do so. And this is the custom of [both] the academies.

Seder Rav Amram Gaʾon, Tefillah: Young Cantors

They further asked Rav Natronai Gaon: If [there is] only one regular prayer leader and he is sometimes busy at work, may youths eighteen or seventeen but not full-bearded be appointed prayer leaders so prayer will be possible?

16. Oxford MS 678, p. 30d.

> What the Sages ruled was the ideal. So while a full bearded
> [prayer leader] . . . is preferable . . . even [a prayer leader who is]
> thirteen [is permitted].

Teshuvot Ha-Geʾonim Ha-Hadashot, No. 15: Young Cantors

> They asked Rav Natronai Gaon: Is it possible to appoint as can-
> tors youths who are eighteen or seventeen years of age who have
> not yet grown full beards to fulfill the obligations of the congre-
> gation in a place where there is only one [prayer leader] who
> regularly leads the congregation in prayer and sometimes that
> man is busy at work [and not available to lead prayers] and thus
> allow the congregation to pray without interruption?

And he answered:

> We note that the sages (b. Meg. 24a; b. Hul. 24b) said only he
> who has grown a full beard may lead prayers or bless the con-
> gregation. This is the ideal. It is preferable whenever possible to
> have a mature man [lead] rather than a child. But surely it is far
> better to have a youth of eighteen or seventeen [lead prayers]
> than omit the Kedushah or the Kaddish. In fact, even a youth
> of thirteen years and one day, if not otherwise possible, can be
> appointed a cantor for it says: "anyone who is not obligated to
> perform an act cannot fulfill the obligation for others." Since a
> youth of thirteen years and one day is obligated [to pray], he is
> thus permitted [to lead].

Tractate Soferim 14:17: Young Cantors

Scholars generally consider this work to be an external tractate, that is,
one that was not part of the canon of talmudic literature. John Townsend[17]
dates this text to approximately the eighth century. The prevailing opinion is that final redaction took place sometime during the Geonic period.
Based on a number of clues, M. B. Lerner[18] speculates that it is a southern
Italian work. Robert Brody[19] however, maintains that it is a composite
work. The consensus of opinion regarding the name of this work is that it
is a misnomer. Rather than "soferim," meaning, "scribes," the original title

17. Townsend, Study of Judaism, 62.
18. Safrai, Literature of the Sages, 1:399.
19. Brody, Geonim and the Shaping, 11n40.

was *Baraita Sfarim* or *Masekhta d'Sfarim*, in reference to "Holy Scriptures," the texts read publicly in the synagogue on various occasions.

Notable is that the minimum age for a prayer leader is raised to twenty, with age eighteen as a possibility for those whose beards had grown in.

> The minor they mentioned—from twelve years old and up he leads the *Shema*. But [the person] who goes down to the lectern and raises his hands [for the priestly blessing]: not until he is twenty years old and bearded. But if he has no beard and he is twenty years old—even though he might be thought to be a eunuch, and some say, if were he actually a eunuch—he is allowed. But if his beard had grown in at age eighteen, he is permitted to pass before the lectern and raise his hands.

Blind Cantors

Although the answer is terse, the first responsum, ascribed to Sa'adiah, suggests that in the ninth century, Babylonia cantors were appointed to permanent positions. On the question itself, there is a difference of opinion. Rav Natronai narrowly construes Mishnah *Megillah* 4:6 to mean that the explicit permission for a blind man to lead *Shema* and read aloud the Aramaic translation of the public Torah reading implies that he may not lead other prayers. Rav Sa'adiah seems to read the Mishnah broadly, inferring that the permission to lead *Shema* extends to other prayers. Neither of these two Geonim expresses the concern that a blind cantor will not be able to recite the liturgy without error.

Teshuvot Ha-Geonim Ha-Hadashot, No. 24: On Blind Cantors

> And as to a blind prayer leader, they sent [the question to him[20]] and he responded: "A blind man is fit and he may not be removed as long as his conduct is appropriate.[21]

20. Presumably, Rav Sa'adiah Gaon.

21. Jewish practice follows the opinion of Rav Sa'adiah. Historically, a number of blind cantors have distinguished themselves. Moishele Soorkis (1900–1974), known as "Der Blinder," was born in Uman, lost his sight as an infant, came to the United States in 1913, learned braille, and served with distinction in congregations in Chicago, Boston, Philadelphia, and New York. A number of recordings survived him. Abe Immerman (1907–2003), known as "The Blind Cantor of South Africa," was a noted educator and cantor.

Teshuvot Ha-Geonim, Sha'arei Teshuvah, No. 245: On Blind Cantors

Rav Natronai ascended to the Geonate in Pumbedita in 719 CE:

> Rav Natronai of Blessed Memory:
> A blind man may go to the lectern and lead *Shema* and translate, but he may not read the Torah portion . . .[22]

Babylonia, Tenth Century:
A Cantor Who Does Not Understand the Words He Says

Rav Sherira took office in Pumbedita in 968 CE. His epistle, despite some inherent difficulties, remains the primary source for the history of this period.

The Mishnah (*Ta'anit* 2:2)—as well as both Talmuds (Babylonian Talmud *Ta'anit* 16a; Jerusalem Talmud *Ta'anit* 2:2, 65b)—requires the cantor to be an expert, well versed in the text. Rav Sherira explains the nature of this expertise by ruling that the cantor must know the meaning of the text as well as the words.

Teshuvot Ha-Geonim, No. 352:
A Cantor Who Does Not Understand

> Rav Sherira, of blessed memory:
> A prayer leader who does not know the "intention" of the prayer is forbidden to lead the service since he cannot fulfill the obligation for others. This applies to the permanent prayer leader. But for another, it is retroactively allowable [for him to lead] since he is not permanent. This is certainly so on fast days and times of need. The "intention of the words" means to know them. Is it not said: "He must direct his heart to gain mercy for his people?"

Babylonia, Eleventh Century

Teshuvot Ha-Geonim, Sha'arei Tzedek, No. 120: A Tardy Cantor

According to the superscript, Rav Hai is the author of this responsum. The author goes to considerable length to excuse a cantor who comes so

---

22. This follows the opinion of the anonymous authority in Mishnah *Megillah* 4:6.

late to the synagogue prayer service that he misses the private recitation of the *Amidah*. It is not clear from the responsum whether the morning service or afternoon service was intended. If the former, the cantor had missed a substantial part of the service. Rather than castigating the cantor for tardiness, the author finds a way of accommodating him. Reviewing the *Amidah* aloud would include fulfillment of the cantor's obligation for private prayer so long as the cantor intends it so. The author also deflects talmudic principle that criticizes a private worshiper who prays loudly— which the cantor would certainly do—by arguing that this is an allowable exception. Here we have a fine example of how the early medieval rabbis sought to defend cantors against complaints.

> You asked whether a prayer leader is obligated to recite the silent *Amidah* afterwards when he [belatedly] entered the synagogue to find the congregation already reciting the silent prayer and he needs to go to the lectern and lead the repetition immediately. Or, shall we say he fulfills his obligation [for private prayer] through the public recital?
>
> And he responded: This is your answer.
>
> There is no need to go back and pray silently since he has already fulfilled his [private] obligation through the prayer he recited publicly. If he was mindful to fulfill the obligation for others, he surely fulfills the obligation for himself. And we do not say 'He who causes his voice to be heard in prayer is considered among those of weak faith (*b. Ber.* 24b)'[23] since he does so in exceptional circumstances. And since it is for the public good, it is not at all considered of weak faith.

Babylonia, Tenth Century: The Requirement of a Pleasant Voice

Israel Abrahams[24] has argued that, "The singing Precentor was not tolerated without a struggle, though he eventually became a marked feature in the synagogue." But the evidence shows otherwise. As early as the Geonic Period the musical abilities of the cantor were desirable and sought after.

23. RaShI explains that one who raises his voice believes that God would not hear him otherwise. This is a weakness in belief. See also Shimoni, *Dov Hyman*, Yalk. Ketuvim 1056.

24. Abrahams, *Jewish Life*, 31.

Teshuvot Ha-Geonim, Sha'arei Tzedek, No. 178: The Need for a Pleasant Voice

The following excerpt was published under the heading: "Ten Examples of Piety Manifested by Rav That His Successors Were Unable to Maintain Entirely But Would Keep in Part."

> Tenth, that his voice was pleasant and he would routinely go down to the lectern as well as translate for his master—and anyone who needed [his services]—and to fulfill what it says 'Honor God with your treasure' (Prov 3:9). And Rabbi Hiyya bar Adda followed after him, as it says: "Rabbi Hiyya bar Adda, the son of Bar Kappara's sister, had a pleasant voice and when he went down to the lectern, he would say: "'Give pleasure to your Creator with what He has blessed you. Thus it says: 'Honor God with your treasure.'"[25]

Tractate Soferim 3:10

Certainly by the tenth century, a musical tradition pervaded the synagogue. With the expectation that the Torah reader and prayer leaders would be singing, appointing officiants who would do it well became an imperative:

> Said Rabbi Shaftai in the name of Rabbi Yohanan: The verse that says: "Even I have given them bad statutes" (Ezek 20:25) is applied to him who does not read sweetly or repeat without melody.

Tractate Soferim 14:9: A Sweet Voice

The person who recites the supplementary reading approaches immediately, holds the Torah, and says the first verse of *Shema* sweetly, with the people answering after him.

---

25. *Pesiq.* 23 and *PDK* 10:3, ed. Mandlebaum, Vol 1, p. 164. See also *Mid. Tan.* Re'eh 9. Aaron Heyman (*Toldot Tanaim v'Amoraim*, 2:441) surmises that based on this Midrash, RaShI comments on the verse in Proverbs "With all that God has granted you, even with a pleasant voice. (Do not read with your treasure [*honekha*] but with your throat [*garonkha*]."

MS Oxford 659, 11[26]: Cantors Who Add Words

That the liturgy was fixed by the earlier rabbis and should remain inviolate is a recurrent Geonic concern. It indicates that as early as the ninth century, cantors were tampering with the prayer service for musical, vocal, or other reasons. The frequency of cantorial expatiation is reflected by the intensity of the objection and the severity of the penalty.

> From Rav Natronai son of Rav Hilai, head of the academy in the city of Mehasia:
> You asked about cantors[27] who appear as if they are careful but do wrong by adding to the formula for prayer coined by the scholars and change [the words].
> So we see that they are acting improperly, changing the custom of both academies and of all Israel.

She'iltot of Rav Ahai, Parshat Yitro, ed. Mirski, p. 140 in Commentary of Rabbi Yohanan ben Rav Reuben of Ochrida[28]

She'iltot formed a collection of homilies following the pattern of the Torah reading cycle. Each homily followed a four-section structure introducing a particular commandment and then presenting two alternatives to a legal question arising therefrom. The classic formulation concludes with a resolution.[29] Little is known of Rav Ahai. Either Sherira Gaon or his son, Hayya, first connected Rav Ahai with the She'iltot.[30]

> And, similarly, Rav Amram, of blessed memory, said: Rav Nahshon said in the academy that in every location where there is a rabbi we do not change at all the prayers that were fixed by the sages nor do we say piyyut, and neither do we admit into the synagogue a cantor[31] who knows piyyut. And a synagogue that includes piyyut testifies that [the congregants] are not scholars. And Rav Amram said: we do not change from what the rabbis of the Talmud instituted [whether for weekdays] or for festivals.

26. Cited by Ta-Shma, "On the Beginning," 285–88, and in Sperber, *Minhagei Yisrael*, 4:36.

27. *Hazzanin* in Aramaic.

28. Sperber, *Minhagei Yisrael*, 4:35.

29. Cf. Brody, *Geonim and the Shaping*, 202–15.

30. Brody, *Geonim and the Shaping*, 207.

31. *Hazzan* in Hebrew.

And should we find ourselves in a place where the cantor says something that was not coined by the scholars, we dismiss him. The great authority Rav Zemah ruled that a prayer leader who adds to the fixed liturgy is subject to ostracism and must be dismissed.

MEDIVEAL SOURCES

Spain/North Africa: Eleventh Century

Born in Fez in 1013, Rabbi Isaac ben Ya'akov HaKohen al-Fasi, known by his acronym RIF, studied with Rabbenu Hananel in Kairouan as well as with Rav Nissim before the latter was elected Gaon. His *Sefer Halakhot*, now appended to every standard printed version of the Talmud, summarized and discussed talmudic sources. He shows a preference for anonymous talmudic sources over the accepted principles of adjudication and he disputes the Geonim in many passages. His decisions became the basis for Maimonides's *Mishneh Torah*. He died in Lucena, Spain in 1103. His responsa were originally written in Arabic.

In the first responsum, al-Fasi offers a procedure for determining what—if anything—should be done when a cantor's honesty is in question. The first step, he argues, is to determine whether or not the testimony against the cantor is reliable. This requires a background check of the witnesses as well as an investigation of the facts. The next step is to determine whether the testimony against the cantor is current. For example, past misdeeds are overlooked if the cantor has changed his behavior since he was observed swearing falsely. Interestingly, if the testimony proves to be reliable, al-Fasi only disqualifies the cantor from serving as a witness but not from serving as a prayer leader.

In the second responsum, al-Fasi considers two separate questions. The first question concerns the possibility of a local resident opting out of his communal obligations, refusing to pay his share of the cantor's salary. On this matter al-Fasi rules that the payment of the cantor's salary is a universal communal requirement analogous to purchasing a Torah scroll or religious texts for which residents compel one another to participate. The second question concerns the disqualification of a cantor who sings popular songs. Al-Fasi calls singing Arabic songs an obscenity" that is grounds for the cantor's dismissal. The language of the text suggests that the Arabic songs were not sung in synagogue yet even so, were symptomatic of behavior so reprehensible that the cantor could no longer be retained as a religious leader. Al-Fasi suggests that there are other similar indiscretions that require a cantor's dismissal, but does not name them.

In each of these responsa, al-Fasi uses the word "*hazzan*," suggesting that by his day the term was already in vogue as the official designation of the synagogue prayer leader, although he also lapses into use of the phrase "prayer leader."

She'elot U'Teshuvot Ha-RIF, No. 164: A Cantor Who Swears Falsely

Question: A cantor about whom two witnesses testified that he swore falsely, and two [other] witnesses testified that he repented and is careful about his oaths.

Answer: We must see whether these [first] witnesses are careful not to testify gratuitously but only as necessary, if and when they swear they do not swear falsely to confirm their testimony. Therefore, we investigate them [to determine] when they heard the cantor swear falsely. If [he did so] a while ago and repented, his repentance is complete and he is fit. But if they heard him after he repented, he is disqualified as a witness. And if these witnesses are not careful in swearing but swear falsely, their testimony is invalid.

She'elot U'Teshuvot Ha-RIF, No. 281: A Resident Who Refuses to Contribute to the Cantor's Salary, A Cantor Who Sings Secular Songs

. . . May a person who refuses to pay the salary of the synagogue cantor be compelled to pay? And may the congregation dismiss the cantor who was rumored to have acted wrongly, for example, sang Arabic songs and the like?

. . . [H]e who refuses to pay the cantor's salary may be compelled to pay according to the law of cities and the law [requiring] the residents of a city to compel one another to pay for a Torah scroll and [books of] the prophets and writing. A cantor who uttered obscenities and sang Arabic songs is [to be] dismissed, as well as for all other similar things. It is said: "She raised her voice against Me, therefore I have rejected her" (Jer 12:8).[32]

Spain: Twelfth Century

Teshuvot Rav Yosef ibn Migash, No. 95: A Cantor With a Damaged Reputation

Rabbi Yosef ben Meir Ha-Levi ibn Migash, probably born in Seville in 1077, was a disciple of and successor to al-Fasi at the age of twenty-six. His career was centered in Lucena, Spain. He died in 1141.

Rabbi Judah's statement in the Talmud that a cantor's youthful indiscretions are held against him is interpreted by ibn Migash to mean only in circumstances where the cantor was unrepentant. Only persistent sinfulness is grounds for dismissal. In addition, rumors alone are insufficient. Accurate, valid, and reliable testimony is necessary before any challenge to the cantor's position can be considered. Further, ibn Migash limits the mishnaic requirement of an unblemished reputation from youth to leading the service on fast days. He thus takes issue with Rav Amram Gaon. So important was the position of cantor that even individual wayward cantors had to be given every legal advantage.

> Question: "Re'uven" was a prayer leader in a city and another city sent for him to be their prayer leader (and he is suitable since he possesses most of the qualifications that our rabbis, of blessed memory, remind us that any prayer leader must have). Yet one of the elders of the congregation objected, saying it is inappropriate to appoint him because of the damage to his reputation from his youth. Any appointment is "contingent on his good stature" as understood by the Talmud to mean that his reputation has been undamaged since his youth. And one of the teachers taught that he is allowed to be a lector since the damage to his reputation was merely a rumor without verification by two witnesses, and it is possible that the rumor was false. He brought proof for his view from what they said about this matter: "He whose reputation was damaged [by what he allegedly did in his youth]: what is this bad reputation like? For instance, two witnesses come and tell us that 'he made a false claim against them.'" But no wrong can be ascribed to him by rumor alone. Another teacher disputed him and said it is forbidden to

---

32. Cf. *b. Ta'an.*16a.

appoint him prayer leader and showed us a responsum of the Geonim, of blessed memory: ". . . and you asked: a lector who is subject to evil complaints, may he be dismissed and replaced by another, *etc.*" just as it is written in Seder Rav Amram. The first teacher dismissed this proof, saying that the ruling of the Geonim applies to someone about whom a rumor persists. And in this case, the complaint is not about what he does now but what he did in the past. May our master instruct us and may his reward be doubled.

Answer: If the complaint against the prayer leader relates to current behavior, it is appropriate to dismiss him because the persistence of the rumor verifies his disqualification. And they have already said: "The gossip of a place must not cease for a day and a half" (*b. M.K.* 18b; *b. Yeb.* 25a). And if the prayer leader were suspected of being unfit, it would be inappropriate to respond to his prayers. And the rabbis, of blessed memory, already interpreted "She raised her voice against me" (Jer 12:8) *etc.* to apply to an unfit lector.

Nevertheless, if the complaint is against what he did in the past and he is not suspect [now] and we see signs of penitence and rectitude, we do not dismiss on account of what happened in the past. He has repented and corrected his ways. We do not take into consideration what was.

The key factor in what we need in a prayer leader—that there be no damage to his reputation in his youth—applies only to the case of one who goes to the lectern on a public fast day, as they said (*b. Taʿan.* 16b): "And they explained: 'Good reputation': that no damage was done to his reputation as a youth." Aside from [fast days], for prayers we do not take this into consideration so long as we see him now walking on the right path and he seems to be repentant, responding to his prayer is allowed. We ignore what is past since repentance is acceptable to Him, as it says: "Return, O rebellious children, I will heal your afflictions" (Jer 3:22).

Teshuvot Rav Joseph ibn Migash, No. 180:
A Cantor Who Prolongs His Prayers

On a practical note, ibn Migash counsels cantors to be alert and sensitive to the congregation, particularly when it comes to needlessly lengthening the service. Yet he comes to the defense of cantors who do so when there are congregants who also do so.

Will our master inform us if there is any reason to inhibit a
prayer leader who prolongs his prayer so that it becomes a supplication or so that it corresponds with some of the people in the
congregation who also do so?

Answer: A prayer leader who stretches out his prayer—if
there is someone in the congregation who similarly prolongs
his prayer so there is a need for the congregation to wait for
them [to finish]—commits no wrong. Yet if there is no one in
the congregation who delays and prolongs his prayer but him,
it is fitting for him to show some manners and etiquette toward
the congregation and not stretch out his prayers, imposing upon
the congregation, and making them wait for him. As they [the
rabbis], of blessed memory, have said: "It was said about Rabbi
Akiva that when he prayed with the congregation he would
shorten and proceed."

Spain/North Africa: Twelfth Century

Rabbi Moses ben Maimon, or Maimonides, was born in Cordova, Spain
in 1135, and died in Fustat (Old Cairo) in 1204. Marvin Fox[33] calls him
"the greatest and most creative Jewish Thinker since the close of the Talmud," adding: "No one has made contributions to Jewish learning, Jewish
law, and Jewish thought equal in depth or originality." In his *Introduction
to the Code of Maimonides*, Isidore Twersky[34] asserts that his works represent "an unprecedented conjunction of halakhic authority and philosophical prestige." Three inscriptions, Abraham Joshua Heschel mentions
near the end of his seminal biography of Maimonides,[35] marked his burial
space in Tiberias. The first, a tribute to his genius, read: "Here lies a man
and yet not a man; If you were a man, then heavenly creatures created
you." The second, a statement of the controversy surrounding his influence, read: "Here lies Moses Maimuni, the banished heretic." The third,
and the one that persists, tersely depicts the high regard in which he was
held: "From Moses to Moses, there was no one like Moses." His Hebrew
language compendium of Jewish law, *Mishneh Torah*, was, according to
Twersky, "designed as a standard manual, a ready, steady and uniform
reference book for practically all issues."[36]

33. Fox, *Interpreting Maimonides*, x.
34. Twersky, *Introduction to the Code*, 1.
35. Heschel, *Maimonides*, 147.
36. Twersky, *Introduction to the Code*, 18.

In the following three passages from his code of Jewish law, Maimonides includes several disparate laws regarding the role of the cantor and the cantor's qualifications incorporating many of the talmudic statements. Noteworthy is the fact that while his code is arranged thematically, for Maimonides, the subject of the cantor did not warrant its own section. Instead, the laws regarding the cantor are included incidentally in his presentation of the laws of prayer.

According to Maimonides, the role of the cantor is to fulfill the prayer obligations of the untrained. Those who are capable of praying on their own must do so, with the exception of the Days of Awe. Since worshipers are less familiar with the liturgy of Rosh Hashanah and Yom Kippur, and given the literary complexities of some of the specific prayers, even those who are generally capable of reciting the liturgy on their own may rely on the cantor's prayers. As to the qualifications of a cantor: Maimonides rules that the cantor must be erudite and of high character. Having a pleasant voice and familiarity with the words are of some importance, but cannot compare with maturity. Maimonides stresses that the inarticulate are excluded from serving as cantors. And a cantor must be properly attired. In chapter 10, Maimonides addresses what to do should a cantor err, particularly in the *Amidah*. This central prayer requires mindfulness. An error in its recital requires another, correct recital. The place to which the worshiper must return when making the correct recital depends on where, in the *Amidah*, the error occurred. But the rules for the cantor are different. Should the cantor err in such a way that requires him to repeat all or part of the *Amidah* correctly, the congregation would be forced to endure a longer service. To avoid imposing this hardship on the congregation, Maimonides rules that when the cantor repeats the *Amidah* aloud he would also fulfill his own personal obligation for its silent recital provided that his public recital is correct. This is an innovation.

Finally, Maimonides considers the case of a cantor who, having made an error, is so agitated and confused he does not know where and how to continue.

Rabbi Moses ben Maimon, Mishneh Torah, Laws of Prayer,
Chapters 8, 10, 11: The Rules for a Cantor

Hilkhot Tefilah (*Laws of Prayer*) Chapter 8

(9) The prayer leader fulfills the obligation [of prayer] for the public.[37] How so? When he prays [aloud] and they listen and answer 'Amen' after each and every blessing, it is as if they were praying [themselves]. To whom does this [rule that the prayer leader fulfills the obligation for the public] apply? [It applies] to [any]one [among them] who does not know how to pray. But one who knows how to pray must fulfill his obligation with his own prayer.

(10) When does this [rule that the prayer leader fulfills the obligation for others] apply? [It applies] to all days throughout the year except the New Year and the Day of Atonement during the Jubilee year. On these two days the prayer leader fulfills the obligation for one who knows how to pray as well as for one who does not since [on these days] the [*Amidah*] blessings are long and most do not know them [so] they [all] can concentrate on them as the prayer leader [recites them]. Thus, the one [who knows how to pray] has permission to rely on the prayer leader on these two days so that the prayer leader fulfills his obligation.

(11) We do not appoint a prayer leader unless among the congregation he excels in learning and merits. If he is old, [appointing him] is most praiseworthy. We try to find a prayer leader who has a pleasant voice and is well versed.[38] One who is not full-bearded—even though he is a great scholar—may not be a prayer leader because of the dignity due the congregation, but he may lead the *Shema* from the time he reaches puberty after thirteen years.

(12) The inarticulate—for instance, he who reads an "ayin" as an "alef" or an "alef" for an "ayin," and anyone who cannot enunciate the letters as they are intended—may not be appointed as a prayer leader. The rabbi may appoint one of his students to pray before the congregation.[39] The blind may lead the *Shema* and serve as a prayer leader. However, one with exposed shoulders—even though he may lead the *Shema*—may not serve as a prayer leader until he is covered.

Hilkhot Tefillah (*Laws of Prayer*) Chapter 10

(1) He who prays mindlessly must go back and pray mindfully. However, if he prayed the first blessing [of the *Amidah*]

---

37. That is, for the congregation.

38. That is, well versed in Scripture.

39. It is not clear whether Maimonides is ruling that a rabbi may appoint one of his students even if the student is inarticulate. See *b. Meg.* 24b and *b. B Metz.* 85b.

mindfully, he need not [go back].[40] He who errs in one of the first three [blessings] goes back to the beginning. If he erred in one of the last three [blessings], he goes back to the beginning of the last three. If he erred in one of the middle [blessings], he goes back to the beginning of the blessing in which he erred and then goes on to complete his prayer as it is arranged. Similarly, a prayer leader who errs when he prays aloud goes back accordingly.

(2) If a prayer leader erred in the silent recitation of [the *Amidah*] prayer, I say he does not go back and repeat it because of the imposition on the congregation. Rather, let him rely on the [*Amidah*] prayer he recites aloud, provided that if he errs in it, he must go back as any individual must go back.

(3) A prayer leader who errs and is so flustered that [he] does not know from where he should begin, [should be given an hour[41] to collect himself]. [But] after an hour, he should be replaced. If he erred in the prayer that curses heretics, we do not wait for him. Instead, a replacement should take over immediately since [we suspect that the prayer leader] might have been thrust into heresy,[42] that is, unless he had already begun. In that case, we wait an hour. [When a replacement is solicited] the replacement should not refuse.

Hilkhot Tefillah (Laws of Prayer) Chapter 11

(4) ... and when it is time for the prayer leader to lead prayer, he stands on the ground [level][43] at the lectern with his face toward the ark the same way as the people [are facing].[44]

---

40. In Laws of Prayer 4:15, Maimonides rules that any prayer recited mindlessly is not a prayer. By making a distinction between the first blessing and the others, Maimonides avoids contradiction.

41. Since Maimonides is concerned with avoiding the lengthening of the prayer service, it is most unlikely that the word "*sha-ah*" (hour) actually means sixty minutes. Rather Maimonides uses the word both here and *supra* to convey a short, but respectful moment.

42. Underlying this rule is the assumption that heretics would be inappropriate prayer leaders. But determining who is a heretic is not so simple. The assumption is that heretics would be reluctant to express a sentiment antithetical to their heresy. Hence, the error is a subconscious reluctance on the part of the prayer leader to repudiate his beliefs. However, sometimes an error is just an error and not an indication of anything more insidious. Thus, if the prayer leader immediately resumes his prayer with the proper correction, any suspicions would be allayed.

43. And not ascend the elevated platform called the *bimah*.

44. Rabbi Mano'ah of Narbonne says this is the custom there. Cf. Rabbi Abraham

In 1960, Jehoshua Blau published Maimonides's Arabic responsa in three volumes. Blau edited and corrected Geniza fragments, manuscripts, and previously published material. Emended Arabic texts of over four hundred responsa were published alongside Blau's annotated Hebrew translation. Noteworthy is the number of questions put to Maimonides regarding cantors.

Teshuvot Ha-RaMBaM, No. 177: A Beardless Cantor

In his *Mishneh Torah*,[45] Maimonides rules that a cantor who is not full-bearded demeans the dignity of the congregation and consequently may not serve as a cantor. In the following responsum, Maimonides clarifies what the talmudic sages meant by a full-bearded prayer leader.[46] The concern was not over hair *per se,* but upon the maturity that comes with the age when beards could grow. Maimonides deduces this from the language of the text. The questioner is not identified.

> A question: May you instruct us regarding a man who has reached more that twenty years of age, that is, forty, and has not grown a single whisker. Rather, wherever hair might grow, his face is as smooth as a ten-year-old or younger. Is he permitted to be a prayer leader, to go to the lectern, and should he be prevented from doing so if he has the temerity to go down to the lectern [on his own accord]? May our glorious master[47] instruct us and may his reward be doubled.
>
> The answer: We only wait for hair to grow on one for whom this is possible. But [as to] the one you mention, the rule for him is like the rule for the monorchid[48] or for the one whose illness caused the loss of his hair because their intent regarding this rule is not the presence of hair or its absence. Rather, the intent is that even a youth who reaches puberty may not go down to the lectern until he reaches full maturity and reaches the threshold of growing a beard. As they taught: "The sale of his father's estate [is deferred] until he reaches the age of twenty" (*b. B. Bat.* 155a). Had the intention of this rule been the presence of hair or its absence, they should have said: 'He who has no beard.' The

---

ben David of Posquieres, *ad loc.*

45. Laws of Prayer 8:11
46. Cf. *Tosef. Hag.* 1:3; *b. Hul.* 24b; *y. Suk.* 3:12, end.
47. "Our glorious Master" is an honorific for Maimonides.
48. *S'ris hamah,* in Hebrew: a neutered male.

law would then have been more general and clear, as they said: "He who has not seen the luminaries . . ." (*b. Meg.* 24a) and other such examples.

The end of the matter: He is permitted to be a prayer leader without doubt or equivocation.

So wrote Moshe.

Teshuvot Ha-RaMBaM, No. 167: Drunken Cantors

The Talmud does not mention drunkenness as a disqualifying factor for cantors. Maimonides considers the case of cantors whose drunkenness resulted in public embarrassment. Though he cites no text for his opinion, it seems that Maimonides would categorize drunkenness as an indication of talmudic "bad character," making him unworthy to serve until he reforms. Living in the Muslim world, Maimonides is likely to have been influenced by the Muslim ban on wine and alcohol consumption.

> A question: Let our master instruct us with regard to prayer leaders who enter the synagogue on some Sabbath days during prayer time or the time for the reading of the Holy Torah while drunk and not sober enough to lead prayers or read Torah. And as happens when a minor reads the *haftarah*, they stand on the pulpit to sing something as is customary, causing people to talk jestingly and with great mockery until it reaches a point where the community reprimands them for this.
>
> Let our master instruct us, what do they[49] deserve to receive for their maliciousness in this matter and may his[50] reward be doubled from heaven.
>
> The answer:
>
> They are required to take an oath in public that they will not enter the synagogue after drinking intoxicating beverages until after their drunkenness abates. And anyone who violates his oath will be removed from his communal appointment.
>
> So wrote Moshe.

49. The prayer leaders.

50. The reference is to Maimonides, who is referred to in the third person as a matter of respect.

Teshuvot Ha-RaMBaM, No. 165:
A Repeatedly Drunken Cantor

That a second question on drunkenness is addressed to Maimonides is an indication that the problem was not isolated. Maimonides also is the first authority to discuss the status of a drunken cantor.

> Question: May our rabbi teach us [what to do] in the case of a prayer leader who gets drunk and does inappropriate things in his drunken stupor, for example: when he entered the synagogue and saw another prayer leader leading prayers he said: 'Such a man is a prayer leader?" and when he held a Torah scroll on one of the festivals—when he was in a drunken state—he dropped it and broke a filial; and when the congregation said to him: 'What is this thing that you have done!' he said to them: 'This is a Torah scroll??' all as a result of his severe drunkenness. Is he permitted to serve as a prayer leader or to hold a Torah scroll or to perform any other such function? (He did not do this once or twice but many times!) May our master instruct us: What is the ruling according to the law as it applies to him and is he liable for any punishment . . . ?
>
> The answer: It is absolutely forbidden to allow a man like this to serve as a prayer leader or lift a Torah scroll. And anyone who relies on his prayers when he goes to the lectern—the moreso anyone who abets him or does not try to stop him—is someone who dishonors the Torah and is counted among those who themselves defile the Torah and profane it; someone who himself is assured of being a profanation to others.[51]
>
> So wrote Moshe.

Teshuvot Ha-RaMBaM, No. 67: A Cantor in Mourning

Cantors were more than prayer leaders in the days of Maimonides. They were also teachers and preachers. Maimonides distinguishes between leading prayers—which is permitted all mourners, including cantors—and public teaching, which is precluded during mourning. Maimonides addresses a question that was not considered in earlier sources.

> Question: Let our rabbi instruct us regarding a permanent cantor[52] who wished to lead public prayer during the seven days

---

51. Cf. *m. Avot* 4:6.
52. The questioner uses the word *hazzan*.

of mourning. Is he permitted to do so in that there is no need since there are many prayer leaders in the city? And how should we behave toward someone who preaches and cites scripture to teach the public ethics and to avoid prohibitions when the death of his wife is weighing[53] on him? Let our rabbi explain to us what the law is and may his reward be doubled.

Answer:

Each man who is obligated to pray may pray in public. Now since he is obligated to pray [even] during the day of mourning, he can fulfill the obligation [of prayer] for others. However, teaching people ethics or to expound a verse is not permitted during mourning, that is to say, during the [first] seven days. [54]

So wrote Moshe.

Teshuvot Ha-RaMBaM, No. 258: How Cantorial Innovations Spread

This responsum is of great value in understanding how local community or synagogue practice extends to a larger audience. Other cantors will quickly adopt a practice initiated by one cantor who receives public acclaim, irrespective of propriety. From the historical perspective, the practice of "*heihkah kedushah*," as it is called in the Ashkenazic tradition,[55] is dated as early as the twelfth century.

> Question: With regard to this custom to which cantors[56] are growing accustomed in their leading of the prayer: While the congregation prays silently, the cantor, on Sabbath and festivals, will say aloud from "May the Lord open my lips" to "may it be Your will . . ."[57]—without [including] the *Kedushah* or the Priestly Blessing—as a kind of reading so that they may follow along and then afterwards, return to the beginning, from "Blessed are You . . ." according to the custom of the public prayer leader, and include *Kedushah* and the Priestly Blessing. This custom—that the cantor reads in an undertone from "May the Lord open my lips . . ." until the end—is a new custom of recent origin that was initiated by one cantor, which proved

53. *Sh'ruyah l'fanav*, literally, "saturating him."

54. Cf. Maimonides, MT, Laws of a Mourner 5:16.

55. *Hoikha* means "loud" in Yiddish. Thus *heikha kedushah* consists in reciting the *Amidah* aloud through the *Kedushah*.

56. *Hazzanim* in Hebrew.

57. That is, from the beginning to the end of the *Amidah*.

popular and was [subsequently] claimed by other cantors. It is too demanding on a cantor to recite aloud during silent prayer and then, afterwards, go back and pray again with *Kedushah* . . .

Let his holy honor instruct us in accordance with his extraordinary wisdom, and let his reward from Heaven be double

Answer:

What is appropriate and authoritative is what the sages, of blessed memory, enacted,[58] and that is that all pray silently—fulfilling the obligation of all those who prayed including the prayer leader and congregation, and afterwards, let the prayer leader go back and pray aloud with the *Kedushah* in order to fulfill the obligation [to pray] for those who are not capable . . .

But this custom that you mention—reciting the *Amidah* aloud twice—is a complete mistake according to all and a profound disturbance to all those who are expert in their prayers [to now be forced to] to listen to the sound [of the prayer leader] during their [own] prayer. This is, without doubt, an act of ignorance . . . And if people will not pray at all silently, but will follow after the prayer leader reciting one prayer aloud with the *Kedushah* with each knowledgeable person praying along quietly and every non-expert listening, all bowing together with him and all the people being attentive, then all will have fulfilled their obligation and everything is ordered and proper and without lengthening the repetition and thus eliminate the desecration of God's name among the non-Jews who see Jews spitting and coughing up phlegm and talking during their prayers.[59]

This is what seems appropriate to me in these times[60] by virtue of the reasons I have given.

So wrote Moshe.

Teshuvot Ha-RaMBaM, No. 181:
A Cantor Changing the Words of the Liturgy

Though the pronouns are inconsistent, Blau[61] maintains that a cantor addressed this question to Maimonides and the inconsistency lies in the fact that only a part of the answer has come down to us. Maimonides rules

58. Cf. *b. Rosh Hashanah,* 34b.

59. An extended service results in a lack of attentiveness manifested by idle conversation and profane activities.

60. Maimonides intimates that legal allowances are acceptable as circumstances demand.

61. Maimon, *Teshuvot Ha-RaMBaM,* 2:330.

that the formulae of the blessings are fixed and may not be changed.[62] Nevertheless, here he rules that congregational unity is more important than loyalty to the established text. But what Maimonides implies is also of great significance: it is the cantor's role to lead the congregation's prayers, even when their prayers do not follow the proper format.

> Instruct us on changing the language of the blessings on Friday nights and Saturday nights and may your reward be double.
>
> Changing the wording of the Shabbat blessings and liturgical hymns is a mistake without a doubt. However, since the congregation is attached to these [variations, not reciting them] would cause controversy. So it is fitting to let him (*i.e.* the cantor) recite them . . . They will recite them anyway even if you do not. So it is better for you to lead them . . .

Teshuvot Ha-RaMBaM, No. 111: Is a Rumor Sufficient Grounds to Remove a Cantor?

In this responsum, Maimonides vigorously defends the status of a cantor who is vilified by a rumor of wrongdoing. Maimonides maintains that a mere rumor cannot result in the dismissal of the cantor, but can result in the punishment of the rumor-spreader.

> Question: We ask the indulgence of our master, Light of the World, our Master and Teacher, Rabbi Moshe ben Maimon, the great rabbi, eminence of this generation whose renown is world wide, may his praise increase, for an answer regarding a well-known cantor and scholar. A rumor is circulating that he committed a sin too terrible to mention. However, there are no proper witnesses to the deed and he is known to have enemies. Shall he be removed from his cantorial position or not? For what is he liable? And if the "testimony"[63] is upheld and he accepts the penalty imposed, should he be removed or not? If only one witness testifies against him what shall be done? May our master instruct us and let his reward from Heaven be doubled.
>
> Answer: Any wise man needs to know that no office-holder may be removed from his position on account of rumor alone,[64] even if he has no enemies . . . If the "testimony" is upheld, it would

---

62. MT, Laws of Prayer 1:1.

63. Not formal or legal testimony, but the acceptance of the accuracy and truthfulness of the rumor.

64. Cf. MT, Laws of Sanhedrin 17:8–9.

be inappropriate to remove him if he accepted the penalty since
we do not remove a person from any rank of sanctity, whether a
member of the Great Sanhedrin or whether a synagogue cantor
unless he committed a public violation [of the law].[65] If [merely]
some rumor is spread about him, it is inappropriate to remove
him or even publicize [the purported misdeed][66] . . . As to the
person who spoke against this scholar without having witnessed
[the misdeed] with his own eyes, is subject to the ban[67]—there
is no greater defamation than this. He is further subject to flogging because of committing slander.[68]

Take care in respecting the Torah since "the commandments are a lamp and the Torah is light."

Moshe.

Germany: Twelfth Century

Rabbi Judah ben Rabbi Samuel, known as "Judah the Pious," (ca.
1150–1217) was the preeminent moralist of the Rhineland in the twelfth
century. Born in Speyer to an esteemed family of rabbis, he went into
self-imposed exile in Regensburg when, according to legend, his wife inadvertently handled the treasured family documents when she was men-
struating. Rabbi Judah was revered for his profound piety, renouncing
worldly pleasures and fasting on Shabbat and for "two days" of Yom Kippur. He wrote books on the laws of prayer, the writing of a Torah scroll,
the laws of ritual slaughter, scriptural commentaries, and numerology.
But he is best known for *Sefer Hasidim*, the Book of the Pious, widely
known in his day, but first printed in Bologna in 1538 and republished
dozens of times thereafter. The passage that follows is a translation of the
Reuben Margoliot edition, published by Mossad Harav Kook in 1973.

Judging by the discipline Rabbi Judah seeks to impose, cantors in
his day were assumed to be egotistical artists who put their vocal performance ahead of the needs of the congregation. They also were lacking in
personal hygiene.

---

65. *y. San.* 2:5.

66. *b. M.K.* 17a; MT, Laws of Torah Study 7:1.

67. MT, Laws of Sanhedrin 26:5.

68. Cf. *b. Pes.* 113b.

Sefer Ha-Hasidim, Section 251: The Cantor's Excesses

In the beginning, the prayer leaders would only go back to the place [in the prayers] where the worshipers ended. There they would begin. For instance, the congregation would say "*na'vah tefillah*" [in the morning service for Shabbat] and he who stood at the rostrum would begin [the next line] "*b'fi y'sharim.*" But when the degenerates raced through the blessings and prayers, rather than continuing from where the congregation left off, he would go back to the top because he did not want to race, with the outcome that when they finished, he did not. But when they were good and did not race through, saying the prayers as prescribed, he did not go back to the top. And now, it is sinful when they [cantors] go back to the top since they do so only to hear their own sweet voices.

Further, it is tedious for the congregation since it is unnecessary to repeat what the congregation has already said when they say the words without speeding. It is proper for the cantor to say only that which will fulfill the obligation of the congregation. If he (*i.e.*, the cantor) begins above in order to fulfill the obligation of someone who does not know [the prayers], then he must start at "*Nishmat kol hai.*" However, [when that is not the case] cantors who start at "*Nishmat* do so only to make their own sweet voices heard. A reverent person should not act this way.

He who has a sweet voice should sing for God and not sing other songs, as Scripture says (Ps 33:1): "Sing forth, O you righteous, to the Lord," to the Lord, and no other kind of singing. "The tents of the righteous resound with the joyous songs of deliverance" (Ps 118:15). But the text does not explain what kind of songs. Therefore, [another verse] comes to say, "Sing forth, O you righteous, to the Lord," meaning, to the Lord and no other kinds of singing . . .

The singer must not interrupt the melody so that if he has to blow his nose, after he wipes, he must pick up from the place he stopped.

If someone is reciting blessings aloud and a fly enters his open mouth, he must stop and spit forcibly to discharge the fly from his throat and then continue from where he stopped.

Responsa of Rabbi Eliezer of Boeheim to
Rabbi Judah the Pious: The Cantor's Importance

The passage that follows was printed in *Or Zaru'a*, Laws of a Prayer Leader, No. 113. The author worries that Rabbi Judah's opposition to local ordinances allowing for supplementary collections of funds to pay for professional cantors would jeopardize the spiritual survival of poor Jewish communities in central Europe. Although there is no evidence in *Sefer Hasidim* that Rabbi Judah was so opposed, his somewhat antagonistic attitude to cantors is reflected in the previous passage. What is of considerable historical interest is the fact by the twelfth century the cantorate was professionalized, with cantors serving as teachers and mentors as much as prayer leaders. To assure that cantors were retained, communities were compelled to resort to unusual ways and means of fundraising. The author refers to assessments at weddings when, in the joyful spirit of the moment, guests were more amenable to giving. Collections were also made on Purim and even on Simhat Torah, which was, apparently, not classified as a holiday that imposed restrictions on the use of money. Smaller Jewish communities today face similar issues and offer similar solutions.

> . . . the early authorities cared about the [financial] distress of the community: not every community had the means to hire a cantor from out of their own pockets. They enacted by-laws to collect from wedding guests who, in joyful celebration, eating and drinking, would not refuse to give, thus one mitzvah lead to another,[69] while you[70] condemned this as unjust. And they also enacted [the procedure on] Simhat Torah and Purim for collecting [funds] for synagogue support, akin to the half shekel [collected] for service in God's Temple,[71] so that the community would not be overly burdened, having no means to pay the cantor's salary all at once. Were it not for these by-laws, he[72] would not agree to subjugate himself to the community without much compensation. They learned from the ways of our Creator who organized twenty-four kinds of [priestly] gifts[73] and did not impose the onus of making all payable at once from the granary

69. Cf. *m. Avot* 4:2.
70. Rabbi Judah.
71. Cf. Exod 30:13.
72. The cantor.
73. Cf. *Tosef. Hallah* 2:8, cited in *b. B.K.* 110b and *b. Hul.* 133b.

and storehouse. Our predecessors were wise to anticipate the future. Should you decide to void the [allowance of] collections on Purim, Simhat Torah, and wedding feasts, then most places in Poland, Russia, and Hungary—where they have no Torah teachers as a result of their poverty and hire for themselves a knowledgeable man as best they can afford who serves as a prayer leader and ethical guide who teaches them and is promised [payment] for all this—would no longer have the means to adequately pay him to keep them going. These communities would decline and remain without Torah, without prayer, without ethical teaching. Even if you should change your mind, I worry that your original words have already been heard and disaster awaits.

Sefer Hasidim, Section 238: Using Non-Jewish Melodies

The passage that follows only indirectly applies to the cantor but is an important early example of the antiquity of Jewish liturgical music. By the twelfth century, some melodies were quite familiar; so familiar, in fact, that Jews were likely to sing them casually. Around the same time as Rabbi Judah the Pious, Maimonides[74] ruled that Arabic melodies have no place in Jewish life. Rabbi Judah comes to the same conclusion regarding Christian melodies. He adds that melodies used in synagogue worship are reserved exclusively for synagogue worship.

> He who has placed a small child in a cradle so that he does not cry should not sing to him Christian songs or hymns, neither should he sing Jewish melodies reserved for the Holy One, Blessed Be He. But if he sings scriptural phrases or passages from the Talmud so that he remembers them and does not forget them, even though the child is quieted by them and enjoys them, it is permitted.
>
> A man must neither teach a [Christian] priest Hebrew letters nor sing in his presence a pleasant Jewish melody lest the priest use the same melody in his foreign worship. And any melody used in the presence of non-Jews should not be used in the synagogue prayer service.

74. Maimon, *Teshuvot Ha-RaMBaM*, No. 224, 2:39.

Germany: Thirteenth Century

Born in Worms, Rabbi Meir ben Rabbi Barukh of Rothenburg (ca.
1215–1293) stands out as one of the luminaries of medieval Ashkenaz.
He fixed Jewish practice for central European Jewry through his substantial literary legacy and through the great scholars that were his disciples,
including Rabbi Asher ben Yehiel, Rabbi Shimshon ben Rabbi Zadok,
and Rabbi Mordekhai ben Hillel. When captured for ransom, he refused
to be ransomed, since, he argued, it would only encourage further taking
of captives. He died in prison.

These responsa reveal that communal life in Germany was fraught
with considerable difficulty: internal disputes, fickle and interfering rulers, and personal animosities. In the first two selections, Rabbi Meir uses
the word "*hazzan*" for the officially appointed prayer leader. As indicated
in the first selection, the *hazzan*, or cantor, was distinguished by a special
hat.

In his rulings, Rabbi Meir makes the appointment of the cantor an
exclusively internal Jewish communal decision in which secular authorities ought to have no legitimate role. The cantorate is a matter of divine
service. He carefully balances the impracticality of dismissing a cantor on
the complaint of a single individual with ensuring that the cantor serves
as the representative of the entire congregation, at least during the Days
of Awe.

The responsa cited appear in the three-volume critical edition of
Rabbi Dr. Yitzhaq Zev Cahana, published in Jerusalem by Mossad Harav
Kook in 1957.

Teshuvot of Rabbi Meir of Rothenburg No. 20: A Cantor's Mandate

Aside from the ruling on the issue, the question intimates that cantors
did not necessarily enjoy universal approval, and the divided community
was not easily reconciled. Rabbi Meir's personal recollection also reveals
that cantors wore a special hat as the symbol of their office. That the local
ruler would take an interest in who served as cantor in the Jewish community is an indication of the status the cantor had earned by the twelfth
century.

Response of our teacher, Rabbi Meir to Rabbi Isaac of Würtzburg:

You asked about the circumstance of the cantor—who had the approval of the majority of the congregation but the disapproval of the minority who were unable to reconcile with him. His appointment was by the decree of the duke who asked the dissenters to reconcile, and [you claimed] they acted improperly to appoint God's lector according to the duke['s wishes].

In our land they were very insistent in these kinds of matters. A situation like this occurred in Cologne during my father's time. A cantor was appointed, and a certain Jew intending to [dis]honor him caused the local ruler to pursue him and remove his hat. He gave it to the rabbi and said: 'You be the cantor.' He[75] grew very angry even against the ruler and said: 'My lord, it is not my right to accept from you [an appointment for] divine service.' And did not accept the cantorate, even though he did initially. I think he fined the Jew. And so in this case, the cantor must make good.

Peace![76]

Teshuvot Rabbi Meir of Rothenburg, No. 21: How Many Critics Does It Take to Dismiss a Cantor?

... It seems to me that if he is acceptable to the majority, there is no cause to prevent him from praying occasionally on account of one congregant who hates him, except on the New Year and the Day of Atonement when the custom prevails that they only appoint a cantor who is acceptable to the entire congregation. The same rule applies on fast days. My proof is based on what it says in Chapter Two of the tractate Ta'anit,[77] that on fast days and meeting days we only appoint an elder who is well versed, enjoys a good reputation, is acceptable to the people, etc. [Signed,] Meir B'Rav Barukh, may he live.[78]

Teshuvot of Rabbi Meir of Rothenburg, No. 23: A Blemished Cantor

The only kind of physical disability for a prayer leader considered by the Talmud was blindness, which, as noted, was subject to dispute among

---

75. The rabbi.

76. Rothenberg, Teshuvot, P'sakim, U'Minhagim, 1:51.

77. b. Ta'an 16a.

78. Rothenberg, Teshuvot, P'sakim, U'Minhagim, 1:52.

the Geonim. Rabbi Meir was petitioned to resolve the issue related to other physical disabilities, in particular a person who is armless. In his allowance for the disabled person to serve as a cantor, Rabbi Meir makes two important points. First, the disabled are especially valued. He learns this by analogy from a scriptural verse. If a broken heart is dear to God, then so is a broken body: a particularly progressive view for his day. And second, any comparison between cantors and *kohanim* (priests) is misguided:

> You asked if a man who has been visited by divine punishment [and lost his arms][79] is fit to be a cantor. It is obvious that he is. In fact, it is the choicest way to fulfill the obligation since the King of Kings desires using broken vessels unlike human rulers, as it is said: "A broken heart . . ."[80] Only priests in sacrificial service are disqualified on account of blemishes.[81]

Austria: Thirteenth Century

Rabbi Isaac ben Moses of Vienna (ca. 1180–ca. 1250) was born in Boeheim and studied in some of the storied academies of Franco-Germany. He traveled extensively and became familiar with the customs and languages of the Rhineland. The teacher to whom he owes the greatest debt is Rabbi Eliezer ben Rabbi Joel Ha-Levi, whose literary structure—and much of his content—he follows. The first edition of his masterwork *Or Zaru'a* (*Planted Light*)—the title of which is taken from Psalm 97:11—was published in Zhitomir in 1662.

In outlining the rules pertaining to the cantor, the author relies heavily on the Talmud and Geonic tradition. The first consideration is that of the age of the cantor, followed by his qualifications. Familiarity with the words of prayer is not only essential for a cantor, but a sure sign that God will accept his prayer. Appended to his compendium is the Geonic approval of a blind cantor and a skilled cantor over a mature one.

---

79. Rabbi Solomon Luria suggested this interpolation. See also Gumbiner, *Magen Avraham*, OH 53:8.

80. Ps 51:19: "You will not despise a contrite and crushed heart."

81. Rothenberg, *Teshuvot, P'sakim, U'Minhagim*, 1:53.

Or Zaru'a, Part 1, No. 116: Laws of the Prayer Leader

The rabbis taught:[82] "If his beard is full he is worthy to be a lector and to go to the lectern and offer the priestly blessing." That is to say, to be a permanent prayer leader, his beard needs to be full, but [to be a prayer leader] occasionally, so long as he is [at least] thirteen years and one day old, he may go to the lectern and fulfill the obligation [of prayer] for the public, as it is taught:[83] "A minor may rise to read and translate but may not lead *Shema* or go to the lectern," meaning, a minor specifically, but someone thirteen years and one day old may lead *Shema* and go to the lectern and fulfill the obligation [of prayer] for the public. That is to say, only occasionally. To be a permanent prayer leader requires a full beard, even if he is not yet used to it. However, during a time of calamity, like a drought or marauding wolves or other such things that endanger the public—and the same goes for Rosh Hashanah and Yom Kippur—[the prayer leader] who goes to the lectern must be mature. As it is taught:[84] ". . . When they stand in prayer they bring to the lectern an elder who is fluent and has children and whose house is empty so that he is wholehearted in prayer," so long as he[85] possesses all the virtues that we learnt. As the Rabbis taught: "They stood in prayer—even though an elder or a scholar is present, the only person they send to the lectern is the regular one [who leads prayer].

"Rabbi Judah says: one who works but has nothing . . ."[86] RaShI[87] interpreted: "*M'tupal*—he has minor children yet he has nothing to support them so that he worries about them. 'He has toiled in the fields'—so that his prayer for rain would be more sincere. *Pirko na'eh*—explained later. *Shafel*—so that they agree to let him pray. *Ne'imah*—with a pleasant voice that stirs the heart. *Ragil*—so that he is familiar with the words of prayer. *Reikan*—that there is no violence or robbery in his house. *U'firko*—even if his reputation from his youth were examined, his reputation would be found to be without blemish. *Eino hagun*—wicked; God hates him more than anyone, and yet he[88] gives voice to Him?" Until here: RaShI. And the law inti-

82. *b. Hul.* 24b.

83. *b. Meg.* 24a.

84. *b. Ta'an.* 16b.

85. Returning to the topic of the permanent prayer leader.

86. *b. Ta'an.* 16a.

87. *b. Ta'an.* 16a.

88. Referring to a wicked prayer leader. It is incongruous for one who is wicked

mates that we do not send to the lectern anyone who is unsuited (*i.e.* wicked) since an accuser cannot become a defender, as we say in the chapter 'The Court saw him' in [the tractate] Rosh Hashanah:[89] "Rav Hisda said: why is it that the High Priest does not wear golden robes in Divine service? Because a prosecutor cannot be a defender." And further, if the prayer leader is unworthy, the entire congregation is punished since his prayer stirs God to anger above.

"The rabbis taught:[90] if the person who goes to the lectern errs, another should replace him and [the replacement] should not refuse. Whence does he[91] begin? From the beginning of the section in which he (i.e., the first lector) erred." "The Rabbis taught: the person who goes to the lectern must refuse . . ." Rabbi Nathan interpreted:[92] "*Mesarev*—[means] refuses, that is, objects. The Aramaic translation [of] *va'y'ma-en* [is] refuses. The Rabbis taught: there are three things that are mostly hard yet partly good. They are: leaven, salt, and refusal."[93]

It was taught:[94] "It is a bad sign for someone who prays and errs. And if he is the lector, it is a bad sign for those who appointed him since the agent of a person is like the person himself . . ."

And Rabbenu Hananel[95] interpreted: Someone who prays and notices his lips were flowing[96], it is certain that his prayer will be accepted, as it is written (Isaiah 57:19): ". . . creates fruit of the lips."[97] End of Rabbenu Hananel's words.

In *Sefer HaMiktzo'ot*:[98] Whenever there is a case of a cantor about whom bad things were said in complaint, he is removed.

---

to represent the congregation to the Almighty.

89. *b. R.H.* 26a.

90. *b. Ber.* 34a.

91. The replacement.

92. In *Sefer Ha-Arukh*, a dictionary of unusual or difficult words that appear in the Talmud and Geonic literature compiled by Rabbi Nathan bar Yehiel of Rome and published first in Venice in 1553. Earlier versions were circulated and well known.

93. *b. Ber.* 34a.

94. *b. Ber.* 34b.

95. Not on the printed page of the Talmud.

96. That is, his prayer was fluent.

97. "and I (that is, God) will heal him," suggesting that God will answer that prayer.

98. This book is ascribed to Rabbenu Hananel of Kairouan, although M. Margaliot believes the ascription is without foundation. Simhah Assaf published a critical edition of this eleventh-century book in Jerusalem, 1947.

Brought in to replace him is another who is acceptable [as a mediator] between Israel and their Father in Heaven. And he[99] must be righteous, saintly, and bodily clean. If this is not the case, about him the verse (Jer 12:8) is applied: "She raised her voice against Me, therefore I have rejected her." "Present it now unto your governor, will he be pleased with you?" (Mal 1:8)[100] Rav Yudai Gaon[101] taught that a blind prayer leader is fit and may not be dismissed so long as his conduct is proper. And [when it comes to choosing between] a prayer leader who does not understand so well but his voice is pleasant and the people like him [versus] an advanced student who can navigate [texts] but his voice is not pleasant, Rav Yehudai Gaon says that surely the advanced student is preferred since he knows what he is saying while the one with the pleasant voice cannot enunciate properly. From this we learn that when there is a suitable and worthy cantor,[102] we do not bring to the lectern youngsters who are not full-bearded or who do not understand too well. However, [in the case of a man] one hundred years old and he does not know what he is saying, and present is a youth thirteen years and one day old who does, [the latter] goes to the lectern. End of *Sefer Miktzo'ot*.

And in the response he wrote: "As you asked, may a blind prayer leader or an old man whose eyesight is failing on account of age but they know how to pray properly go to the lectern to fulfill the obligation [of prayer] for the public? We saw that they go to the lectern and do fulfill [the congregation's obligation of prayer] . . . but they do not read Megillah nor read Torah even though they know the text since reading Megillah and Torah require reading from the text and not by memory, as they taught with regard to Megillah, "Read it by heart—he did not fulfill the obligation."[103] And with regard to a Torah scroll, it is written: "And they read from the book of God's Torah (Nehemiah 8:8)" explicitly . . ."

Thus our rabbis the Ge'onim interpreted.

---

99. Any prayer leader.

100. The first part of the verse reads: "When you offer the blind for a sacrifice . . .," serving as an introduction to the laws regarding a blind cantor.

101. In Emanuel, *Teshuvot Ha-Geonim Ha-Hadashot*, No. 24, this view is ascribed to Rav Sa'adiah Gaon.

102. The author uses the Hebrew term *hazzan*.

103. b. *Meg.* 17a. However, Cf. *Mishnah Berurah* 690, subparagraph 7, allows reading some of the Megillah by heart. See his reasons there.

Or Zaru'a: Part 1, No. 112: Laws of the Prayer Leader: May a Man-slaughterer Be a Cantor?

While the details of the episode are lacking, it appears that a certain named cantor was responsible for the inadvertent death of a baby. Rabbi Isaac rules that intention matters. Even the greatest of rabbis err, but their reputations remain intact because they were repentant. So it seems that cantors who show some evidence of remorse are not subject to dismissal, no matter the gravity of the sin. This restrictive interpretation of "a compromised reputation" allows for broad latitude in the behavior of cantors thus securing their positions:

> May an accidental homicide be a cantor?
>   . . . I have thought deeply about your letter in order to respond. It appears to me that the father of the baby has no power to prevent you from praying with this [cantor] Matityahu. Rather, the matter is a communal decision to make. To be sure, had he intentionally killed—even if there are no relatives[104] of the victim [to object]—we would bar him from leading the congregation in prayer. The community itself must distance themselves from him, as Rav Sherira Gaon, may the memory of the righteous be a blessing, wrote, we have no power to do anything—not to kill, beat, or exile—someone who kills a human being these days. All we can do is to stay away from him and not fraternize with him or to look at his face. So the sages said: "It is forbidden to look upon the face of the wicked.[105] And he is disqualified from [giving] any testimony."
>   There is no difference between intentional homicide and accidental homicide: the person who commits either must be avoided unless he has fully repented. But if he repented fully, he is considered entirely righteous immediately, even though no trial was yet to take place . . .
>   Now even though I have explained that all penitents require immersion, nevertheless, [absence] of immersion does not foreclose repentance. Whether in violation of negative commandments or whether in violation [of commandments] for which the punishment is excision or execution by the court, whether intentional or unintentional, as soon as he considers repentance, he is [considered] as if he is wholly right [with regard] to

---

104. Literally, "redeemers."
105. *b. Meg.* 28a in the name of Rabbi Yohanan.

the entire Torah. (However, he must punish himself and afflict his body to atone for what he has already done.) . . .

[The author cites the examples of the sons of Korah and King Ahab.]

We learn that repentance retroactively annuls the punishment decreed against them previously. Henceforth, the thought of repentance alone—along with an immediate confession—is all that is necessary for God to show him good will and grant him peace, as it says in *Pesiqta*:[106] "The ministering angels said to the Holy One, praised be He, it is written: 'show no favoritism.'[107] But how can you show favoritism to Israel, as it says: 'May God lift up His face to you?'[108] He said to them: 'How can I not lift up my face [to them] when they confess to me and say 'We have sinned, we have dealt treacherously, we have robbed, etc.'" Therefore, when he confesses—although he has not undergone any judgment—even so, God grants him peace and he is called a penitent, as it is written: 'Peace, peace to the far and near,'[109] [meaning] to the one who was far and is now near . . .

Therefore, it has been clarified to us that all those who have sinned—even those who warrant excision and execution by the court—as soon as they consider repentance—even as of today— are considered fully righteous. He must afflict his body for what he had done previously in order for him to achieve atonement. Now since he is righteous as of today, it is certainly [fine] to pray with him even though he has not yet received his judgment. [This applies] even the moreso [to] this Matityahu who has already accepted what the rabbis imposed on him in that he was in one city and exiled himself to another. There are no grounds for apprehensiveness. As it says:[110] "Rav Judah said: Exile atones for three things, as it says, "Thus says the Lord: He who lives in this city shall die by famine, sword, and plague. But one who leaves and falls away from the Chaldeans shall live . . ."[111] Thus we learn from this verse that exile atones for sin . . .

Therefore, since this Matityahu was exiled and made known that on account of this sad occurrence that happened to

---

106. A midrashic collection dated sometime between the seventh to ninth centuries. Buber published a scholarly edition. Cf. *PDK*, 156a.

107. Deut 10:17.

108. Num 6:26.

109. Isa 57:19.

110. *b. San.* 37b.

111. Jer 21:9.

him he went into exile and he lived and was employed there, it is considered [true] exile that satisfies our Sages, as it is taught:[112] if people in a city of refuge want to honor a homicide who fled there, he must say to them 'I am a murderer.' If they say to him 'even so . . .' he may accept [the honor] from them, as it says: "This is the matter of the homicide."[113] Therefore, this Matityahu as well, since he went into exile on account of this occurrence, even though others treat him with a measure of respect, it is still real exile. Even if he earns a living, the law is on his side, as it is written: "He flees to one of the cities and lives"[114]—he does something so that he lives.

As to the matter of making him a prayer leader, it seems to me that were he—in this case—treated as a *kohen* who is disqualified from officiating at the altar, he similarly would be disqualified from officiating as a prayer leader based on what Rabbi Joshua ben Levi said:[115] "Prayers were formulated as a substitute for sacrifices." Supporting Rabbi Joshua ben Levi is the teaching: "Why did they say that the morning prayer [may be recited] until midday? Because the regular morning sacrifice could only be offered until midday, etc." and they[116] also interpreted "The God whom you serve so regularly will save you (Dan 6:17)" "and is there sacrifice in Babylonia? Rather, this refers to prayer." Hence, since prayer is in place of sacrifice, he would not be fit to be a prayer leader.

But nowadays, in this case a *kohen* is fit to officiate at the altar, he too would be fit to officiate as a prayer leader. Whence do we know that in this case a *kohen* is fit to officiate? It says:[117] "If he deliberately slaughtered [to an idol]—Rav Nahman said: His sacrifice [yields] a pleasant aroma[118] and Rav Sheshet says: his sacrifice does not [yield] a pleasant aroma. He became an attendant[119] to idolatry. Rav Nahman said: What is the source of my view? From that which was taught: If a priest officiated before idols yet repented, his sacrifice [yields] a pleasant aroma. How so? If you say [he officiated before idols] inadvertently, then

112. *b. Mak.* 10b.

113. Deut 19:4.

114. Deut 4:42.

115. *b. Ber.* 26b.

116. *y. Ber.* 4:1, 26a.

117. *b. Men.* 109a.

118. That is, the sacrifice is acceptable to God.

119. *Kumar*, also an acolyte, Cf. *b. Kid.* 20b.

what is the point of 'yet repented?' He was always repentant! Obviously, it must be where he officiated deliberately. Moreover, if he sprinkled, it is of no benefit even if he had repented since he officiated [before an idol]. It can only be by slaughtering [before it]. Rav Sheshet would say 'I still maintain that he officiated inadvertently, and it means: if he had always been repentant, that is to say, when he officiated he did so inadvertently, his officiating [yields] a pleasant aroma; otherwise his officiating does not [yield] a pleasant aroma. Thus you learn that Rav Sheshet concedes to Rav Nahman that when inadvertent, the officiating yields a pleasant aroma and he is fit to officiate even though when deliberate, he becomes an attendant to idolatry. If he sprinkled to idols, he becomes impaired. Yet even so, inadvertent slaughter is valid. [This applies] with greater force [to] this Matityahu, who is still fit to be a prayer leader even though he inadvertently [caused the death] of this baby.

. . . With regard to murder and other trespasses, we do not find any source that says a *kohen* is blemished. Further proof: As it says:[120] "A priest who killed a person may not lift up his hands [to recite the Priestly Blessing], as it says: 'When you spread out your hands' and I received from my master and teacher *Avi Ezri*[121] that this applies only when he was unrepentant. But if he repented, he lifts up his hands and blesses Israel, as it is [found] in the Jerusalem Talmud in [the chapter] 'Compensation for damages:'[122] "So he doesn't say: this *kohen* committed adultery and murdered and he blesses me? Said the Holy One, praised be He: Is it he who blesses you? I am the one who blesses you, as it says (Num 6:27): "They shall link My name [with the people Israel and I will bless them]." And so that we can reconcile this [passage from the] Jerusalem Talmud with our Talmud, we do not say they dispute one another.[123] We must therefore maintain that the passage in *Berakhot* [refers to a case where] he was unrepentant, while the passage in the Jerusalem Talmud [refers to a case where] he repented.

Therefore, this Matityahu who acted unintentionally with this baby is fit to be a prayer leader and there is no difference

---

120. *b. Ber.* 32b.

121. The popular name by which Rabbi Eliezer ben Joel Ha-Levi (1140–1225) was known.

122. Jerusalem Talmud, Gittin 5:9, 47b.

123. The leveling and reconciling of the two Talmuds was a standard rabbinic approach in the premodern period.

with what RaShI raises[124] with regard to the qualifications of a
prayer leader that ends with 'full-bearded' saying that no evil report has come forward about him since there is no question that
an inadvertent act is not the same as an evil report. Were this
so, you would have difficulty with the first chapter of [the trac-
tate] *Makkot*[125] where it is taught: "Said Rabbi Judah ben Tabbai:
May I never see consolation for Israel if I did not put to death
a plotting witness to refute the Sadducess who used to say that
plotting witnesses are executed only after the falsely accused had
been executed. Simon ben Shetah said to him: May I never see
consolation for Israel if you have not shed innocent blood, etc.,
and all his life, Judah ben Tabbai used to go to prostrate himself
on the grave of that [plotting] witness, and so forth." And Rabbi
Yishmael[126] read [on Shabbat] and tilted [the lamp]. And here
you have these righteous men who inadvertently committed an
act requiring execution by the court yet even with this, would
you say that their reputation was not intact—God forbid! A
"compromised reputation" means that the act was deliberate and
they were under warning. But a person who acted inadvertently
and regrets [it] is entirely righteous in accord with the Torah.

May you merit the day that is all light. To the crown and
diadem for whom I long,

Isaac ben Rabbi Moses, who has gone deeply in the matter.

Or Zaru'a, Part 1, No. 114:
The Appointment of a Cantor Requires Unanimous Consent

Rabbi Isaac concludes that the appointment of a cantor requires unanimity even when he possesses all the desirable attributes. Ultimately, the
cantor is a servant of the community and it is inconceivable that he would
officiate without the endorsement of the community as a whole. Accordingly, the cantor must work at gaining and retaining universal support by
being principled though congenial.

> Another responsum from the rabbi author, may the memory of
> the righteous be a blessing, to Rabbi Hezekiah ben Rabbi Jacob,
> may the memory of the righteous be a blessing.

---

124. *b. Ta'an.* 16b.

125. *b. Mak.* 5b.

126. *b. Sab.* 12b. By tilting the lamp he would be liable to bring a sin offering.

I met a young man who has succeeded his father. Myrrh and aromatics drip from his lips.[127] His letters are a living glory to Israel. His deeds are recognized through his intentions. His questions are sweeter than honey for his paths lovingly lead to the right and the good, the treasured Rabbi Hezekiah ben Rabbi Jacob (may the memory of the righteous be a blessing):

It is true and certain that my teacher, Rabbi Simhah, may the memory of the righteous be a blessing, taught me that the operative law is that an individual can veto [an appointment to] the cantorate so that no one may become a prayer leader without communal unanimity. It is also well known throughout the Rhineland that the minority may compel the majority to appoint a prayer leader. I have seen many instances in the Rhineland where the minority imposed upon the majority. However, I never questioned my teacher the rabbi whether this was [a matter of] custom or law. So I say the rabbis disapproved of anybody who is to be appointed as a prayer leader without unanimous consent, as it is taught:[128] "Rabban Gamliel says: the lector fulfills the obligation for the public." And it is taught: "Rabban Gamliel said to them: According to you, why does a lector go down to the lectern? They said to him: to fulfill [the obligation of prayer for] those who are not expert. He said to them: Just as he fulfills [the obligation for prayer] for those who are not expert, he fulfills [the obligation for prayer] for those who are." If he stands and prays without community unanimity—the others not having made him a prayer leader—how could he fulfill their obligation when they have not agreed to his prayer? And the rabbis taught:[129] "They stood in prayer—even though there is an elder scholar present, he is not brought down [to the lectern] when there is someone fluent. Rabbi Judah says . . . and acceptable to people"—RaShI,[130] may the memory of the righteous be a blessing, explains "acceptable to people—they agree to his prayer." Hence, a prayer leader whose prayer is agreed to be for all. Even if there are twice as many who agree than those who do not, how can this prayer leader include them? Even if he intends to include them, they do not agree to his prayer! Even if he possessed all the virtues mentioned in the *baraita*,[131] we still need universal consent. And the person who goes to the

127. Cf. Song 5:13.
128. *b. R.H.* 34b.
129. *b. R.H.* 16a.
130. *b. R.H.* 16a.
131. *Baraita* is the term for a Tannaitic passage, extraneous to the Mishnah.

lectern described in the *baraita* applies to during the year. For even were you to say it applies only in a case of drought, Rosh Hashanah and Yom Kippur are days when [God's] mercy [is required] no less than times of drought. And further, it is logical to conclude that "acceptable to people" refers to all year round because how could their obligation [for prayer] be fulfilled through his prayer when they do not agree to his prayer? Know that a Jew who set aside a required offering to sacrifice and a *kohen* came along and offered it when the propitiant did not want him to do so and should you think that it atoned for his sin, then why does it deal with [the question of] why did they establish staffing divisions? Because it says: "instruct the people Israel that these are My sacrifices (Num 28:2)." "How is it possible for a man's sacrifice to be offered with him not standing over it? So the early prophets ordained twenty-four watches."[132] From this you learn that even if the propitiant wants the *kohen* to make the sacrifice on his behalf, he does not fulfill his obligation unless he, the propitiant, is standing over it. If the propitiant does not wish the *kohen* to sacrifice on his behalf then he certainly does not fulfill his obligation. And the passage in the Jerusalem Talmud[133] that a man can slaughter the paschal lamb of his colleague without his consent applies to a case when, at the time of slaughter, he does not know [if he approves]. But if he does know, then he must want his slaughter and service. So then we learn that just as a *kohen* cannot sacrifice without the consent of the propitiants, here, too, the prayer leader may not pray without universal consent. And when he prays, it is tantamount to a public sacrifice since prayer is like sacrifice, as it is written: "Your God whom you serve so regularly will deliver you" (Dan 6:17, 21). "And can sacrifices be offered in Babylonia? Rather, it must refer to prayer."[134] Rabbi Yossi ben Hananiah already disputed Rabbi Joshua ben Levi[135]—whereby Rabbi Yossi said prayer was established by the Patriarchs whereas Rabbi Joshua ben Levi said prayer corresponds to the sacrifices—and we follow him. Further, they conclude that Rabbi Yossi ben Hananiah also agreed that the rabbis based prayer on the daily sacrifices. Thus you learn that when the prayer leader prays, he is, in effect, making a sacrifice for the public. So if a minority does not want his service, how can they fulfill their obligation

132. *b. Ta'an.* 27a.

133. *y. Pes.* 8:1, 50a.

134. *y. Ber.* 4:1, 26a.

135. *b. Ber.* 26b.

[for prayer]? After all, even a person who wants his service does not fulfill his obligation until he is standing over him, and you have learned that a *kohen* is not allowed to sacrifice his offering unless he knows that the propitiant wants his service. Here, too, the prayer leader cannot be a prayer leader unless he knows the public agrees to his service, that is, as it is taught in the *baraita*, that he is acceptable to all, as RaShI explained, that they agreed with his praying.

Should you say: 'Let those who do not agree get another prayer leader,' how can two pray as one? Or: this at the south and the other at the north. Can something like this be possible? Or by what power can they force them from the synagogue to form a different one, when scripture cries out: "Their heart is divided, now shall they bear his guilt" (Hos 10:2), from which you learn that the rabbis disapprove of any prayer leader who arises who does not have communal unanimity.[136] They must find someone who is acceptable to them all. And the saintly Rabbi Judah the Pious, my teacher, taught me that the prayer leader must be beloved to the public. Were this not so, when he reads the peroration, there is danger to one who does not love him. So he said to me that someone who knows the cantor does not love him, if he is called up to the Torah for the peroration, he should take care not to go up lest he meet some grief should he do so.

Therefore, it is wrong for a prayer leader to be appointed unless there is unanimous agreement. Once a prayer leader is appointed and enters to pray, if afterwards one, two, three, or four should object saying 'We don't want him,' without any indication that he had violated any of those things whose violation is deemed wrongful, he is not subject to removal since they already accepted him. In any case, the prayer leader must work at being loved by them by flattering them and behaving leniently toward them, as it is taught, "[one who is] humble."[137] However, when it comes to religious matters, he is forbidden to flatter them. Rather, he must adjure them.

May God renew your strength in Torah and good deeds. Warm regards from your friend,

Isaac ben Rabbi Moses, who has delved into the matter.

---

136. Cf. *Sifre*, Naso 42.

137. *b. Ta'an.* 16a.

Spain: Thirteenth Century

She'elot U'Teshuvot Ha-RaShBA, Part 1, No. 300: *Replacing an Aging Cantor*

Rabbi Solomon ben Abraham, RaShBA, was born in Barcelona in 1235. He was a celebrated student of Rabbi Yonah Gerundi and Rabbi Moses ben Nahman. The Spanish sources refer to him as Adret so that name has been appended to his patronymic. By the time he was twenty he was already responding to questions addressed to him from disparate parts of the Jewish world. In 1272, we find him acting as Chief Rabbi of Barcelona. One chronicler[138] reports that he authored over 6,000 responsa. Just over 3,000 are extant. His influence and scholarship earned him the title "*el Rab de España*" (The Rabbi of Spain). One century later, Rabbi Yitzhaq bar Sheshet[139] asks rhetorically about him: "Who is greater for us among all the later scholars than he?" He died in Barcelona in 1310.

Historically, the following responsum is of immense interest for several reasons. Adret attests to a Jewish presence in somewhat remote regions of Spain. He refers to a sizable community of at least 150 Jews in the northeastern Spanish city of Huesca. Jews seem to have settled there many generations earlier and established a community large enough to require the services of a cantor. He also attests to the fact that the community engaged their cantor contractually. This is likely the earliest mention of such an agreement with a good deal of its provisions listed. From Adret's response, cantorial contracts, as well as the rights of succession of the office of cantor from father to son, seem to have been the norm in Spain. While the cantor was obligated to perform certain unspecified other duties, reading Torah was expected. There is no mention of any monetary compensation for the cantor and likely there was none since Adret makes no mention of who would pay the replacement if the cantor could not perform his responsibilities. The responsum also reveals that no more than ten complainants caused the strife in this community.

Legally speaking, Adret breaks no new ground. His response offers little by way of citations and their interpretation. His resolution—that the current cantor of thirty-eight years' tenure, despite his declining skills, must remain, with his son as an assistant when necessary—is based primarily on a close reading of the contractual document, as well as a

---

138. Conforte, *Korei HaDorot*, 22a.

139. *She'elot U'Teshuvot Ha-RIBaSh*, No. 146.

reliance on local custom. Nevertheless, he does include a novel twist on the talmudic requirement that a cantor ought to have a pleasant voice. Adret understands that to mean that a cantor does not need a great voice, only one that is not offensive.

Stylistically, Adret follows the usual pattern of using assigned, generic names for the principals in order to protect anonymity. He also uses the words "prayer leader" (Hebrew: *sheli'ah tzibbur*) and "cantor" (Hebrew: *hazzan*) interchangeably. It is a style followed by Rabbi Joseph Karo[140] and others.

> You asked: "Re'uven" claims against "Shimon" saying: 'You were our prayer leader in the synagogue in Osca (Huesca)[141] for thirty-eight years and now you have grown old and you can no longer fulfill your duties as you once did. You have given us your son in your stead and he is not so capable because his voice is not pleasant. I, and some of the other worshipers in the aforementioned synagogue, do not want him to pray. If you can pray: very well. But if you cannot, be so good as to stay home.' "Shimon" replied: 'It is possible that some of my strength has failed and my eyes have dimmed from aging and I cannot focus and read Torah as I once did. But in all other matters a cantor is obligated to perform, my strength now is as my strength was then. I appeal to the community who regularly pray in the synagogue that they treat me with kindness for the remainder of my years as they did with my ancestors, for my father and my father's father were cantors for many generations [who served] for their entire lives and no deficiency was found [to issue] from their lips. And my previously mentioned son—even though his voice is not pleasant—he fills the role of my ancestors in all other ways. My son will read Torah in my stead and he will serve as the communal secretary and by so doing the community will not violate the official appointment that I have inherited from my ancestors, may their memory be a blessing. Those who appointed me to serve over them as a cantor for life did so with an enforceable agreement and no one else can serve in any cantorial capacity but me (or my designated substitute) as the enactment document states. Besides, it is the desire and will of most of the community—some 150—to treat me with kindness and mercy for the sake of my ancestors who were cantors for them and their ancestors and they want my son to assist me

---

140. Cf. *Shulhan Arukh*, OH 53:1.

141. Located in Aragon in northeastern Spain.

in all previously mentioned duties for the rest of my life. And the people you represent number no more than ten.'

This is the text of the communal ordinance: 'The entire congregation of the great synagogue in Osca—known as the *Patzaltat*[142] congregation—are in unanimous agreement without any dissenters who wholeheartedly appoint over them from now on, a cantor who would serve them in all matters of the cantorate—from minor to major—so-and-so, son of so-and-so, from today and for his lifetime, etc. and the congregation may not appoint another cantor to assist the previously mentioned cantor in any of his previously mentioned duties except whom the previously mentioned cantor appoints. And no other cantor nor another man may be appointed in his place or to replace him in any of the previously mentioned duties without his consultation and permission, etc. and to certify all the above-mentioned terms, the entire congregation confirmed them under threat of ostracism standing in solemn assembly with a Torah scroll, *etc*.'

Answer: The law is on the side of "Shimon," the prayer leader, for several reasons. One, strict law [holds] that someone who sets a condition with a congregation to serve them in a certain capacity is not limited only to what he himself can do unassisted, there being times when he cannot [perform his duties without assistance]. Rather, both the intention of the congregation and the person serving the congregation is that the person serving the congregation serves most of the time. Yet, if sometimes he needs assistance from others, he can place another in his stead for a short time. We learn this in Tosefta: "A public bath attendant, a barber, a baker, a money-changer: when there is no one else except him and the festival is about to begin and he wants to go home [to prepare] he may be prevented [from going home] until he appoints a replacement. But if he set terms in court or if he suffers from traveling, he has permission [to appoint a replacement]."[143] If so, this cantor who sometimes needs help from his son has permission since this was the stipulation from the outset.

Further, it seems that from the language of the communal ordinance itself they explicitly agreed to this stipulation, for the text says: 'The congregation may not appoint another to assist the previously mentioned cantor nor may another man be appointed in his stead to perform any of the previously mentioned

142. This meaning of this name is not clear. It appears to be Spanish, perhaps a play on the word *paz* (peace).

143. Tosef. *B. Metz.* 11:13.

duties without his advice and consent.' From the plain meaning
of these words it seems that the congregation's intent from the
outset was that occasionally the cantor would need an assistant
in the performance of his duties. And logic leads [us] to deduce
that the congregation would never have thought that he would
serve in the same way for his entire life, that he would not take
sick or that he would never succumb to any human affliction.
With all this, they explicitly agreed to the stipulation that even if
he needed assistance, the congregation did not have permission
to appoint someone else to assist him and also no one else could
volunteer to help him: only one appointed with his advice and
consent.

Also, if he fell ill for a year or he left the city for a year the
congregation may not appoint anyone else; only someone he
appoints since this is the wording of the communal ordinance.
And if, God forbid, he took ill or needed to leave on a journey,
they must wait a year until he returns or recovers. After the year
the congregation must judge if they will wait longer for him or,
based on their judgment, how [else] they should behave toward
him. From this language it seems that even if he should fall ill
for a full year they are not allowed to appoint another to assist
him, except one appointed by the cantor or by the cantor's ap-
pointee—even though this is not explicitly explained in the text
of the ordinance as we said. I say that even though it is not so
clear but questionable, since there is a penalty attached, we follow a strict reading [of the ordinance] and not a liberal one, and
no one may appeal against him in these matters.

Now if the son is suitable for this—even though his voice
is not pleasant, that is, his voice is not strange—if he is of good
character and not guilty of any personal transgressions, it is fitting that his son be given preference over anyone else based on
what I see from the custom of those places where sons of cantors
are appointed by congregations to succeed their fathers. In this
case—his father and father's father were cantors, according to
the wording of his claim—and [our sages] of blessed memory
articulated an important principle that if the son is worthy he
takes precedence over all other men.[144] Even the High Priest,
if his son were worthy—though there are others as great as or
greater than he—the son takes precedence. And surely now that
the father is living and performing his duties but needs help for
a few days, the law is on his side that his son takes precedence
over all other men.

---

144. Cf. *Sifra*, Ahare Mot, Parshata 5, Chapter 5.

She'elot U'Teshuvot Ha-RaShBA, Part 1, No. 215:
What Mood Should a Cantor Generate?

Adret informs us that, as early as the thirteenth century, some cantors tried to impress their audience with their musical talent. The questioner expresses annoyance with two aspects of the cantor's singing. First, the cantor makes the prayer service longer than it should be. And second, the cantor's happy music seems to contravene the talmudic requirement for solemnity in prayer. Adret answers both these concerns. He rules that it all depends on the cantor's attitude. There is a vast difference between thinking his voice to be a vehicle for serving God through his musical talent and using his voice in a kind of exhibitionism. The former is praiseworthy; the latter is not. Moreover, cheerful music is not an indication of a lack of solemnity. Second, Adret rules that the thrust of the Talmud is to shorten the time at prayer rather than lengthen it.

> You asked further about a cantor whose voice was agreeable and pleasant to listeners, who embellishes his prayer so that the people will hear his pleasant voice and he takes pride in this and rejoices in his voice, and does so intentionally when he prays. And he[145] says this is fitting since it is good for him to feel happy. Is it appropriate to prevent him [from leading prayers] because it is better to make his prayer more sober, and how can he pray soberly [when he prays] out of joy?
>
> Answer: These matters follow the heart. If the cantor feels happy in the fact that he offers praise and thanks to God in a pleasant and sweet voice and rejoices out of awe, may he be blessed! For one of the qualities that one who goes down to the lectern needs to have is a sweet and pleasant voice. As it is taught in the tractate Ta'anit, Chapter "Order of the Fast Days:"[146] "They stood in prayer. Even if there is an elder or a scholar present, only one who is well versed is brought down [to the lectern] . . ."[147] However, one must pray solemnly, as it is taught: "One stands to pray only in solemnity."[148] So one should stand in awe as someone standing in God's presence, for it is recorded there[149]: "Rabbi Hama bar Bizna said in the name of

145. Referring to the prayer leader in question.

146. b. Ta'an. 16a.

147. "One who possesses a sweet and pleasant voice" is one of the criteria included in this passage listing the qualifications of a lector.

148. b. Ber. 30b.

149. b. San. 22a.

Rabbi Shimon Hasida: 'The worshiper must see himself as if God's presence is before him,' as it is written: 'I am ever mindful of the Lord's presence.' (Ps 16:8)." And it is taught:[150] "We do not stand to pray after conversing, after laughing, or with light-headedness or [discussing] trivial things." Therefore, if this cantor stands in awe and, as it is written: "Serve God in awe and rejoice with trembling (Ps 2:11)," he is praiseworthy. However, if his intent is to make his voice heard and rejoice in his voice—that the people will hear it and praise him—then he is to be condemned and to him and all like him we apply the verse: "She raised her voice against Me, therefore I have rejected her (Jer 12:8)." In any case, anyone who embellishes his prayer does a disservice since in some places they required shortening [prayers] on account of the burden [imposed] on the congregation. And Rabbi Judah said: "This was Rabbi Akiva's custom: when he prayed with the congregation he would shorten; when he prayed alone, one person would leave him in one corner and find him in another because of all the kneeling and bowing he would do."[151]

She'elot U'Teshuvot Ha-RaShBA, Part 1, No. 450:
A Paid Cantor?

This responsum was also published in an abridged form in Part 3, No. 439. In contrast to the responsum (No. 300) above, Adret considers the merits of employing a professional cantor. He argues that a paid cantor is preferred since that assures a higher-quality prayer leader—particularly when the liturgy is complicated and the words are unfamiliar to the masses. A paid cantor would act professionally, that is, prepare more intently than one whose livelihood was not at stake. Adret also reveals that the custom in Jewish communities everywhere in his day was to engage paid cantors. Thus any ruling against the custom would result in an unintended yet undeniable criticism of the prevailing custom and the congregations that adopted it. This he was not about to do.

You asked: Which is better: a paid cantor or a volunteer?

Answer: It is more appropriate to be a paid prayer leader because when he is paid, it is clear to the community without trespass or complaint that there is no other appropriate person

150. *b. Ber.* 31a.
151. *b. Ber.* 31a.

so bold as to pray. If he were a volunteer, all would have the option, and with no boundaries, an unfit man may just as likely come forward as a fit man. Due to this [worry] we had to enact [a provision] that during the Days of Awe, like the penitential services as well as the New Year and Day of Atonement, no person had permission to go up to the platform to pray without the approval of the community. And, similarly, with shofar blowing: since the experts in the city saw that many [wanted to perform] this [function], they had to enact [regulations] and circumscribe [its performance].

Further, according to the dissenters' opinion, all the congregations everywhere who pay cantors would be deemed wrong. Also, a paid cantor would be more careful in his prayers and preparation.

She'elot U'Teshuvot Ha-RaShBA, Part 5, No. 283: When Can a Cantor be Replaced?

Ostensibly, the responsum that follows limits the terms of cantors to three years, following the local custom that is determinative. Yet Adret also includes cantors in the list of communal professionals, lending status to the office. The recipient of this letter is unknown, but Adret confirms his conclusion: cantors are public servants and, as such, customarily considered contracted for a three-year term.

On the Law of dismissing a cantor only on the grounds of disqualification—and proofs for this.[152]

You wrote well and reasoned well. Further, we learned: "An 'eruv[153] should always be placed in an old house[154] in the interests of peace."[155] And the Gemara holds that [the reason

152. This heading is in error. The actual subject, as evident from what follows, is the custom of limiting the term of any public servant (including cantors) to three years.

153. Literally "mixture." An 'eruv is a rabbinic enactment that allows residents sharing a common courtyard to freely access each other's premises on Shabbat by depositing a measure of food in which all the residents have a share on the property of one of residents. Cf. m. 'Eruv., chs. 6–8.

154. That is, in the same location.

155. b. Git. 60b. Were the deposit not set in the same place, people entering the courtyard might think the residents had neglected the mitzvah. They would be suspected of violating a rabbinic enactment. To promote peace among members of the community it is important to be consistent, that is, doing things the customary way.

for this ruling] is to avoid suspicion.[156] The entire Gemara is binding and, if so, still should be applicable.[157] Today, however, all communities are accustomed to appoint public servants for a specified time. When the time expires, these [public servants] leave [service] and others enter [into service]. This [system applies] to food [distribution], community chest,[158] taxation, and other communal offices, whether they are paid or unpaid. If the custom is not to specify any term, that custom is followed as well. Custom is tantamount to law and all these things are contingent on custom. Since [cantors] are accustomed to have replacements, [the worry over] suspicion[159] disappears. Capable individuals in every generation take on the onus of serving the public for a specified term and are replaced afterwards. There is no worry here over money or suspicion.[160]

She'elot U'Teshuvot Ha-RaShBA, Part 3, No. 381: Who Pays the Cantor's Salary?

How a community spends its money is often controversial. In thirteenth-century Spain, there seems to be an issue regarding who pays the cantor's salary. Some argue that that since the role of the cantor is to fulfill the obligation of prayer for all Jews, he should be paid from the communal treasury. Others, however, argue that a cantor is a kind of luxury, the cost of which ought to be assessed proportionately, with the rich covering the bulk of the expense. Adret argues that if the proportionate view prevailed, then the bulk of the expense ought to be imposed on those who are illiterate and need the cantor to fulfill their obligation for reciting the prayers they are unable to read. But this would be preposterous. Hence, the cantor must be paid from communal funds, particularly from some unspecified "Cantor Fund" to which additional money might be added if necessary.

---

156. Suspicion of failing to observe the laws of 'eruv.

157. RaShBA intimates that previous practice remains in force. There was no stipulated term for cantorial service during the time of the Talmud, and it would be fair to assume that same attitude should prevail in his day. He then proceeds to dismiss this inference.

158. For the distribution of alms to the poor: kupah in Hebrew.

159. That replacing a cantor violates established practice.

160. This ruling is accepted by Rabbi Joseph Karo, Shulhan Arukh, OH 53:26.

With regard to a prayer leader you also asked: Does a man hired
from communal funds fulfill [the obligation of prayer] for the
poor and rich alike? According to the community rule, each
member of the community pays on a sliding scale. The poor
cannot afford as much as the rich. So the rich pay a dispropor-
tionate share [of the cantor's salary].

In most cases there are special funds set aside for paying
prayer leaders [and there are] places where they add to them so
when they pay out, they pay out from community funds. If you
dispute this and [argue that] instead, payment should be shared
by all equally because each receives the same benefit, then we
ought to say that those incapable of prayer (*i.e.*, the illiterate)
should pay it all since he (*i.e.*, the cantor) fulfills the obligation
[of prayer] for the incapable and does not fulfill the obligation
for the capable.[161]

She'elot U'Teshuvot RITVA, No. 97: A Blind Cantor

Rabbi Yom Tov ben Abraham (al-Ashbili is a family nickname)[162] was a
student of RaShBA and Rabbi Aaron of Barcelona (mentioned by name
below) but his style is considerably different. Unlike RaShBA, RITVA—as
he is known by his acronym—includes flowery expressions and oblique
references to Scripture, rabbinic sources, and popular expressions of his
day. Always modest and deferential, RITVA denies any pretense of authority. Yet his command of all the sources belies any need for modesty.

Much of this repsonsum is a detailed textual analysis of the talmudic sources cited by a certain Rabbi Dan of Toledo in which the latter
argued that a blind man may not serve as a prayer leader. Rabbi Dan
then sought confirmation of his opinion from RITVA. RITVA exposes
the weaknesses of the questioner's interpretation and, in addition, cites
a number of post-talmudic sources that explicitly rule the opposite way,
that is, that a blind man may lead prayer services. RITVA shows that
prayer today is a rabbinic requirement, although there are certain prayers
that are scripturally required. A blind man is obligated to perform the
rabbinic obligation for prayer like everyone else. Hence, theoretically, a
blind man can fulfill the obligation of prayer for the congregation. Yet
RITVA finds this problematic. When people depend on the cantor to

161. *Cf. b. R.H.* 34b.

162. See Rabbi Yosef David Kafah's introduction in Al-Ashbili, *She'elot U'Teshuvot
RITVA*, 9.

recite the scripturally required prayers that they themselves are incompetent to recite, the cantor must be in a position to fulfill that obligation. He reveals that in his day, many Jews were so ignorant they could not even recite the most basic of Hebrew prayers. Consequently, the cantor must be scripturally obligated and a blind cantor is not. Ironically, even though he disputes Rabbi Dan's analysis, he agrees with his conclusion. RITVA, however, leaves open the possibility that a blind man may be an occasional cantor.

Readers may infer from this responsum that despite the flourishing of many great scholars in thirteenth-century Spain, the Jewish community was largely unlettered. The position of cantor was, as a result, transformed from one of providing a musical component to prayer to one of becoming the agent for prayer. The responsum begins with RITVA's self-deprecation.

> ... I will answer according to the portion I have learned from my teachers' benefactions and I shall put forward my opinions not as a teacher of Jewish law or a decisor but only as a student reviewing his lessons before his teachers since this is the way men of the Talmud acted, being a student making comments before his teacher—even though, in the end, in matters of dispute Jewish law does not follow [the opinion of] the students in the place of the teacher. Therefore I said I would "approach the subject"[163] as if his statements were holy anointing oil and I will suffice to "draw out"[164] some strands from them . . .
>
> These are the words of the student:
>
> Thus I received from the mouth of my master, Rabbi Aaron Ha-Levi (may God protect him!): a blind man may lead the *Shema* and go to the lectern. And even though in the tractate Megillah does not mention—in any of our editions—whether the teacher of this Mishnah says whether or not he goes to the lectern [to lead prayers, we infer] the reason is that a blind man is rabbinically required to recite the *Shema* and the *Amidah*. The blessings connected to the *Shema* and the public recitation of the prayer is also rabbinical. 'The rabbis come and exclude,'[165] as in the case of a woman and the blessing of [thanks after eating] food where we come to prove that it[166] is scripturally required

163. See *b. Shev.* 47b.

164. See *Shir HaShirim Rabbah* 1.

165. *b. Ber.* 20b. The rabbis determine what prayer obligations apply.

166. The blessing of thanks after eating food.

since the text says "in truth they said a son blesses for his father and a wife blesses for her husband" which we apply [the principle] to a case when, for example, the husband ate a rabbinically determined measure [of food]. The rabbis come and the rabbis exclude.

That the Mishnah in Megillah does not mention [anything] with regard to a blind man and going to the lectern, is because it did not have to: it is obvious that since he can lead the *Shema* because 'the rabbis come and exclude' the same applies to going to the lectern, for what is the difference? For just as a minor cannot go to the lectern to lead the *Shema* [so can he]. And with regard to the improperly dressed for whom it is necessary to teach that he does not go to the lectern on account of the dignity for the congregation, with regard to the blind man it is unnecessary. And the [only] reason why it (*i.e.*, the Mishnah) includes leading the *Shema* is because of the dispute in which Rabbi Yehudah takes the position that "he never was able to see." This is the approach of my teacher—may the Merciful One protect him and keep him!

Rabbi Moshe ibn Maimon (May the memory of the righteous be a blessing!) also wrote that a blind man may be a prayer leader.[167] And I am but dust and ashes to include myself among these great authorities.[168]

For clarification, RITVA goes on to consider possible qualifications to the principle that the rabbis have the authority to determine the parameters of obligations through a careful examination of talmudic passages. He concludes that Rabbi Dan follows a legitimate, but contrary opinion.

I see that Rabbi Dan (May God protect him!) bases [his view] on [the passage from the tractate] *Pesahim*[169] from which he learned that nowadays prayer that is rabbinic is held to be Scriptural and the rabbis do not come to exclude. And Rabbi Dan would say that *Hallel*, *Shema*, and *Megillah* differ from the prayer of [thanks to God after eating] food in that for the latter [mentioned prayers] we say that one who is rabbinically obligated may fulfill the obligation for others even according to the

167. MT, Laws of Prayer 8:12.

168. Literally: "to place myself between these great mountains." The reference is to Rabbi Aaron Ha-Levi and Maimonides, who both rule that a blind man may serve as a cantor.

169. *b. Pes.* 116b.

rabbis—and certainly according to Rabbi Yehudah. However, it is not clear to us what good reason the rabbis had to make a distinction between the prayer of [thanks to God for food] and *Megillah, Shema,* and prayer . . .[170]

And now, let us return to the [issue of the] blind man. We have already learned from our teacher (May God protect him!) that our sages, the Tosafists,[171] of blessed memory, expressed in writing three opinions on this matter. There is someone who says that a blind man—even according to the rabbinical definition—is exempt from the commandments even in the case of the sighted man who goes blind. And there is someone who holds that even though [a blind man] is scripturally exempt, the rabbis make him obligated. For although with regard to women [we say] they are scripturally exempt and similarly rabbinically exempt, as stated in the passage that women are obligated to recite *Kiddush* according to the Torah, it is different there since it is a positive commandment they are required to do, and customarily do. But in this case (*i.e.,* the blind man) who is scripturally exempt from all positive commandments and all negative commandments, if he is exempted even from rabbinical commandments he would be made into a gentile! As Rabbenu Tam, of blessed memory, and Rabbenu Yitzhak the elder, of blessed memory, wrote (and as others say): A blind man from birth was never obligated by the Sages at all; only a sighted man who became blind. It goes without saying someone who lost his vision as an adult after already having become scripturally obligated [to observe the commandments] when he had his sight—even when he lost his vision when he was a minor . . . is put under an obligation by the rabbis as much as possible. Accordingly, the rabbis unqualifiedly impose upon him the obligation. The legal reasoning is that the rabbis come and the rabbis exclude *viz.* everything whose source is rabbinic (like reading the *Shema* and prayer—but not [with regard to eating] *matzah* and similar such cases) or whose source was scriptural at the time the Temple stood and whose obligation is rabbinic today (as a remembrance of Temple times as I wrote above): [all Jews are equally obligated to perform].

However, it puzzles me how a blind man can be made a permanent prayer leader today, fulfilling the requirements of others, to recite the blessings before the *Shema*, and to go to the

---

170. RITVA continues his analysis of the difficult passages mentioned above.

171. *b. Eruv.* 96a, *s.v. dilma.*

lectern. For isn't *"emet v'yatziv"* a scriptural requirement[172] on account of *"emet mi-mitzrayim"* that includes the requirement for a man to mention the Exodus from Egypt in the daytime? And even though a man fulfills this obligation in [reciting] the passage on fringes, is it not the case that in our sinfulness nowadays there are many ignoramuses who do not know [how to read the passage about] fringes? And even the first verse of the *Shema*—according to all—is scriptural yet there are many ignoramuses who do not recite it, instead relying on the cantor who says it aloud! Also, the essence of prayer is a scriptural obligation, as we say ". . . and to serve Him with all your heart—this is prayer,"[173] although its formulation is rabbinic, the product of the enactment of the prophets and the men of the Great Assembly. Yet there are many ignoramuses who do not pray at all and the cantor fulfills their obligation. Because of this, it appears to me, in my poor estimation, that Rabbi Dan (May he live!) came to the true conclusion: that today, in our sinfulness, with the spread of ignorance it is not appropriate to appoint a permanent cantor who is blind, either from birth or who was born sighted but became blind. I suspect that this is why the teacher of the Mishnah was silent and did not teach anything about a blind man going to the lectern, neither did he specifically say that he may not go to the lectern because in the places where the worshipers are scholars he may, while in places where the worshipers are ignoramuses he may not. However, with regard to reciting the *Shema*, the law is explicit on account of the dispute with Rabbi Yehudah. Further, when it comes to leading the *Shema* whereby he recites only the blessings before the *Shema*, there is no Scriptural obligation [involved] so there is no reason to be concerned.

This is what I suggest to my master, Rabbi Dan (May he live!) and to my teachers and my eminences[174] the students of his academy (May the blessed God protect them!) based on what I have deduced through my meager intellect. And my master, the great rabbi, and the students of his academy will use their fine filter to sift through the chaff and take out the kernels and bring the matter to light. And the blessed God in His compassion will transform the dark before us into light and make the crooked straight and bring us the righteous teacher to instruct us in truth and righteousness, amen and amen!

172. See *b. Ber.* 21a.

173. *Sifre*, Deut 11:13.

174. A title of respect.

And to you, my master and teacher, the great rabbi, and to all my teachers, the exalted lords and great and wise eminences, the elders of Toledo, the Holy City, its nobles and all who turn to your teachings and heed your Torah, may they follow you as a living river. Much honor and great peace to you forever as you desire and as I, your servant's servant, desire for you,

I am a worm and no-person,

Yom Tov ben Rav Avraham (May God protect him and save him!) ben al-Ashbili.

Provence: Thirteenth Century

Born in Perpignan in 1249, when Barcelona dominated southern France, Rabbi Menahem ben Solomon Ha-Meiri was also known as Don Vidal Solomon. He was a brilliant student of Rabbi Reuben ben Hayyim of Narbonne and took up the defense of science and philosophy. His principal work, Bet Ha-Behirah (The Chosen House, another name for the Jerusalem Temple), was a multivolume summative exposition of the Babylonian Talmud, purposely eliminating the discursive elements. Largely unknown in his day—it was published serially beginning in Amsterdam in 1769—it has become one of the most popular tools for the study of Talmud. He died sometime around 1310.

Rabbi Judah explicates the Mishnah and lengthens the list of qualifications for a prayer leader. Ha-Meiri presumes that Rabbi Judah's view is adopted as a talmudic rule that extends the requirements of a prayer leader from public fast days to year round. Even so, the mandate to appoint a worthy prayer leader is particularly pressing during times of peril when the prayers of a worthy man would be most efficacious. To emphasize this idea, Ha-Meiri adds an extra-talmudic, midrashic element—an interpretation of the parable in Ecclesiastes 9:14–15: "There was a little city, with few men in it; and to it came a great king, who invested in it and built mighty siege works against it. Present in the city was a poor wise man who saved the city with his wisdom . . ." The parable was intended to prove that there is no better quality than wisdom. Ha-Meiri cites the seventh-century[175] Ecclesiastes Rabbah (9:15:7) that shifts the context and intent of the parable demonstrating that a worthy synagogue cantor can change God's decrees. "Wisdom" is taken to mean "skill" as in Exodus

---

175. According to Townsend, Study of Judaism, 70.

35:31. It is likely reflective of the esteem in which worthy cantors were held in thirteenth-century Provence.

Bet Ha-Behirah on Babylonian Talmud Ta'anit 16a: The Benefit of a Worthy Cantor

> The Gemara explains that even throughout the year we need to appoint a worthy man but it is especially the case in a time like this[176] that we must take particular care. And in the Midrash they said: 'A small city'—this is the synagogue; 'and few people in it'—this is the congregation; 'and a great king came to it'—this is God; 'and present in it'—*etc.*, 'and he spared the city by his skill'—this is the cantor.

Italy: Thirteenth Century: The Qualifications of a Cantor

Rabbi Zedekiah ben Abraham Ha-Rofeh is reputed to have studied in Germany and Austria as well as in his native Rome. He was an honored correspondent of Rabbi Meir of Rothenberg. His family traced their lineage back to the exiles taken to Rome by Titus following the destruction of the Second Temple in 70 CE. It seems that the title "Ha-Rofeh" refers to his father, a doctor. His principle work, *Shibbolei Haleket* [Sheaves of Gleaning], hints at the purpose it was intended to serve, as the author's introduction states: "I have gleaned from the intellectual fields of the Geonim, of blessed memory, and I have arranged the laws, one after another, like aromatic garden beds . . ."[177] The Geonim, claims Rabbi Zedekiah, were the giants upon whose shoulders we—mere dwarfs—sit. Yet the very same Geonim—who, for him, include Rabbi Isaac al-Fasi, Rabbenu Gershom, Rabbi Solomon Yitzhaqi, Rabbenu Jacob Tam, and Rabbi Eliezer ben Yoel Ha-Levi, among others—left their successors room to distinguish themselves. Thus *Shibbolei Ha-Leket* cites from and builds upon classic rabbinic sources and serves as a window that provides a glimpse into early medieval Jewish practice. The Buber edition, from which this passage is translated, was first printed in Vilna, 1887.

Marshaling sources from the Babylonian and Jerusalem Talmud, responsa, and Midrash, the author summarizes the rules regarding the age,

---

176. That is, during a time of drought and famine when divine relief is needed.

177. Ben Abraham, *Shibbolei Ha-Leket Ha-Shalem*, 17.

dress, character, and physical abilities of the cantor. Particularly interesting is his citation from *Pesiqta Rabati* that extols the value of the cantor's voice in the service of God and the duty the cantor has in using his vocal gifts accordingly. The Midrash also indicates that perhaps as early as the second century, Jews would make special efforts to hear a gifted cantor. Hiyya bar Ada was arguably the first identified cantorial celebrity. The fact that *Shibbolei Ha-Leket* is the first source to cite this Midrash in articulating the laws of the cantor is most probably a reflection of the high value placed on voice in the Italian tradition.

Shibbolei Ha-Leket Ha-Shalem, Law of Prayer, Section 10 (ed. Buber 6a, 11): The Law of the Cantor Who Is Suitable to Lead Prayers?

A minor and a slave are not suitable[178] to lead prayers,[179] as it is taught [in the Mishnah[180]]: "Anyone who is not obligated in the matter does not fulfill the obligation for others." And it is taught in the Tractate *Soferim*, Chapter 13:[181] "A minor reads from the Torah and translates but does not lead the *Shema* to say 'Creator of Light,'" meaning [in the presence of a quorum] of ten, "nor may he pass before the Ark nor lift up his hands [for the priestly blessing]. The poorly dressed, whose sides are showing or whose clothes are torn, or someone whose head is uncovered may not lead the *Shema*. And some say: [Someone whose] sides are showing and clothes are torn may lead the *Shema*, but is not allowed to utter God's name with an uncovered head. And in either case, he may translate, but not read from the Torah, etc."

Jerusalem Talmud, Chapter 'The Stolen Lulav':[182] "A minor who knows how to shake a *lulav* is obligated for [taking] a *lulav*; knows how to wrap, is obligated for *tzitzit*, knows how to talk, his father is obligated to teach him Torah; knows how to guard his hands: others may eat *terumah*[183] [he handles]; [knows how

178. Neither minors nor slaves are legally competent. The slave lacks the liberty to serve as an agent for others and a minor lacks understanding and experience.

179. Literally "go before the Ark."

180. *m. R.H.* 3:8.

181. *Sof.*, Vilna edition, 14:15.

182. *Suk.* 3:12 end, 15a.

183. *Terumah* is a priestly emolument that an ordinary Israelite is required to give from each annual harvest in accordance with Deuteronomy 18:4. It is holy food (Cf. Lev 22:10) that must be guarded from impurity by casual contact.

to guard] his body: others may eat holy foods [he touches]—but
he may not lead the service and may not raise his hands and may
not go up to the dais [for the priestly blessing] until his beard is
full. Rabbi says: all [age thresholds for majority] are [calculated]
from twenty years and older, as it is written: 'And they appointed
the Levites from the age of twenty and older to supervise the
work of the House of the Lord forever' (Ezra 3:8)."

And in the responsa of the Geonim,[184] blessed be the
memory of the righteous, I found: "They asked Rabbi Natronai,
blessed be the memory of the righteous: a congregation that
has only one regular cantor who is sometimes busy at his work
and there are youths seventeen and eighteen years of age whose
beards have not filled out—may they be made prayer leaders
to fulfill the obligation of prayer for others?" And he answered
thus: "We note the sages' requirement that he may neither pass
before the ark nor raise his hands until his beard fills out. That is
the ideal; whenever possible, an adult is preferable to a youngster. But when it comes to omitting 'Borkhu', 'Kaddish', and 'Kedushah', it does not matter whether he is seventeen or eighteen
since even those [of] thirteen years and one day [old]—when
necessary—are allowed [to lead] because they [too] are obligated as it is taught [in the Mishnah[185]]: 'A thirteen year old [is
obligated to observe] the mitzvot' and one who is obligated for a
matter fulfills the obligation for others."

And [regarding] a blind man[186] and someone whose deeds
are [morally] deficient—may they pass before the Ark or not?
This was asked of the [members of the Geonic] Academy.[187]
And they answered: a lector about whom bad behavior was reported—need this question be asked?—surely the law requires
replacing him with someone more acceptable [to mediate]
between [the people of] Israel and their Heavenly Father. Certainly he must be righteous and upstanding, pure in body from
any failing, and if not, the sages already said: "She raised her
voice against Me, therefore I have hated her (Jer 12:8)"—this
applies to an unworthy lector.

And indisputably, if on weekdays it is forbidden [to be led
by an unsuitable cantor], then certainly on Rosh Hashanah, Yom
Kippur and on a fast day (a day when prayers of supplication

184. Cf. *Seder Rav Amram*, Laws of Prayer; Emanuel, *Teshuvot Ha-Ge'onim Ha-Hadashot*, No.15.

185. Avot 5:21.

186. Cf. *Teshuvot Ha-Ge'onim Ha-Hadashot*, No. 24.

187. Cf. *Teshuvot Ha-Ge'onim Shaarei Teshuvah*, No. 51.

and mercy abound so that the prayer leader must be, as Rabbi Yehudah says, someone whose reputation was unsullied since his youth) we would dismiss any cantor about whom there is complaint now, even if the indiscretion was committed in his youth.[188]

And in *Pesiqta Rabbati*[189] on the phrase "You shall surely tithe . . ." (Deuteronomy 14:22): "Honor God with your treasure (Prov 3:9)." "With your treasure" [means] if your voice is pleasant and you are sitting in the synagogue, arise and honor God with your voice." Hiyya,[190] the nephew of Rabbi Elazar Ha-Kappar,[191] had a pleasant voice and it was said to him: Arise, and honor God with what he has graciously bestowed on you! Nabot had a pleasant voice and went up to Jerusalem and all Israel gathered together to hear his voice. Once, he did not go up and some mischief-makers testified against him and he died. What caused him to not go up to Jerusalem to honor the Holy One, praised be He, with what God had graciously bestowed upon him? The Torah had already assured that "no one would covet your field when you go up to Jerusalem to be seen by God"[192] and had he gone up he would not have died, but [he worried about] the coveting of his field.

Spain: Fourteenth Century

Rabbi Isaac ben Sheshet Perfet (or Barfet) was a student of Rabbenu Nissim Gerondi, Rabbenu Perez, and Rabbi Hasdai Crescas. Born in Barcelona (or, according to some, Valencia) in 1326, he resisted entering the rabbinate although he was a recognized scholar and authority. Instead, he went into business. Rabbi Isaac gives sparse details about his imprisonment along with other prominent Jews following false accusations (Responsa, No. 376), but shortly after his release he took a series of rabbinic positions, culminating with his tenure in Valencia. In the aftermath

188. *Teshuvot Ha-Geʾonim Ha-Hadashot*, No. 24.

189. Chapter 23. *Pesiqta Rabati* consists of homiletical traditions on the festival Torah readings. The collection is commonly dated after the mid-ninth-century. M. Friedmann published the first critical edition in 1880. See also Mandelbaum, *Pesiqta D'Rav Kahana*, 1:164—a slightly earlier work—where the same story appears in a shortened form.

190. bar Ada.

191. This relationship dates him to the last third of the first century.

192. Exod 34:24.

of the anti-Jewish riots of 1391, Rabbi Isaac fled to Algiers where he served—not without controversy—until his death in 1407. While Rabbi Isaac wrote a commentary on the Torah and novellae on several talmudic tractates, he is best known for his responsa. An initial collection of 517[193] responsa was published in Constantinople in 1547, followed by a smaller collection published in Munkacz in 1901.

This case may be the first written description of a contractual dispute between a cantor and his congregation in Jewish history. From what can be inferred from Rabbi Isaac's response, the story is as follows. A small Jewish community appointed a search committee to engage a cantor. Their task was met with success and the cantor served without complaint for an initial term of three years. At the time of his hire the cantor expressed the desire to be exempt from communal taxes—a benefit the poor cantor needed—and the search committee seems to have assured him that this would be the case. While there was some written account of the salary to which they agreed there was no written statement regarding a tax exemption. When it came time to renew the cantor's contract, the new search committee did not include the tax exemption, insisting that the cantor pay the required sum just like any other member of the community. The cantor demurred. Relations worsened. The leaders of the congregation pressured the cantor to accept, yet he continued to refuse. The two sides finally agreed to submit the matter to Rabbi Isaac for adjudication. Rabbi Isaac, applying talmudic precedents and the regnant custom in Spain as mentioned by Rabbi Solomon ben Adret, ruled that the cantor was entitled to the same exemption. The congregation disputed his ruling, prompting Rabbi Isaac to write a second time. Rabbi Isaac repudiates the contention that a cantor's contract should be treated differently from other categories of employees. All oral contractual stipulations are valid. Moreover, the congregation cannot claim that what the initial search committee promised is not binding on its successors or on the congregation. The search committee had an obligation to inform the leadership. If they failed to do so, the cantor still has every right to expect that the congregation as a whole accepted the promises made to him by the agents of the congregation. Moreover, the oral stipulation was made in the presence of the rabbi of the congregation who came to the defense of the cantor. Finally, even if the cantor might have offended some of

---

193. No. 518 is an exhortation for Spanish Jews to attend synagogue and not actually a response.

the leadership during the contentious period of renegotiation, that is no reason for treating him unfairly.

The entire scenario is remarkably familiar and continues to be played out with minor variation in the contractual negotiations between congregations and ritual professionals to this day. What is of particular interest to the history of the cantorate is that this account confirms three important historical facts. First, even small Jewish communities secured cantors for their synagogues. Second, cantors were not particularly well paid in fourteenth-century Spain. Third, the custom in Spanish communities of the thirteenth and fourteenth centuries was to exempt cantors from certain communal taxes as a standard fringe benefit.

She-elot U'Teshuvot Ha-RIBaSh, No. 476:
A Dispute Regarding the Cantor's Contract

To the judges of al-Kolaya,[194] again, nobles of Israel, judges, your letter has reached me, and I see in it that you were greatly amazed that I said in my response that if a cantor made a condition with the original selectors that he would be exempt from the tax and there were witnesses [to this fact] or they concede that he is legally exempt since that is what they promised him orally, and even though it is not written in his contract, this needs no documentation or validation since an employer must fully compensate the employee who does his work. Yet you said the cases are not alike. What you say is the law applies to a day laborer who is hired by oral agreement and not to a contracted employee who requires formal agreement. This is the gist of your contention.

I presently will continue to amaze you in this obviously clear case in which there is no difference between day laborers, weekly workers, monthly or annual hirelings or contract workers for harvesting grain or collecting grapes for in all these things no formal agreement is required. Rather, the agreement itself is effected by the onset of the work, even though the worker has the option to quit at any time, as it is written: "For

194. Alkolinia, according to She'elot U'Teshuvot MaHaRYTaZ, No. 104. It is probably a reference to Alcoy, a town situated approximately fifty kilometers south of Valencia. According to the account of Jeronimo de Zurita, two Jews from Alcoy took part in the Disputations at Tortosa in 1413 (Cf. de Castro and Kirwan, *History of the Jews in Spain*).

the people Israel are my servants"[195] and the householder may
not opt out . . .[196]

And I say even in this case it is one entity, that is, the community, that the original selectors and the current officers are
both agents of the community and it is the community that hires.
Further, there is no doubt that when the original selectors hired
the cantor and exempted him from taxes they reported this to
the community or its leadership thereby fulfilling their mandate
as would any agent, as we say regarding a *get*.[197] Accordingly,
the congregation should have told the later selectors explicitly
that he would not be exempt henceforth. Also, if the original
selectors did not inform the congregation, they should have
informed the second selectors or the second selectors should
have asked the first. So the cantor's original exemption stands:
he was of the opinion that the congregation was informed and
surely the selectors [were]. [So] why would he need to renew the
condition with the second selectors? . . .

. . . From what I know, according to the testimony of the
sage Rabbi Shem Tov Hakham (the wise),[198] this cantor is exempt since he testified that when they appointed him the cantor
said that the congregation pays the *modinis* tax [199] and [other]
taxes since he could not afford to do so. And the selectors who
hired him said he should not fear that they would alter [the
terms] with some new thing. He would be like all other cantors.
If so, it appears that at the time of his hire the cantor orally stipulated that he would not have to pay any of these things and they
assured him that he need not worry, *etc.* If so, they conceded to
his stipulation that he would be exempt even though it was not
recorded as his salary was recorded . . .

The end of the matter all things having been said . . . I say
according to what is possible for my heart to know, the cantor—over the course of the three years he was employed—was
exempt from all taxes. I am amazed by how the selectors and

195. Cf. Leviticus 25:55.

196. While the worker can. *b. B. Kam.* 116b.

197. *b. Git.* 24a.

198. It is unclear whether Hakham was his name or an honorific.

199. See Epstein, *"Responsa" of Rabbi Solomon*, chapters 2 and 3 for an extensive
discussion of the variety of taxes Jews in Spain were responsible for paying around this
time. Yet there is no mention of any such tax called *modinis*. Perhaps an emendation
to *merínos* is in order here, with the Hebrew *dalet* often mistaken for a *resh*. *Merínos*
was the title of the district tax collector who transmitted what he collected to the royal
Chancellor (22).

the congregational leadership have pursued and besieged him, particularly after they saw a number of witnesses who have come to his aid, especially the testimony of Rabbi Shem Tov Hakham (May God protect him!) without any clear testimony against him. And even if they had some doubt in the matter, it was appropriate for the congregation to give up their own resources rather than have the money stolen from the poor in their homes.[200] Yet I must judge them favorably: perhaps this cantor troubled the congregation or its leadership and verbally abused them and on account of this they wanted to press him with the builder's cubit[201] in their hands. In any case, true judgment is God's and there must be no favoritism or mercy in judgment.

Germany/Spain: Fourteenth Century: The Cantor's Qualifications, Age, and Importance

Scholars and historians consider Rabbenu Asher ben Yehiel (ca. 1250–1327) one of the foremost legal authorities of the thirteenth century. With a pedigree traced back to Rabbenu Gershom, the esteemed founder of Rhenish Jewish tradition, he was a disciple of Rabbi Meir of Rothenberg and a grandson of Rabbi Eliezer ben Nathan. The deteriorating political status of Jews in central Europe compelled Rabbenu Asher to relocate first to Savoy, then to Provence, and ultimately to Spain in 1305.[202] His scholarly reputation preceded him. Appointed as the presiding officer of the Jewish court in Toledo, the dean of the local academy and the chief rabbi, his influence extended throughout Castille. His commentary on the Talmud and his responsa reflect on both the Ashkenazic and Sephardic traditions.

In the first responsum, Rabbenu Asher agrees with the anonymous questioner that Spanish cantors do not meet the standards of integrity, but takes issue with the questioner who wished to limit cantorial appointments to the *grandees* (Spanish noblemen of high rank) alone.

200. That is, it is far better to use congregational funds to pay the amount the cantor would be charged in taxes otherwise, rather than to spread the fiscal burden among all the members of the community, which would include those least able to pay.

201. See Shabbat 31a. Shammai uses a "builder's cubit," i.e., a measuring stick, to chase away a person making a frivolous demand.

202. Louis Ginzberg attributes a more personal motive for his relocation: attempted government blackmail to deprive him of his fortune. Cf. Louis Ginzberg, *Jewish Encyclopedia*, s.v. *Asher ben Jechiel*.

Appointments, he argues, should be based on competence and character, not class or vocal pyrotechnics. At the same time he reveals that in fourteenth-century Spain, it was not uncommon for Christians to convert to Judaism and even become synagogue professionals. He cleverly plays upon Isaiah 57:19 to make his point.

In the second responsum, he returns to address the specific issue of the age of a cantor based on the requirement of being full bearded. The anonymous questioner assumes that "full bearded" refers to someone who shaves regularly and has the capability of regrowing a beard. Rabbenu Asher rules that "full bearded" is a requirement for any permanent appointment, but is not required for an occasional prayer leader. Notably, his answer discloses, first, that the cantor's position was by virtue of communal appointment, investing the cantor with the exclusive privilege of leading the congregation in prayer, and second, the cantor's appointment entitled him to appoint a subordinate.

In the third responsum, Rabbenu Asher ranks the relative value of a cantor versus a rabbi, concluding that a rabbi is more valuable to a community only when the rabbi is a scholar. Otherwise, the cantor who fulfills the congregation's obligation for prayer is preferable.

She'elot U'Teshuvot Ha-ROSh, Section 4, Number 22

A thirteen year-old boy may occasionally lead prayers but may not be appointed a permanent prayer leader until he grows a beard.

And what you have written that it is customary in these parts to appoint someone from a lesser family[203] as a prayer leader, and that there is in this matter a denigration of the mitzvah as if it is inappropriate for the distinguished families of Israel making it like other mere appointments. God forbid that Divine service be considered an ordinary occupation; it is, rather, a crown. Even I complained against the cantors of this land since the day I arrived here.[204] But I did not object on the grounds you mention with regard to family pedigree. This is not so in God's eyes. If he is from a distinguished family but is wicked, what benefit is his pedigree before God? And if he is from a Christian family but righteous, 'Peace, Peace to the

203. Perhaps this is an interpretation of *m. Ta'an.* 2:2, referring to economic distress but applied to lower social status.

204. In Spain from Germany.

near from the seed of the distant!' Rather, I complained that the cantors of this land perform for their own pleasure, to hear a pleasant voice. Even if he is completely wicked, they only care that he has a sweet voice. Yet God says (Jer 12:8): "She raised her voice against me, therefore I have rejected her."

She'elot U'Teshuvot Ha-ROSh, Section 4, No. 17

Can a person who has not re-grown his beard several times lead prayers on occasion?

Know that he may lead prayers on occasion just like any other townsfolk [who may lead] when it occurs to them, provided that he was neither appointed by the congregation nor by the cantor who appoints an assistant to ease his load and lead prayers for him on occasion.[205]

She'elot U'Teshuvot Ha-ROSh, Section 6, No. 1:
A Rabbi or a Cantor?

That you asked: If a congregation has only enough [resources] to pay a rabbi or a cantor, which one takes precedence?

If he (*i.e.,* the rabbi) is a brilliant scholar and great in Torah and expert in religious instruction and the laws, there is no doubt that the study of Torah takes precedence. But if [the rabbi is] not [a brilliant scholar], a cantor is most preferred [in order] to fulfill the obligation [of prayer] for the many.

Germany: Fourteenth Century

Born in Mainz around the year 1360, Rabbi Jacob ben Moshe Ha-Levi Moellin emerged as the preeminent authority of his generation in central Europe, especially on the customs and practices of the Jews of Germany, Austria, and Bohemia. He did not publish any works in his lifetime, but one of his students, Zalman of Sanegor (Saint Goar) gathered together the disparate customs approved by Rabbi Jacob and published them under the name *Sefer MaHaRIL*, an acronym for Morenu Harav Ya'akov Levi. The popularity—and authoritativeness—of the first printed edition that appeared in Sabionetta in 1556 led to many additional printings.

---

205. In these two last cases, a mature cantor is required.

Rabbi Jacob died in Worms in 1427, and, as an indication of the esteem in which he was held, was buried beside Rabbi Meir of Rothenberg.[206] Several passages in *Sefer MaHaRIL* (28a; 49b; 55a–b; 82b) attest to the musical ability of Rabbi Jacob, who served as a cantor on occasion.

Sefer MaHaRIL, Laws of Prayer, Section 8:[207] *May an Underage Boy be a Cantor?*

Said Rabbi Jacob Segal[208] when asked whether a boy who turned thirteen on Shabbat is allowed to be a prayer leader on the eve of that Shabbat:

And he responded: even though MaHaRaM [of Rothenberg][209] made an allowance to count [a boy] who had not yet reached the age of majority to lead [the blessings of thanks for food] with adults, we do not hold this view. And even though on Friday we add from the ordinary to the holy, this applies to the sanctity of the day, but it does not apply to adding to the age of the boy. And since we pray on Friday evening while still daylight, he may not be a prayer leader. Yet they reported to him that in the province of Saxony boys are made prayer leaders one month before reaching the age of thirteen and he said that this is not our practice.[210]

She'elot U'Teshuvot MaHaRIL, No. 62: *Who Pays the Cantor's Salary?*

As to the matter of cantorial payment: In my opinion it seems that it should be collected from communal funds used for all

---

206. See above.

207. Moellin, *Sefer MaHaRIL*, No. 18a. This passage also appears in New Responsa of MaHaRIL, No. 18a.

208. Segal, an acronym for *Se*Gan Lakohanim (priestly deputy, i.e., Levi), was also a name by which MaHaRIL was known.

209. Shlomo Spitzer (*Sefer MaHaRIL*, 442) suggests an emendation here. Rabbi Meir of Rothenberg is on record opposing counting a minor in a prayer quorum or in the invitation for the prayers for thanks for food (Cf., e.g., Rothenberg, *Teshuvot, P'sakim U'Minhagim*, No. 161, 1:191; *She'elot U'Teshuvot TaShBaTz*, No. 309). Perhaps the reference here ought to be to Rabbenu Peretz who does count a minor in a quorum. See Spitzer for the sources and his reasons.

210. Rabbi Moses Isserles agrees. See *Darkhei Moshe* on Tur 53 and gloss in *Shulhan Arukh*, OH 53:10.

other [needs]. And the proof is from the response of RYZBA (Rabbi Yitzhaq ben Avraham) and MaHaRaM who both wrote that it is necessary to appoint to overseeing the community chest all contributors on whose authority all allocations are assigned and they mention the cantorate along with other matters put up for funding in the community. So I wrote and previously ruled. So is the custom in these communities. Yet I know of a teacher who taught that some of the cost must be imposed on [wealthy] individuals but I do not know the reason. Rather, what appears to me [to be correct] is as [I have stated] above. And similarly, a cantor and a ritual slaughterer and all other such community expenditures Rabbi Meir ruled that half the cost should be borne by the wealthy and half by [other] individuals the reason being that requiring only one of these two resources would endanger the community so that the cost was imposed on both. And on this no expatiation is needed.

Majorca/North Africa: Fourteenth Century

Isidore Epstein was convinced that the hero of the legend regarding the miraculous escape of a Spanish rabbi following his imprisonment and death sentence in 1391 and his subsequent acceptance and fame in North Africa was Rabbi Shimon ben Zemah Duran, who was born in Majorca in 1391 and died in Algeria in 1444. Descended from a family noted for its scholarship and married into a family that traced its ancestry to Nahmanides and Rabbi Yonah Gerondi, RaShBaZ, as he is known by his acronym, mastered mathematics, logic, astronomy, history, philosophy, grammar, and languages, as well as rabbinics. Intending to pursue a career in medicine, he was compelled to accept a rabbinical position since the superstitious Algerians took no liking to doctors.

She'elot U'Teshuvot RaShBaSH, Part 4
(Hut Ha-Meshulash), No. 7:[211] The Cantor's Successor

While authorship remains a mystery, four points emerge from the content of this responsum. First, it describes how synagogues were

---

211. The Lemberg [1891] edition, called *Sefer TaShBaZ*, shows the signatory to this responsum is Shlomo ben Zemah Duran. Yet controversy persists over who this is. Mordechai Margaliot claims that the Shlomo ben Shimon—not Zemah—whose responsa are appended to those of Rabbi Shimon ben Zemah under the title *Hut*

sometimes thought of: as the private domains of the builders yet open to other members of the community. Over time, congregants seem to have forgotten the origins of the synagogue and assumed that every synagogue was a communal institution. Accordingly, the author of this responsum addresses the issue of whether a synagogue built privately is public property. He rules that so long as the conditions under which a synagogue was built privately still apply, the synagogue remains private property.

Second, the questioner assumes that the position of cantor was inheritable. The respondent seems to agree. Cantorial dynasties seem to have developed as early as the beginning of the eleventh century. Joseph Albaradani of Baghdad (d. 1006), known as "the Great Hazzan," left sons and grandsons who succeeded him in the office. Nevertheless, the respondent rules that all sons have an equal say regarding the disposition of family property, even when one son is not a dynastic successor.

Third, the questioner describes the key traits of the cantor as if they were long established and accepted. Good character and knowledge are the most important factors.

Finally, the questioner mentions in passing that the minimum age for a cantor is twenty-eight, perhaps reflecting the local understanding of what "mature" means when considering a cantor. The respondent offers no contrary view. It would seem, then, that by the fourteenth century the ambiguity surrounding the issue of the maturity of the prayer leader—to which the early sources refer as "full-beardedness"—was resolved. The specific age necessary to receive cantorial appointment was twenty-eight.

Not to be overlooked is the expression the respondent uses to clarify his explanation: "like a set table." That expression becomes the very name Rabbi Joseph Karo gives to his popular sixteenth-century compilation of Jewish law: *Shulhan Arukh*.

Ha-Meshulash is actually a scholar of the late fifteenth and early sixteenth-century, six generations removed from Rabbi Shimon (*Encyclopedia L'Toldot Gedolei Yisrael*, 4:1308). Professor Boaz Cohen disputes this view, writing that Shlomo was Shimon's son (*Kuntras Ha-Teshubot*, 55). Moshe Sobel, in his annotated edition of *She'elot U'Teshuvot RaShBaSH*, 11, agrees with Cohen, writing that Shlomo was born in Algiers in 1400 and died there in 1467. This is highly unlikely since reliable reports fix the birthdate of Shimon at 1391, making him a father at the age of nine! Some revision is necessary. The postscript attests to the endorsement of the father of the son's written opinion, indicating that the father was Shimon, the authority whose endorsement would carry great weight. Yet the name that appears as the endorser in the Lemberg edition is Zemah ben Shimon, son of another rabbi whose acronym is unknown. Margaliot may likely be correct.

You asked a question: "Jacob" divided off a piece of land from his courtyard and built on it a synagogue where he could serve as cantor, and the community used it during his lifetime for more than twenty years. When he died, he left three sons: "Re'uven," "Shimon," and "Levi." Re'uven, the eldest, took over from his father and served as cantor in the previously mentioned location and filled his father's place, since he, like his father, was of good character. Shimon died and Levi, the youngest, has neither the learning nor the manners to fill his father's position. As time passed and the congregation aged, and having no one fit to succeed as cantor, Re'uven wanted to appoint his eldest son Hanokh as cantor in his stead. But his brother, Levi, came to protest, saying that his brother cannot appoint his son to replace him. "If you want to stand, stand [but not your designate]." So there was a quarrel between the above-mentioned brothers. Reuven, the older, says: 'I have the rights of the firstborn since I am the oldest and, besides, I filled the place of my ancestors for a number of years and on the strength of this I shall appoint my son in my stead in that he is also fit for this [office]: he is over twenty-years-old and good to God and to people.' And Levi says: 'No. You and I and have equal rights of inheritance. If I am unfit to serve as cantor, I shall bring my son-in-law in my place until my own son grows up and then he will be in my place.'

The question is twofold. What becomes of the property [upon which the synagogue is built], namely, is it considered holy since it has been used by the community as a synagogue, or does it revert to Reuven's estate and may be divided among the heirs? And who has control over the property? Should you say they share control, may Levi appoint his son-in-law until his son comes of age or does it remain the domain of Hanokh ben Re'uven who serves in succession of his father?

And may peace ever increase to the master and may his light never be extinguished.

Answer: May your peace also increase and may you be like a fortress and a tower . . .

The property dedicated for a synagogue was not dedicated forever but only so long as Re'uven was the prayer leader. Hence, it does not qualify as public property. Neither is there any support for the claim of Re'uven, brother of Levi, to appoint his son to succeed him. He has a legal presumption, serving in his father's stead for a number of years as we hold in *Ketubot* 103b (See also *Horayot* 11b) which the rabbis ascribe to the verse (Deut 17:20): ". . . to the end that he and his descendants may reign long in the midst of Israel." As cited by Maimonides and as appears in *Sifre*: "He and his son: should he die, his sons succeed him. How do we know that their sons succeed all Jewish officials? In that it says 'in the midst of Israel'—all who are in the midst of Israel." And it is taught in *Torat Kohanim*: "'And they had no sons' that is, had they sons, the sons have preference."

In our case, since the property belongs to an individual, Levi can prevent Re'uven from appointing a man not to his liking—whether a relative or not—since he has a share in the property. And if the congregation does not like the cantor Levi appoints, they are free to go to any synagogue they want. They cannot force Levi to [renounce his portion and] assign it to his brother Re'uven to appoint his son in his stead. This is certainly the case if the congregation—may our Rock and Redeemer protect it—likes the man Levi appoints with his portion [of the inheritance]. Re'uven would surely have no room to disagree.

And this is all clearly explained to you like a set table.

May those who know you be blessed. May you merit eternal life.

The answer as you requested from one who loves you greatly in whose good fortune he rejoices.

Shlomo, son of the honorable Zemah Duran. (May the compassionate one protect him and save him.)

She'elot U'Teshuvot Ha-RaShBaZ, Part 3, No. 171: A Minor As a Cantor

Simon Duran holds that while a minor may recite the *haftarah* on an ordinary Shabbat, he may not do so on festivals, neither may he lead prayer services. Since Jewish law defines the threshold of adulthood to be puberty, that threshold can only be crossed with eyewitness testimony to the presence of two pubic hairs. Here some sensitivity is in order. Physically examining a boy can be, at the very least, embarrassing. So Rabbi Shimon, for the purpose of leading prayers, is content to rely on the attestation of the father who, presumably, could honestly report on his son's maturity. Of particular interest is the fact that the respondent indicates that he "tries" to arrange for the adult recital of the *haftarah* on festivals, leaving room for the possibility that if his attempt proves unsuccessful, a minor might be called upon.

I do not allow a minor to take on any of the required rituals [of Shabbat] except for reciting the *haftarah* that is not a required ritual. But when it is a required ritual—on days when two Torah scrolls are taken out—I try to ensure that the *maftir* is an adult since anyone who is not obligated to perform a mitzvah cannot fulfill the obligation for others . . .

By law, he is to be examined to see if he has two pubic hairs as it appears in the Talmud[212] with regard to the prayer for [after eating] food, and as the commentators, of blessed memory, said. But I was not overly scrupulous in this since it might be distressing. Besides, the father is reliable to say he (*i.e.*, his son) has two pubic hairs [for the purpose of qualifying him] for [leading] prayer, even though he is not authorized to attest to this for the sake of marriage, as the author of *Sefer Ha-Terumah* says. But if he were under the age of thirteen years and one day, I would not let him.

She'elot U'Teshuvot Ha-RaShBaZ, Part 3, No. 113: A Cantor Who Is Hard of Hearing

A blind cantor did not strike earlier authorities as a thorny problem since prayer was a vocal activity. One need not see in order to sing or recite, particularly when prayers were largely recited by heart. So for the Geonim, on days other than those whose liturgy was largely unfamiliar and a reliance on reading a written text is essential, a blind cantor was acceptable. Blindness, as a physical disability, was not a disqualifier. Moral defects were of paramount concern, not physical ones. But deafness was qualitatively different. Rabbenu Asher (*She'elot U'Teshuvot Ha-ROSh* 85:13) had ruled that the person hard of hearing is competent to engage in business or marry and that the "*heresh*" of rabbinic literature refers exclusively to a person born a deaf-mute. In the following responsum, Duran considers whether being hard of hearing is a disqualifying factor for a cantor.

From the question posed there is evidence that some people intuited that this was precisely the case. The question was generated from an incident in which the cantor made a liturgical mistake in full view of a large congregation. But it was not the mistake itself that triggered the inquiry. Even the most highly trained and experienced professional could make a mistake. The fact that the cantor could not hear the correction signaled that he might make uncorrected mistakes in the future, to the detriment of the congregation in fulfilling its individual and collective obligations.

212. *b. Ber.* 47b.

The intuition was probably related to the fact that a deaf priest was disqualified from temple service[213] and a deaf judge was disqualified from serving on higher court since deafness was considered a defect.[214] Surely the judge needs to hear testimony. The analogy seems to be inescapable. Duran, however, disabuses the questioner of this notion. The absence of any specific mention of the disqualification of a cantor who is hard of hearing leads to the conclusion that the rabbis had no concern about prayers led by such a cantor.

Besides, he argues, since worshipers in the congregation pray independently, only relying on the cantor for his musical abilities rather than for his agency, they will fulfill their obligations for prayer no matter who is leading.

Why Duran does not cite the view of Rabbi Shimon ben Gamaliel,[215] who rules that a hearing person who goes deaf is treated like the fully hearing, is hard to explain. He was certainly aware of the Jerusalem Talmud and cites from it at the end of this responsum.

> You further asked about a prayer leader who went to the lectern on the second night of Rosh Hashanah and when he recited *Kiddush* on the cup [of wine] he omitted "*She-he-heyanu*" and the elder there scolded him [demanding] that he recite the blessing. But he (*i.e.*, the lector) did not hear him. Hence, the elder insisted that he (*i.e.*, the cantor) is [then] disqualified from leading prayers because he is hard of hearing.
>
> Answer: This disqualification is not mentioned. And since his conduct is upright and his household is devoid of sin, and he has no children who are robbers or thieves or informers, why should he be disqualified? If he wanted to disqualify him on the basis that the hard of hearing are exempt from the commandments and one who is exempt cannot fulfill the obligation for others, I do not know of any such disqualification for the hard of hearing other than in the matter of blowing *shofar*.[216] A person who cannot hear at all—even when they shout in his ears—is exempt from blowing shofar because it is the hearing for which we recite the blessing and not for the blowing. Since he cannot hear at all, he is exempt from it. Since he is exempt, he cannot

213. *m. Bekh.* 45b; Maimonides, MT, Laws of Temple Service 5:16.

214. Cf. *b. Yeb.* 101a.

215. *y. Ter.* 1:1.

216. Cf. OH, Laws of Rosh Hashanah, The Rule of Blowing Shofar 8; *Kol Bo*, Section 64.

fulfill the obligation for others. But for the other commandments, he is not disqualified since he is obligated to [perform]
them based on the ruling of Rabbi Judah (*b. Ber.* 16b) who said
that if he recited the *Shema* but did not hear it, he has fulfilled
his obligation since one who has the ability to hear but did not
hear fulfills his obligation. This fellow who does not hear at all
fulfills his obligation even from the outset since his condition
is identical to others after the fact.[217] This is also confirmed in
the Jerusalem Talmud in the tractate *Megillah*[218] with regard
to reading Megillah. Now all this applies to the case where he
fulfills the obligation for others through his reading when they
hear [but do not recite] on their own. This surely, then, is the
case when today everyone customarily recites *Shema* and *Hallel*
[on their own] so that this fellow can go to the lectern and begin
the blessings and recitals that they can then complete.

She'elot U'Teshuvot Ha-RaShBaZ, No. 404: A Deaf Cantor

In this reponsum, the son takes further the opinion of his father. Duran
the elder had ruled that hearing loss is not a disqualifying factor for a
cantor. Duran the younger (known as RaShBaSh, by his acronym) subsequently rules that deafness is not a disqualifying factor either, with the
exception of the public reading of the Scroll of Esther (Megillah).

> You[219] further asked: May a deaf prayer leader fulfill the obliga-
> tion to pray for others since he himself is obligated to pray?
>   Answer: You[220] have spoken well.[221] Since he is obligated in
> the matter, he fulfills the obligation for others because the deaf
> to which the sages refer always refers to "someone who neither
> speaks not hears," as in the tractate *Terumot*[222] and yet he still

217. By analogy, Duran infers that if a person who has the ability to hear but does
not hear the recital of *Shema* still fulfills his obligation to recite the *Shema*, then a
person who does not have the ability to hear should be able to similarly fulfill the
obligation to pray.

218. *y. Meg.* 2:5.

219. The unidentified questioner.

220. The unidentified questioner.

221. As evidenced by the reasoning embedded in the question: a person who is
obligated to perform a commandment can fulfill the performance of the commandment for others. If a deaf cantor is obligated to pray, then a deaf cantor can fulfill for
others the requirement of prayer.

222. *m. Ter.* 1:2. Cf. also *m. Hag.* 2:2 and RaShI in his commentary there. The

fulfills the obligation for others in all things except in the reading of the Megillah in accordance with Rabbi Yosi, as it is taught:
"All are fit to read the Megillah except the deaf, an imbecile, and
a minor."[223] And the Gemara proves it according to Rabbi Yosi.
And the deaf in this passage is one who can speak for if he could
not speak, how could he read Megillah?[224]

But with regard to reciting *Shema*, since—after the fact—if
he read it without hearing it, he fulfilled his obligation, as the
rabbis of blessed memory ruled,[225] it seems that he can fulfill
the obligation for others because his "at the outset" is like "after
the fact." Even according to Rabbi Yosi—who said that if he did
not fulfill the obligation it appears that he can still lead *Shema*,
since he disagrees with Rabbi Yehudah regarding a blind man
and said he cannot lead *Shema* if he did not see the heavenly
bodies since his birth[226] and since the rabbis and Rabbi Yehudah
also agree on the deaf man, it may be deduced that he can lead
the *Shema* and recite the blessings beforehand and afterwards
since these blessings were not formulated as the fulfillment of
the commandments. Even according to Rabbi Yosi who said
that if he cannot hear it with his own ears he did not fulfill the
obligation, it certainly is the case with the ruling of the rabbis, of
blessed memory, who say 'if he read but did not hear, he fulfilled
the obligation.' Further, all Israel is already accustomed to recite
Shema on their own and, as it is stated in the Jerusalem Talmud:
"It is the law that everyone recites his own."[227]

Therefore, in all matters he is fit to go to the lectern and
fulfill the obligation for others—except for the reading of the
Megillah according to Rabbi Yosi. And there are those who rule
like Rabbi Yosi (so it appears from the words of the author of the
Ittur, of blessed memory in the Laws of Megillah[228]). The commentators have already considered these matters at length in
the second chapter of [the tractate] *Berakhot*. And my father my
teacher and Rabbi Shlomo ben Avraham, of blessed memory, in
the explication of the laws he composed, and al-Fasi, of blessed

---

explanation for this attitude seems to be that deafness was concomitant with speech-
lessness, and the inability to communicate was tantamount to an absence of reason.

223. *m. Meg.* 2:4 (19b).

224. See Tos. Meg. 19b, *s.v. hutz*.

225. Cf. *b. Ber.* 15a.

226. That is, he was born sightless. Cf. *b. Meg.* 24a.

227. *y. Ber.* 3:3.

228. Abba Mari, *Sefer Ha-Ittur*, Laws of Megillah 113:3.

memory, in his straightforward statement of the law in the tractate Megillah: all agree with Rabbi Yosi.[229]

Provence: Fourteenth Century

Both the author and the date of the first edition of *Kol Bo* (*All in It*)—a
popular compendium of the laws of Jewish holidays, prayer, mourning,
and some of the dietary laws—remain a subject of scholarly debate. Some
have ascribed it to Rabbi Isaac ben Sheshet, others to Rabbi Shemariah
ben Simhah. There is, however, no dispute that the content reflects much
of the material published in *Orhot Hayyim*, written in the fourteenth century by Rabbi Aaron ben Jacob Ha-Kohen of Lunel and Narbonne. The
second edition was published in Constantinople in 1519.

The author considers two separate tests of cantorial worthiness.
First, he weighs whether fornication and denunciation of others fall under the category of a bad reputation the Talmud considers disqualifying
grounds for a cantor. Second, he evaluates what constitutes ignorance
since the Talmud requires that lectors possess knowledge, fluency, and
expertise.

The author gives the cantor every advantage to retain his position.
No matter what the failing, should the cantor reform, his status is preserved. If the complaints are not supported by valid testimony, the complaints are dismissed, not the cantor. Further, procedures are in place that
must be followed before any cantor is relieved of his position. Corporal
punishment, official reprimand, and suspension are imposed prior to
final dismissal. It seems that by the fourteenth century, the institution of
the cantorate was so entrenched in southern European communities that
each individual cantor could expect to have his tenure ensured because
his contribution to Jewish communal life was deemed essential. Nevertheless, there is clear evidence that some cantors were less than competent. Their tenure was assured because of the scarcity of better cantors.

---

229. Cf. further, Rabbi Moses Sternbuch, *She'elot U'Teshuvot Teshuvot V'Hanhagot*,
No. 101, who rules that hearing aids fulfill the requirement of "hearing what he says"
so excluding a prayer leader with a hearing aid is an unnecessary embarrassment to
him.

Kol Bo, Section 147: Grounds for Dismissal of a Cantor

A prayer leader about whom the people complained that he was caught with a Gentile woman:

If this report that he was caught with her were confirmed by two valid witnesses in a way that would have made him liable for flogging[230] but was not yet flogged and he had neither desisted nor repented, or, if he informed[231] on another Jew and had not yet repented of his wickedness, or, if he threatened another Jew: 'I will go to the non-Jewish civil magistrates and tell them that all the stolen goods in the city are in the hands of this named Jew,[232]' or, if he said to a Jew: 'I am going to David's house and tell him that you stole from so-and-so and the local ruler will hang you' (even though his threats did not result in any harm, for example, when the threatened [person] was saved by miraculous intervention), he is disqualified [from serving as a prayer leader] and [were he already a prayer leader] merits removal. But, if witnesses did not confirm the complaints:[233] he is not disqualified.

A prayer leader who threatens his neighbor with informing to the non-Jewish authorities though he did not act on it: while the conduct is reprehensible—even for someone else[234]—he is not summarily removed.[235] Rather, he should be reprimanded and warned that should he persist in conduct like this, he would be suspended. Should he still persist in his rebelliousness, he would be removed.

A prayer leader who was told by the congregation to wrap in a *Tallit* during prayer and he responds that he does not want to, and when they ask 'Why not?' and he says something like 'Because it is written in the Torah (Num 16:39) "and you shall

---

230. Fornication is penalized with flogging. Cf. Maimonides, MT, Laws of Intimate Relations 1:4, even if the woman is Jewish.

231. The punishment for informing could be a fine and/or imprisonment and even death. Cf. Assaf, *Ha-Onshin*. See also Maimonides, MT, Laws of Assault and Damages 8:10–11.

232. Whether this charge is true or false.

233. That the cantor in question was romantically involved with a Gentile woman. Absent any corroborating testimony, the complaints are dismissed. In contrast, see Bar Sheshet, *She'elot U'Teshuvot Ha-RiBaSh*, Nos. 373, 376 who—perhaps because of his own false imprisonment at the hands of an informer—rules that the legal requirements for proper witnesses are loosened when applied to informers.

234. That is, someone who is not a religious leader.

235. Permanently.

look upon it and remember all of God's commandments and do them" [meaning,] anyone who doesn't perform all of God's commandments does not wrap himself in a *Tallit*,' is worthy of reprimand and to be informed that scripture does not say 'You shall perform all of God's commandments so that you shall make fringes [upon your garments] and look upon them.' Rather, you shall make fringes and look upon them and remember. Scripture does not make the wearing of fringes contingent on the performance of commandments. Rather, the fringes are a reminder so that by seeing them perhaps he will perform all the commandments, just as it says: "So that you will remember to perform them." And if he did so, it is as if he performed them all. And if he performed the commandment regarding fringes but did not perform any others, he is not punished for [failing to do] all. Furthermore, all the while he fails to perform the commandment regarding fringes, he is punished for all the other commandments [he failed to do]. If he did not change his conduct and remains insolent—denigrating the Torah—he is worthy of removal—so long as they do not appoint another as unsuitable as him . . .

Turkey: Fifteenth Century

One of the most respected Talmudists of this period, Rabbi Elijah ben Rabbi Abraham "Mizrahi," was also a mathematician and astronomer. A contemporary, Rabbi Judah ben Bulat, calls him "the chief authority of all diaspora in our generation."[236] Aside from his commentary on RaShI (known as "Mizrahi"), his responsa are his best-known literary legacy. He is reputed to have lived a long life. His date of birth is unknown, although Rabbi David Weisbord Ha-Lahmi[237] claims it to be 1450. He died around the year 1525.

He seems to be the first authority to consider the case of a cantor who had apostasized when young and subsequently returned to Judaism. Since the Talmud disqualifies any prayer leader whose reputation was not without blemish from his youth, the status of a cantor who had once "worshipped idols"—the standard expression for adopting non-Jewish religious practice—needs to be addressed. Rabbi Elijah finds support for his view that youthful apostasy is not grounds for dismissal on the

236. Cited in Margaliot, *Encyclopedia L'Toldot Gedolei Yisrael*, 1:168.
237. Ha-Lahmi, *Hakhmei Yisrael*, 1:27.

basis of what Maimonides does *not* say rather than on what Maimonides does say. He reasons that whatever conduct Maimonides did not explicitly mention as disqualifying is implicitly acceptable. By narrowing the factors that could result in the disqualification of the cantor to the few that are explicitly mentioned, Mizrahi shows a willingness to tolerate a broader ranger of cantorial malfeasance, giving cantors every advantage in retaining their positions.

Teshuvot REM, No. 88:
May a Former Apostate Serve as a Cantor?

About what you asked regarding someone who worshipped idols in his youth and subsequently repented fully and his conduct is for Heaven's sake, whether or not it is appropriate to appoint him a prayer leader to fulfill the obligation for others? I will respond to you according to what is in my heart and in my humble opinion what God has shown me.

In my humble opinion, it seems to me that it is a simple matter that needs little [clarification] and no qualification in that once he fully repented, obviously he can go down to the lectern to fulfill the obligation [of prayer] for others since even the righteous cannot stand in the same place as the fully repentant[238] . . .

Maimonides did not care at all about earlier misconduct. Rather, his concern was only regarding current behavior, and now that his conduct is for the sake of Heaven, we have no concern. That is why [Maimonides][239] did not mention at all in his list of qualifications [for a prayer leader] whether he has earlier committed some infraction and subsequently repented as he does with regard to a *kohen* and the Priestly Blessing[240] . . .

Germany/Italy: Fifteenth Century

The exact dates of the birth and death of the author of this work are unknown. However, from references in his book, as well as the personal information he provides, it is certain that Rabbi Ya'akov Barukh ben Rav Yehudah Landau Ashkenzai flourished in the late fifteenth century. In his 1960 annotated edition of the text, Moshe Hershler ascribes two purposes

---

238. Cf. *b. Ber.* 34b.

239. MT, Laws of Prayer, chapter 8.

240. MT, Laws of Prayer, 15:1–6.

to this book: to collect all the extant opinions, novellae,[241] and glosses on the full range of Jewish practice, and to then render a final decision. The word *"agur"* means "collection" in Hebrew.

In the first passage, Rabbi Ashkenazi refers to the regnant consensus of opinions in his day that presumes universal agreement on the appointment of a prayer leader. In fact, a single objection is sufficient to prevent any candidate's appointment. However, relying on the opinion of a contemporary and their thirteenth-century predecessor, Rabbi Ashkenazi endorses the view that universal consent is not required for the appointment of a cantor. Moreover, a single dissenter is insufficient to remove a cantor from his office.

The second passage recounts an actual episode in which a convert was denied the opportunity to lead prayers. The community construed that the Mishnah barring a convert from reciting the scriptural passage when bringing first fruits ought to be applied by analogy to a convert leading prayers. Since a convert has no biological Jewish ancestors, the person bringing first fruits could not recite the scriptural passage referring to the promise made to his ancestors since they were not Jewish. Because similar such prayers are included in the liturgy, a convert could not legitimately recite them either. A certain Rabbi Yoël, however, rejects this construction of the Mishnah on the basis of a contrary source. The Jerusalem Talmud marshals an opinion of Rabbi Judah that the convert does indeed recite the declaration. The scriptural warrant for his opinion is Genesis 17:5, which asserts that Abraham is the father of all nations. Since Rabbi Judah's view is endorsed by Rabbi Joshua ben Levi and supported by an actual case resolved by Rabbi Abbahu, Rabbi Mordekhai ben Hillel declares it to be binding. It is this last mentioned opinion that the author of *Sefer Ha-Agur* accepts as law.

Sefer Ha-Agur, Laws of Blessings, Section 90:
Is Unanimity Required to Appoint a Cantor?

The spirit of the sages does not approve of anyone who aspires to be a cantor without universal consent and a single individual can forestall [the appointment of] any candidate in [matters of] *hazzanut*. And Rabbi Moshe ben Hasdai disagrees on the basis of [the opinion of the author of] *Or Zaru'a*.

241. *Hiddushim*, in Hebrew.

Sefer Ha-Agur, Laws of Blessings, Section 91:
May A Convert Serve as a Cantor?

[The inhabitants of] the city of Würzburg prevented a convert
from serving as a lector and lead public prayers. The proof [is
adduced] from *Bikkurim*:[242] "a convert may bring but may not
recite [the declaration] since he cannot say 'Who has promised
our ancestors' (Deut 26:3)." But Rabbi Yo'el allows [a convert to
serve as a lector] and he adduces proof from the Jerusalem Talmud.[243] [See the commentary of Rabbi] Mordekhai [ben Hillel],
first chapter of *Megillah*.[244]

Germany: Fifteenth Century

The birthdate of Rabbi Moses ben Isaac Segal Minz[245] is unknown. But
from his principal tutelage under Rabbi Jacob Weil in Erfurt, scholars
place his birth somewhere between 1420 and 1430, but possibly as early
as 1415. He was born in Mainz. He served as a rabbi in Würzburg until
the expulsion of all Jews from the city in 1453, returning to Mainz where
his intellectual reputation grew, reaching as far as Austria and Italy. Persecution forced him to leave Mainz in 1462, and he remained homeless
for seven years until settling in Bamberg. The authorities confiscated all
his possessions, including his library. Even so, he continued to write and
include citations from memory. Near the end of his life, he moved to Posen and died there around 1480, without fulfilling his desire to immigrate
to Israel. The only written works to survive are his responsa, published
first in Krakow in 1597. Included in the collection are 119 responses
(on questions primarily devoted to matrimonial and civil law) and one
exhortation on communal loyalty. His responsa frequently cite local customs and practices. The translation below is of the responsum published
in the 1991 critical edition of Rabbi Yonatan Shraga Domb, based on the
1851 Lemberg edition.

The nature of the question that follows shows that while the office of
the cantor was well established in Germany by the fifteenth century, the

242. *m. Bik.* 1:4.

243. *y. Bik.* 1:4, 64a.

244. No. 786.

245. The first edition of his response indicates his name as Moshe Minz Segal. His
signature appended to the end of each responsum reads: Moshe Levi Minz.

conduct of cantors was uneven. Even though it was the Jewish community in Bamberg that raised specific concerns, Rabbi Moses Mintz's answer tells us that many of the problems were pervasive. Cantors lacked punctuality, showed indifference to the sanctity of the prayer service, were inattentive, poorly prepared and mistake prone, and generally lacked piety. They were often casually dressed, poorly groomed, and intoxicated. Even when cantors were competent, they too often sped through the service. Cantors were prone to leave the pulpit during the service to engage in idle conversation with worshipers and even meddle in their affairs. Rabbi Minz's response was a serious attempt to correct the problems he observed. Noteworthy as well is the fact that cantors were assumed to have the responsibility for public Torah reading.

She'elot U'Teshuvot MaHaRaM Minz, Part 2, No. 81: The Rules a Cantor Should Follow

The holy community of Bamberg, may it prosper, has requested of me, the undersigned, to organize the issues relating to the cantor:[246] how he should conduct himself with the congregation, may it prosper, and what are his qualifications. And further, what is [proper] mindfulness in prayer and the order of the [Torah] reading, and the proper attire during prayer. Connected with this, [I have been requested] to lay out how prayer should be well-organized and internalized so that he may do God's service with due intention and full faith, as it is written (Ezra 9:9) "To exalt the house of our God, repairing its ruins" which is applied [by the rabbis[247]] to a prayer leader who prays mindfully. Here it states: "to exalt" and there it states (Psalms 34:4): "Exalt the Lord with me, let us extol his name together," that is to say, the prayer leader says to the congregation 'Exalt the Lord with me' and it says 'extol,' that is, exalt and extol together, that is to say, all of us with shared intention as one community which will then result in repairing our ruins, and may this be God's will.[248]

　　Here are the rules:

---

246. The text uses the word *hazzan*, indicating that the position was known as such.

247. In his critical edition of the *She'elot U'Teshuvot MaHaRam Minz,* Rabbi Yonatan Shraga Domb notes that he could find no such rabbinic interpretation in the classical sources. He suggests that the rabbis mentioned here were his teachers.

248. As much a reference to the sad circumstances of the Jews in Germany as it is to the rebuilding of the Temple in Jerusalem.

It is proper for the cantor to enter the synagogue first and leave last. And it is a rule that he fulfill the criteria of a lector as they appear in Chapter 2[249] of [the Tractate] *Ta'anit*[250]: "The rabbis taught: we only bring to the lectern one who regularly, etc. Rabbi Judah says: one who has young children he cannot support, etc., his house empty of sin, etc., an elder, full-bearded, humble, pleasant, one who regularly reads Torah and the Prophets, and the Writings, and is expert on the blessings, etc." Also appearing there[251] is: "My own people acted toward Me like a lion in the forest; she raised her voice against Me" (Jer 12:8) . . . Said Mar Zutra bar Tuviah in the name of Rav (Zevid),[252]" and so forth, "This [verse] applies to an unworthy lector who goes down to the lectern [to lead the prayer service]."

It says:[253] "Rabbi Hiyya and Rabbi Simon bar Rabbi were sitting and one opened [the dialogue] and said: 'The worshiper must cast his eyes downwards' as it is written: "My eyes and my heart shall ever be there (I Kgs 9:3)."[254] The other opened and said: 'The worshiper must set his eyes upwards,' as it is written: "Let us lift up our hearts with our hands to God in heaven (Lam 3:4)." When Rabbi Yishmael ben Rabbi Yossi came, he said to them: 'What did you discuss?' They said to him: 'Prayer.' He said to them: 'So said father: the worshiper must cast his eyes downward but direct his heart upwards so that he fulfills both verses.'"

In the first chapter of the tractate *Shabbat*[255] it says: "Rava, the son of Rav Huna, put on stockings and prayed. He said: 'It is written (Amos 4:12): "Prepare to meet your God, O Israel." Rava draped his cloak over his hands and prayed, saying: '[I pray] like a slave before his master' . . . when there was no amity in the world, he would clasp his hands and pray . . . He would say: "Prepare to meet, etc." And nowadays, because of our great sinfulness, there is trouble in the world. Therefore, [the cantor] must stand as a slave before his master. I need not elaborate with

---

249. Domb notes that this is the correct citation and not "Chapter Five" as it appears in the text. The incorrect citation may be attributable to a copyist's error or the result of Rabbi Minz citing from memory.

250. 16a.

251. *b. Ta'an.* 16b.

252. Absent in the standard printed edition of the Babylonian Talmud.

253. *b. Yev.* 105b.

254. God is speaking to King Solomon, looking downward from his heavenly abode.

255. *b. Sab.* 10a.

further examples. My goal is only to arrange a few of [the rules on] how the cantor should behave.

Here is how he should dress: A prayer leader must wear clean clothes without dirt or stains, particularly his *sarbal* or *matron*.[256] And further, his robe must be so long that his legs do not show. If his robes are not long enough, he must wear breeches from his hips to his knees that are called "*knie-hosen*." He should take care not to pray without pants. And his pants must be clean, without excrement. Thus it would be good that he have clean underpants that he wears only during prayer service, and after prayer, change from those special underpants.

He must be expert in the pietistic poems,[257] the liturgical hymns that are said throughout the year. He must review them in advance—in Hebrew and with commentary—so that he becomes fluent in Hebrew and commentary, and likewise with the penitential prayers.

When he rises to pray, he must empty his heart of all extraneous thoughts and worries. And he must direct his eyes downward so that he does not look at any person. And he should not busy his hands with anything. Rather, he should place his hands on his heart under his cloak, his right hand over his left, as a servant stands before his master in fear and in awe. He should not separate his hands unless it is necessary, to wit, to turn pages or to straighten his prayer shawl, and in this manner he will not busy himself with anything else as do some cantors who have hands busy with trivia: fixing the candles while they pray or looking up their customs or the like—which they should not do.

When he prays aloud, he should pray word by word as if counting coins. And he should not remove his *tefillin* until after his prayers are completed and he leaves the pulpit. Rather, all his thoughts should be directed to the intention of prayer and praying deliberately and calmly and precisely in every way, taking a breath between adjoining passages: not like cantors who run through the liturgy by virtue of their fluency but without their hearts in it . . .

It is good to have a permanent cantor who leads aloud the preliminary service in the synagogue and following the customary local melody since it is forbidden to talk from the beginning of the preliminary service . . . [which would] exclude some cantors who exit the synagogue to go out to the courtyard and

256. The *sarbal* was a sleeveless cloak. The *matron* was a cowl: a covering for the head and eyes especially during prayer. Cf. Rubens, *History of Jewish Costume*, 115.

257. *Piyyutim*, in Hebrew.

join with the scoffers who discuss nonsense only to return to the pulpit to lead the morning service . . .

He must also take care that his body is clean and that he need not relieve himself, as it says there:[258] "The rabbis taught: if he needs to relieve himself he should not pray, and if he prayed, his prayer is an abomination."

. . . and it says in *Eruvin*:[259] "Said Rava bar Huna: 'A person impaired by alcohol should not pray and if he prayed his prayer is valid. A drunk should not pray and if he prayed his prayer is an abomination. Who is impaired and who is drunk? A drunk cannot speak before the king." Therefore, he (*i.e.*, the cantor) should not drink too much wine or liquor [over the course of the day] that he cannot lead the evening service, especially on Shabbat afternoons when he is found among many people. In this he must be [especially] careful.

The laws of Torah reading: the cantor must learn the entire portion so that he is fluent in all the linguistic details, correct accents, and all other features of reading. He must read deliberately—word by word—not rushing at all . . . and during his Torah reading, he must stand without support or leaning against the pulpit . . .

Now I come to explain the rules of the cantor and his conduct *viz.* his public. The cantor should take care not to say or do anything—publicly or privately—when there is a quarrel or dispute between householders. This is certainly true as well when there is a quarrel between a non-Jew and a householder—even if that non-Jew is an in-law or relative. He should give no support—orally or in writing—to that non-Jew or to write in other places against any householder—whether that householder is a friend or enemy. Rather, the cantor must take particular care to be acceptable to the entire public, not to cause any enmity or rancor with householders for if he has any hatred or enmity with any of the congregation—male or female—this would be contrary to the virtue the sages ascribed to the cantor and this would also be worrisome since an individual has the power to complain against him and dispute him on several grounds. Moreover, obviously a cantor cannot be a mediator for a person who does not like him, to pray on his behalf since a prosecutor cannot be a defender.[260] So if he has any quarrel or enmity with any of the congregation or if this should happen, the matter must

258. *b. Ber.* 23a.
259. 64a.
260. Cf. *b. Ber.* 59a.

be brought to the rabbi or congregation for resolution to do all that seems correct to them and thus the cantor will have fulfilled his obligation. And if the situation is irreconcilable, the fault lying with his nemesis, he is exonerated. What is there for him to do? The cantor must conduct himself correctly, to be pleasing to the people, humble and beloved. Then his prayer shall be heard, as it is said (Isa 66:23): "'All flesh shall come to bow down . . .' Said Rabbi Judah ben Levi: 'Come and see how dear are the lowly of spirit in the esteem of the Holy One, praised be He, that when the Temple stood, a man brought a burnt offering and received the reward of a burnt offering, a meal offering and received the reward of a meal offering. But as for him who is of lowly spirit, Scripture ascribes it to him as if he has offered all the sacrifices, as it is said (Ps 51:19): 'The sacrifices of the Lord are a broken spirit.' And even more: his prayer is not despised, as it [follows]: 'A broken and contrite heart, O Lord, You will not despise.'"[261]

And so may it be His will that our cantor [remain] a faithful emissary. May he rejoice in that he gains merit for himself along with his holy congregation that they have a faithful emissary and . . . if his prayer below is perfect—that is, wholehearted— then there will be peace above . . . that is to say, in heaven, for when prayer is recited mindfully, an angel comes and makes it a crown and places it on God's head . . . and it is as if he offered a sacrifice on the altar . . . And prayer brings redemption closer, as it says (Isa 56:7): "I will bring them to My sacred mount and let them rejoice in My house of prayer, their burnt offerings and sacrifices shall be welcome on My altar."

May this be His will and may we merit redemption.

Moses preoccupied[262]—Moses Levi Minz.

She'elot U'Teshuvot MaHaRI Bruna, No. 25[263]: The Cantor's Ruined Reputation

Born in the city of Brünn around the year 1400, Rabbi Yisrael son Rabbi Hayyim also was a protégé of Rabbi Jacob Weill and Rabbi Israel Isserlein. He served as a rabbi in Regensburg for a time, and after the deaths of his mentors was considered to be the preeminent rabbinical authority in all

261. *b. Sot.* 5b.

262. *Tarud*, in Hebrew: an indication of his personal situation.

263. In some editions, No. 26.

of Germany. That high station, however, did not prevent him from suffering at the hands of a certain Rabbi Anshel and his students, who saw him as a rival and carpetbagger. Adding to his distress was his imprisonment by Emperor Frederick III for refusing to compel the Jewish community to pay one-third of their wealth to the crown. In 1474, an apostate accused him of murdering a seven-year-old Christian boy for ritual purposes (Blood Libel). Rabbi Israel barely escaped death by immolation when the apostate confessed. Accounts indicate that he left Regensburg for Prague in 1476, and died there shortly thereafter.

Rabbi Bruna considers the case of a cantor whose reputation is sullied by his promiscuous daughter that, according to the Talmud, would merit disqualification.

> I have been asked by Congregation M'Eretz Hagar [264] in Brünn whether to appoint a cantor who was considered defective on account of his daughter who became pregnant while her husband was in Russia for five years.
>
> I responded that this is not right, in my opinion. I just saw in *Or Zaru'a* that a defective prayer leader ought not be appointed but I forgot where. Nevertheless, there seems to me to be proof from the end of chapter "One Who Says" in *Kiddushin* (67b) which concludes that the officiating of a defective [priest] is retroactively null, making it worse than a defiled priest who, while he should not officiate from the outset, still has his officiating valid after the fact. The blemished priest rule is learned from the verse (Num 25:12) "Behold I make with you My covenant of peace (*shalom*)" meaning when he is whole (*shalem*) and not when he is defective. And they ask: 'Is shalom not written with a "*vav*"?' and they answer: 'The letter "*vav*" is split, meaning, the "*vav*" is small, allowing for the interpretation "whole." Now since our prayer is in place of sacrifice, as it is written (Hos 14:3): "Instead of bulls we will pay [the offering of] our lips," if so, it is not right at all to appoint him *ab initio* a permanent prayer leader but occasionally he can [lead prayers] because he is no worse than a blind man who can pray[265] on occasion. Yet when no other person is available, it is wrong to annul our worship on account of this since we all pray individually and prayer is only a rabbinical requirement even though it is written "You will serve with all your heart" (Deut 11:13) which is interpreted (*b. Ta'an.*

264. The meaning of the congregation's name is uncertain. It might mean that it was founded by Egyptian Jews.

265. That is, lead prayers.

2a) "What service is in the heart? One would say this is prayer," this is merely a weak justification or applied scripturally only at a time of distress, as explained by *Sefer Mitzvot Gadol*[266] and *Sefer Mitzvot Katan*.[267]

Indeed, what you asked of me about his daughter who committed adultery, on this it seems to me that we must find from wherever we can find another prayer leader, as it states at the beginning of the chapter "Four Modes of Execution" (*b. San.* 52a): "It is her father she defiles" (Lev 21:9) so that if they used to treat him (*i.e.* the priest) as holy, they now treat him as profane, and there is nothing holier than prayer. This means that if he were a prayer leader, we remove him. It is also implied in RaShI's interpretation "to start first and to bless first,[268]" even though the Tosafists question him on this and prove[269] that what he meant was if he were removed he nonetheless may bless first, here too with regard to our prayer. Thus, if no one else is available, the situation is considered *post facto*, as Rabbenu Asher wrote in the chapter "The Law of Levirate Marriage" in the name of Rabbi Abraham ben David (*b. Yev.* 103a): "A blind man may not perform the Rite of Removing the Sandal. But if only he is present, the situation is considered *post facto* and he performs the Rite of Removing the Sandal *ab initio*. Here, too, the case is considered *post facto*.

Now since the daughter defiles her father, it is no worse than a case of a profaned priest. And a profaned priest's officiating is valid *post facto* as in (*b. Kid.* 66b): "Said Rabbi Tarfon to him: 'It is compared to one who stands and sacrifices on the altar and it is known that he is the son of a divorcee that his officiating is valid'" which is inferred from the very verse (*i.e.* Num 25:12) and Rabbi Yannai infers it from [the verse] "and you shall come to the priests, the Levites in those days" (Deut 17:9), "Shall it ever occur to you that a person would go to the judge who did not live then? Rather, it [means that it] applies to [a case when] he was authorized but then became profaned." From this I learn when there is no one else but him, he may be appointed from

266. Written by Rabbi Moses ben Jacob of Coucy. The first edition appeared sometime before 1480. The second edition was published in Soncino in 1488.

267. Day 1, Mitzvah 11; written by Rabbi Isaac ben Joseph of Corbeill and first published in Constantinople in 1510, it was an abridgment of the previous work with the addition of moralistic teachings.

268. *b. M.K.* 28b based on Leviticus 21:8.

269. Cf. *b. Hul.* 87a, *s.v. v'hayvo*.

the outset, which is considered after the fact, as it says: "You shall come to the judge . . ." (Deut 17:9).

So it appears to me,

Israel of Brünn

Italy: Sixteenth Century

She'elot U'Teshuvot MaHaRaM Mi-Padua, No. 64: May Only One Person Cause the Dismissal of a Cantor?

Rabbi Meir ben Yitzhak Katznellenbogen, the grandson by marriage of Rabbi Yehudah Minz, was born in Katznellebogen, Germany in 1482, and studied with Rabbi Yehoshua Falk in Prague. Following the death of his father-in-law, Rabbi Abraham Minz, Chief Rabbi of Padua, Rabbi Meir Katznellenbogen succeeded to that position and served there until his death in 1565. He was recognized as one of the preeminent Talmudists and legal authorities of his generation.

> A group from the Ashkenazic community of Mantua unintentionally blurted out that a mountain has come between the highly esteemed scholar Hayyim and his son on one side, and the highly esteemed scholar Menahem Rafael Shamash Katz on the other. The highly esteemed teacher Hayyim and his son (May the Rock and Redeemer protect them!) were cantors in that congregation for many years without a trace of complaint. The people liked them. Even Menahem Rafael liked him until now. That they came to a circumstance of enmity on account of unsavory remarks made one to the other was due to the call for payment of a debt to the charity that the highly esteemed scholar Menahem Rafael owed. The highly esteemed scholar Hayyim had volunteered—to the satisfaction of the community—to collect all outstanding debts. And for this, the highly esteemed scholar Menahem Rafael intended to dismiss these men so they would no longer serve as cantors. He relied on what appears in the Mordekhai at the end of the first chapter of *Hullin* (section 597) in the name of Rabbi Simhah that "an enemy is not appointed a cantor." And in the Responsa of Rabbi Yosef Colon, No. 44, these words of Rabbenu Simhah appear, [stating] that even one individual can prevent [the appointment of a cantor].
>
> To me it seems that our case is not the same as the proof [cited] because there, in the previously mentioned responsum, he explicitly concludes: "If there was no initial agreement for

him to serve." Yet here [in our case], the highly esteemed scholar Menahem Rafael had already agreed to them. There was no complaint at all against them until now. Even the words of the Mordekhai prove it, for he says: "An enemy may not be appointed a cantor," and similarly, in the *Agudah*,[270] there, it says: "A man who has enemies in the community may not be appointed as a cantor." But neither says that a cantor may be removed because he has become an enemy to a member of the community. If so, it is plain to see this as a case of increasing [holiness] and not diminishing holiness, that it is inappropriate that the entire community loses out, that they will be left without their favored cantor because of one [objector]. The one [objector] is set aside; particularly since the enmity was caused by the previously mentioned Rafael, who resented that Hayyim was the communal agent assigned to collect charitable funds. Therefore, the community is within its rights to do what they want. And if they desire that he serves as cantor as [he did] previously, then the highly esteemed scholar Hayyim and his son must remove any enmity in their hearts and state in no uncertain terms that he intends to fulfill the obligations of prayer for him, as he does for everyone.

So goes the custom of [our] predecessors. They felt that anyone who served as cantor for the Days of Awe must make such a declaration. And this is what we have done here for many years with our teacher, Rabbi Kopman[271] (May his Rock and Redeemer protect him!) before Rosh Hashanah on account of the fact that there was some enmity between him and the highly esteemed scholar Meir Zarfati (May the righteous be kept in life!).[272] Should the highly esteemed Rafael (May his Rock and Redeemer protect him!) not believe him,[273] he should go to another synagogue in the city, of which there are certainly many.

I wrote what seemed right in my poor opinion,
Signed, Meir ben Isaac Katznellenbogen.

---

270. Suslin, *Sefer Agudah*, Laws of Prayer Leader.

271. Who is also the cantor.

272. The cantor was asked to make a declaration that he intends to fulfill the obligations of prayer for all members of the community, including Meir Zarfati, with whom he had a quarrel.

273. That is, should Rafael not believe that the above-mentioned cantor Hayyim intends to fulfill the obligations of prayer for him as Hayyim declares on account of the enmity between them.

North Africa: Sixteenth Century

She'elot U'Teshuvot HaRaDBaZ, Part 2, No. 809: A Cantor Who Sings Popular Songs

Born in Spain in 1480, Rabbi David ibn Zimra or RaDBaZ, as he is known by his acronym, was a victim of the Expulsion of 1492. He migrated to Jerusalem, where his reputation as a noted scholar grew, and then on to Fez. He settled in Cairo and remained there for forty years until his death in 1574.

> . . . And with regard to a prayer leader with a pleasant voice who sings love songs and popular songs in taverns: we reprimand him. And if he refuses to listen, we dismiss him. For this and other such things, the applicable verse is Jeremiah 12:8. This is what Rabbi Yitzhaq al-Fasi, of blessed memory, answered in a responsum.
>
> I [Rabbi David ibn Zimra] wrote what seemed correct to me.

Poland: Sixteenth Century

She'elot U'Teshuvot MaHaRShaL, No. 20: Removing a Cantor from His Position

Many revered Rabbi Solomon ben Yehiel Luria (ca. 1510–1574) as one of the exceptional scholars of his era. Orphaned at an early age, he proudly attributes his scholarship to the training he received from his maternal grandfather, Rabbi Isaac Klober. As much as his impeccable pedigree, it was his skillful erudition and logical reasoning that made his reputation. He served for a time as a congregational rabbi in Ostrog and later served as the head of the rabbinical academy in Lublin. As intimated in the responsum that follows, Luria was no stranger to quarrels. In 1567, he was embroiled in a dispute with the son of one of the leading sages of Poland, Shalom Shakhna, which resulted in the founding of his own independent yeshiva. He authored many important scholarly works, principally his commentary on the entire Talmud called *Yam Shel Shlomo* (preserved only in part) and talmudic glosses called *Hokhmat Shlomo*.

The question he received on the matter of the cantor of dubious character was written in Yiddish. He cites it in its entirety and then responds in Hebrew. It is a lengthy responsum that includes a close reading of rabbinic texts beginning with the Talmud and a careful analysis of all the extant literature. But of equal, if not greater, interest is his recounting of the events that led up to his response. Luria reveals key information about the underside of communal affairs: secret cavils, broken promises, deceptive practices, slanderous remarks, overt challenges to the rabbi's authority, and underhanded strategies that include taking action when the rabbi is not around to challenge them. Cynics might say that synagogue life has not changed much over the last five hundred years. This responsum also reveals how difficult it was for cantors to support themselves on the cantor's salary alone. Cantors had to supplement their income with other work.

Luria staunchly supports the cantor, Rav Isaac—even though he concedes that cantors as a group may be deficient in good character—implying that without the cantor the community would be deprived of its connection with God. The office of the cantor must be defended and those who hold that office must be protected. A community without a cantor is bereft of its gateway to prayer. And anyone who thwarts the performance of the cantor is cursed.

> The following incident occurred just before Shabbat Nahamu.[274] Rabbi Abraham ben Jacob organized a rabbinic court to sit between the upcoming Rosh Hashanah and Yom Kippur. Meanwhile, several weeks before Rosh Hashanah, the cantor came to see me along with two supporters and said: "My master, I am guilty of an accident: I mixed up non-kosher meat[275] with kosher meat and sold the non-kosher meat [to Jews] on the presumption it was kosher and I sold the kosher meat to non-Jews on the presumption that it was not kosher." I told him that certainly unintentional wrongdoers require atonement. But in a case like this, when the accident was unintentional and the non-kosher meat was recovered [before eaten], no repentance is needed. However, you should be more careful in the future.
>
> The community knew of this incident but didn't care [what I said] since today, in our sinfulness, people do what they want rather than what is in God's name. So those who opposed me took the opportunity to find some infraction to remove the cantor from his post seeing that he behaved respectfully toward me. It was then that Rabbi Abraham convened the aforementioned

274. Shabbat Nahamu is the first Sabbath after the Ninth of Av, mid-summer.

275. Here, "non-kosher meat" means meat from a kosher animal that was slaughtered incorrectly.

rabbinic court and ruled that this cantor may no longer serve as a slaughterer and post-slaughter checker. That was at a time when I was not home. After the ruling, the community tried to compromise with the cantor since they no longer wanted his services. (He had told them that he could not earn a living on his cantorial salary alone.) So they implored him to stay on as the cantor without serving as slaughterer on the condition that the aforementioned rabbinic court would appear before me and accept any direction I would give them. With this compromise, the cantor led prayers on Rosh Hashanah, Yom Kippur, and Sukkot.

But after the holidays, the rabbinic court did not come to see me or even send me any word. Rather, Rabbi Abraham and his following gathered in the synagogue and ruled that the cantor may not lead them in prayer again. I entered deeply into the matter with Rabbi Abraham and asked him: 'Why do you prevent him from leading prayers?' he told me that tomorrow he would send the rabbinic court to me and that I would see why he is not fit to serve as a cantor. But a segment of the community told him that their intention was to resolve the issue of his remaining as slaughterer. But as far as his remaining as their cantor is concerned, they are resolved that he remain their cantor as before. He (i.e., Rabbi Abraham) did not respond. So I asked Rabbi Abraham to report to me what terrible thing this cantor had committed. He said that the cantor had sold meat as kosher from an animal that had an adhesion on one of its ribs but he defended it . . . (In truth, it is kosher according to the decision of Rabbi Mordechai ben Hillel and others. No need to expatiate) . . .

Then Rabbi Abraham told me that he would share a confidence: once this cantor defrauded a woman to annoy her by declaring a goat non-kosher, buying the carcass [cheaply] from her on the ruse that he would sell it to a non-Jewish servant, and then butchered the meat and ate it. And I told him this proves that he committed an immoral act but it does not prove that he is untrustworthy as a slaughterer. He was careful in his observance of kashrut though ultimately answerable to God for his deception. Besides, perhaps the woman might have done something to offend him.

The next day we continued our discussion yet the rabbinic court still did not appear before me. So I said to Rabbi Abraham and his supporters: 'Why allow your contentiousness to subvert prayer? What do you gain when he does not lead prayers and there is no one else to do so? It is better that he leads prayers since

even if you are correct [in your assessment of him], he would be
no worse than a non-Jew whose recital of certain prayers would,
according to the Jerusalem Talmud, require an "amen" response
[thus fulfilling the requirements of prayer by the congregation].
Besides, if you already allowed him by way of compromise to
lead prayers on Rosh Hashanah and Yom Kippur and Sukkot,
you surely should allow him to lead prayers on other occasions.
To avoid further controversy, allow him to serve as cantor until Passover and in the meantime he may find other means of
livelihood and the community might find a replacement more
acceptable. Rabbi Abraham conceded that he, personally, agreed
with me. However, there are others to whom he must answer
and with whom he must consult before agreeing to anything.
The next day they sent me a notice from the Bet Din. The opposition closed the synagogue and did not allow either prayers
or Torah reading there for several days until the civil authorities
ordered its reopening and forbade further closure with the rabbinic authorities of Lithuania charged with resolving whether
the cantor in question is disqualified or not . . .

This is my response: According to all the above, there is
no trace of fault to disqualify [this cantor] from slaughtering
or from checking slaughtered meat, forbidding others from
eating from the meat he slaughtered or checked. However, the
community may choose to be stricter than the law requires and
hire another slaughterer since this one was almost responsible
for a disaster and this is the compromise they had reached with
him. But as far as disqualifying him from serving as cantor and
removing him from his profession is concerned, anyone who
disqualifies him is disqualified and needlessly causes prayer to
be nullified, and chases away God's people from joining in God's
inheritance and all blame will be on his head and he shall be
deprived of children and grandchildren . . .

Here Rabbi Luria provides a logical analysis of all the relevant
sources from the Talmud to his day, concluding that the "wicked" person
excluded from leading prayers must refer only to prayer leaders praying
for rain during the talmudic period, but not to cantors in his own day
because should the same standards of good behavior that applied in the
time of the Talmud be applied in his own day, "how can we justify allowing any of our cantors to lead prayers?" Rabbi Luria finds support for his
view in the writings of his predecessors. He then goes on to address some
other objections.

It may not be argued that [allowing] this [cantor to continue when under some degree of suspicion] disgraces the mitzvah. To the contrary, it is even better that he leads since "the righteous cannot stand . . ."[276] This is precisely what Rabbenu Asher argued when faced with the question of cantors of low pedigree.[277]

If you say that there repentance is denied him unless he goes to another place, as the Talmud[278] seems to imply, then you would be locking the door to penitents since sometimes there are people who cannot go to other places because of their responsibilities for dependants and the duties of the home that are thrust upon them, particularly in our day in exile. [Since they lack the freedom to relocate,] they would have no way to repent. Likewise, in our day there are no contemporary scholars who have taught that the penitent must go to another place and dress in black etc. Rather, they assess penance according to the severity of the sin and the judgment of the scholar . . .

From a legal perspective, he (*i.e.*, the cantor) certainly is fit [to perform his duties] since he is apologetic and he has suffered financial loss . . . He never intended to sell non-kosher food to Jews and he has cried out of regret [for his error] . . . Therefore I declare before God without equivocation that there are no grounds to disqualify or dismiss our cantor, Rav Isaac, even if they wish to pay him now the remaining salary for his tenure as the cantor for the entire community. However, if the entire community unanimously agrees not to keep him on, then he is barred from leading them in prayer. They must, however, continue to pay his salary during the term of his tenure even if he should find other paid employment . . .

God knows that all I have written regarding the fitness of the cantor in question and rejecting his dismissal is well intentioned and is neither provocative nor vengeful. Rather, [my intention is] to demur against those who would undermine synagogue prayer and would rather close the House of God. Hence, I hope that God will support me since I am fighting God's battle even now when I am a wanderer on the earth and I am unarmed against many lawbreakers . . . I have no power to impose a ban . . .

---

276. *b. San.* 99a.

277. Asher, *She'elot U'Teshuvot Ha-ROSh*, Sec. 4, No. 22

278. *b. Kid.* 40a: "Rav Ilai said: If a man finds that his evil inclination has overcome him, let him go to a place where no one knows him, dress and cover himself in black, act as his passion desires but not profane the name of God in public."

> May God bless with peace all those who stand for peace,
> who pursue peace, desire to strengthen God's abandoned House,
> who pursue righteousness and loving kindness. May God allow
> them to find tranquility and [long] life. Honor and peace to all
> judges in Israel! And may the people Israel find eternal peace.
> The words of Solomon Luria.

Levush Ha-Tekhelet, Section 53: Qualifications of a Cantor

Born in Prague in 1530, Rabbi Mordekhai ben Abraham Yaffe could trace his lineage back to Rabbi Solomon ben Yitzha of Troyes and further back to Hillel and thus to King David. He studied under the great Polish rabbis Solomon Luria and Moses Isserles. Returning to Prague, he established an academy that he led until 1561, when the Holy Roman Emperor Ferdinand I banished all Jews from Bohemia. Fleeing to Italy, he took the opportunity to study science, mathematics, and astronomy over the ten years he resided there. Rabbi Jaffe was accepted as the rabbi of Grodno, Poland in 1572, and twelve years later he moved on to serve as rabbi in Lublin, where he also sat as one of the six rabbinical delegates of the Council of the Four Lands, the Jewish communal governing body in Poland for almost two hundred years. He served as rabbi in three other towns before his death in Posen in 1612.

He called his magnum opus *Levush* (*Attire*) based on the verse in the book of Esther (8:15) that described how Mordekhai—thinking of his own name—went out before the king dressed in royal clothing. The ten sections of this work were compiled over a period of fifty years in which he supplemented the contents of Rabbi Joseph Karo's *Shulhan Arukh* with the customs and practices of German and Polish Jewry more extensively than his teacher Rabbi Moses Isserles.

It is difficult to assess how many Christians actually converted to Judaism in sixteenth-century Poland. Reacting to the accusation that Jews were circumcising their Christian servants, King Sigismund I ordered the punishment of Christians who converted to Judaism or knowingly harbored converts to Judaism. In a celebrated case, Katarzyna Malcherowa Weigel, the wife of Kraków councilman Melchior Weigel, was convicted to death for apostasy to Judaism in 1539. The tenth-century Magdeburg law served as the legal framework of Polish cities. After 1658, the *Sejm*, the Polish legislature, officially enacted it. Its provisions demanded death penalties for apostasy from Catholicism.[279] Rabbi Moses Isserles noted in one of his glosses in the *Shulhan Arukh*[280] that: "in these lands [Poland] ... it is forbidden to convert non-Jews." And Rabbi Solomon Luria condemned the acceptance of converts into Judaism: "Should one of Israel accept [a proselyte], he is a rebel, and is responsible for his own death ... let his blood be on his own head, whether he himself engages in proselytization, or whether he merely knows of such."[281] Yet despite the threat of severe punishment from Polish authorities and nonacceptance by Jewish authorities, Polish court records show that conversions to Judaism continued. But given the obstacles to conversion and the inherent dangers, the number of converts to Judaism was likely small. Thus Rabbi Jaffe's ruling was not intended to address a pressing, practical contemporary issue: how to integrate a wave of converts. Rather, his intention was to refine the criteria for serving as a prayer leader. By discounting the opinion he states was already discredited, he affirms that converts may serve as cantors:

> Paragraph 19—Converts as Prayer Leaders
> There are those who prevent a convert from being a prayer leader since he cannot say "Our God and God of our fathers, *etc.*" and when he prays by himself he says 'God of Israel's ancestors, etc.' But their opinion has already been rejected for he can rightly say "Our God and God of our fathers" since God called Abraham the father of a multitude of nations, as it is written (Gen 17:5): "I have made you the father of a multitude of nations" which means that from that day forward he (*i.e.,* Abraham) will be father to all nations, and they can say "God of our fathers" with their intention to include Abraham, Isaac, and Jacob as if he (*i.e.,* the convert) were related to them as God, may He be blessed, had said.

In the paragraph that follows, the *Levush*—as he is known—rejects the opinion of some earlier authorities[282] who argue that prayer takes the place of sacrifice and the cantor stands in place of the priest who cannot offer an individual's sacrifice without his consent. Here the *Levush* declares that it would be impractical to give every member of the community veto power over cantorial appointments. No matter the virtues

279. Cf. Jedlicki, "German Settlement," 133–36.

280. Yoreh De'ah 267:4.

281. *Yam Shel Shlomo*, on *b. Yev.* 4:49.

282. See, for example, Abudraham, *Abudraham Ha-Shalem,* 46.

of any candidate, there will always be a dissenter. With the frightening prospect of communities going without a cantor due to a lack of consensus, the *Levush* rules that a small representative committee ought to make the final decision on the appointment of the cantor even if a significant minority may demur.

> Paragraph 20—May an Individual Veto the Appointment of a Cantor?
>
> . . . These days, in our sinfulness, many people hold onto baseless disputes that are not in God's name. If they had to ask each and every individual—particularly in large congregations—they would never agree on a single cantor, even if he were the finest in his generation, possessing all the enumerated virtues. They would still find 'a blemish in the offering' and, as a result, synagogues would go unserved—God forbid—as it happens on occasion as I have seen. Therefore, it is proper to choose selectors to appoint a prayer leader according to the will of the majority of the taxpayers, even including those who are disqualified and even if many individuals are opposed to him. For the benefit of the congregations, we follow the majority.

Israel: Sixteenth Century

Rabbi Moses ben Hayyim Alshikh (1507–1593) was born somewhere in Turkey before settling in Safed. He was a student of Rabbi Joseph Karo, author of the *Shulhan Arukh*, and the teacher of the kabbalist rabbi Hayyim Vital, and the Talmudist rabbi Yom Tov ben Moses Zahalon. He turned his public lectures into a written commentary on the Torah to prevent some unscrupulous listeners from publishing his insights as their own. Personal piety earned him the nickname of the "Holy Alshikh." The short passage below appears in his commentary on the book of Proverbs entitled *Rav Peninim* (*Multitude of Pearls*), which was published in Venice in 1601.

The "Holy Alshikh" ascribes to a worthy cantor the power to relieve the pain of the congregation he serves. He is the metaphorical cool breeze to assuage those toiling under the hot sun. But the cantor's power is contingent on his good character and attentiveness, qualities that are prerequisites for a cantor, according to the Talmud.

Rav Peninim on Proverbs 25:13: The Power of a Worthy Cantor

> "Like the coldness of snow at harvest time is a trusty messenger
> to those who send him for he refreshes the soul"—The faithful
> messenger is the prayer leader who is devoted to his mission to
> pray with appropriate mindfulness and not transgress with evil
> deeds or absence of mindfulness. So if they are smitten with a
> passel of troubles, like the sun during the harvest, the faithful
> messenger shall heal their pain.

Bohemia: Sixteenth Century

Rabbi Judah (Leib) ben Bezalel Loew was born into a prestigious family
in Poland around 1520. His uncle was the Chief Rabbi of the Holy Roman
Empire. Absent any specific information about his training, scholars suspect he was privately tutored, if not self-taught. His father was independently wealthy, so he had no reason to seek any posting, although he was
well regarded as a scholar with a special expertise in philosophy and mysticism. But in 1553, he accepted the position of District Rabbi of Moravia
at Nikolsburg, and in 1588 was appointed the Rabbi of Prague, the city
with which he is most associated (as MaHaRaL of Prague). In 1592, he
was elected Chief Rabbi of Poland, but served for a short time, returning
to Prague sometime before his death in 1609. He authored many books,
novellae, and commentaries, some of which have not been preserved. He
is also the subject of the legend about how he used esoteric knowledge to
fashion a creature made of clay (*golem*) to defend the Jewish community
of Prague from attack. His collection of explanations of talmudic passages, *Sefer Ba'er Ha-Goleh*[283] (*The Book of the Revealing Expositor*), from
which the selection below is taken, was published in Prague in 1598.

The Talmud implies that the leader of public prayer wraps his head
with a prayer shawl. This was probably what most cantors did then and
in sixteenth-century Europe (and still today.) MaHaRaL contends that
wearing restrictive headwear does not necessarily induce mindfulness in
prayer—a requirement of any cantor. Rather, mindfulness in prayer is the
outcome of spiritual attentiveness. Wrapping the head with a *tallit* might
be a useful tool for prayer for some, but it is not a requirement for the

---

283. And not *Be'er HaGolah* (The Well of Diaspora) as commonly assumed. Since
the intent of the author is to explicate difficult statements, that is, to reveal the underlying meaning and offer insightful expository notes, the name indicated is far more
appropriate.

cantor. It is not intended by the rule that a cantor must wear appropriate clothing. Later authorities[284] disagree.

Sefer Ba'er Ha-Goleh: Section 4, Chapter 12, s.v. umipnei khi: A Cantor's Tallit

> ... if a man concentrates on his prayers and does not turn away from God, may He be blessed, God—may He be blessed—will be with him entirely. And what He[285] said "Be wrapped up like a prayer leader"[286] [means] because the wrapping of a prayer leader is so that he cannot turn neither right nor left—to any side at all (and this is wrapping) so then the reading will be entirely mindful, from the depths of the heart in its sincerity. This is not so without wrapping, for then it is possible for him to turn to other things and the reading will not be sincere, and this is clear. However, the matter is not contingent on wrapping with a *tallit*. When the reading is sincere and mindful it is called 'wrapping' in that he is removed from any other thing and is not turning right or left. This is the quality of wrapping, not one and not the other ...

Germany: Seventeenth Century

Born in Worms, Rabbi Yair Hayyim ben Rabbi Moses Samson Bachrach (1638–1701) was a polymath. Aside from his expertise in classical Jewish sources, he also mastered astronomy, mathematics, logic, history, and music. He even composed a number of hymns. So developed were his philosophical skills, he wrote novellae on Maimonides's *Guide of the Perplexed*. He never managed to revise and publish his commentary on the first section of the *Shulhan Arukh*. He considered *pilpul*—an exercise in arcane rabbinic reasoning—"a waste of time"[287] and the study of kabbalah "dangerous."[288] He bemoaned the paucity of his scholarly output and praised brevity as a virtue. Rabbi Bachrach served as the rabbi of Koblenz and Mainz and subsequently moved to Worms to succeed his father as

284. Cf., e.g., *Mishnah Berurah*, OH 8:4, citing Rabbi Joel Sirkis.

285. The advice God gives to Moses, and Moses to Israel. The mindful cantor will gain God's forgiveness.

286. Cf. *b. R.H.* 17b.

287. Bachrach, *She'elot U'Teshuvot Havat Yair*, No. 123.

288. Bachrach, *She'elot U'Teshuvot Havat Yair*, No. 210.

the rabbi of the city. But the community engaged another rabbi instead. He remained in Worms and devoted himself to scholarship. Following the expulsion of the Jews from Worms by the French in 1689 during the Nine Years' War, he was forced to take up residence in several different communities. But ten years later, when Jews were allowed to return, he was appointed the rabbi of Worms and served there for the last few years of his life.

In his preface he offers four reasons behind the name of his collection of responsa—*Havat Yair*. First, it alludes to the Amorite villages captured by Yair of the tribe of Menasseh (Num 32:41). The unwalled villages (*havot*) were weak and unfortified. Similarly, his self-described modest attempts at resolving contested issues of law pale in comparison to those of his worthy predecessors. Second, *hava* means "life," an allusion to his given name, Hayyim.[289] Third, the numerical value of *Havat Yair* equals the "minimum of 635 responsa ready for publication" (even though only 238 appear in the Frankfurt edition of 1699). Finally, he pays tribute to his paternal grandmother, Hava, a descendant of an illustrious rabbinical family, a scholar in her own right, and a person of impeccable character.

The unidentified cantor in the following responsum is the victim of his own ambition. After an initial three-year tenure—which seems to be the norm—he is offered and accepts a ten-year extension with a raise in pay, six years of which were guaranteed. But after three years he accepts an even more lucrative offer from another community. The dispute between the cantor—who claims the legal right to move on—and the congregation—that wants to hold him to his commitment—is sent to Rabbi Yair Hayim Bachrach for resolution. In rejecting the cantor's claim, Rabbi Bachrach distinguishes between an ordinary workman and the exceptional status of a cantor. Because the cantor fulfills a special musical and ritual role for the congregation, his status falls into a category that is not circumscribed by a three-year limit. Thus a ten-year contract is valid. The irony is that the status the cantor enjoys comes with a limitation on his freedom of movement.

Included in the response that follows is the mention in passing of a customary cantorial search committee composed of twenty-three men, which in small communities would be a remarkably large number. This

---

289. The name Yair was added as a remedy for illness. Adding a name to camouflage one's identity and thus confuse the Angel of Death was a popular strategy to combat illness. Cf. Trachtenberg, *Jewish Magic and Superstition*, 168, 204–6.

would indicate the enormous importance attached to the task and to the position. In addition, by the seventeenth century in Germany, cantors bore the reputation of being failed businessmen and men of limited means who turn to cantorial arts less as a calling and more as an economic necessity. Even so, this did not discourage communities from luring away the best cantors with better terms.

She'elot U'Teshuvot Havat Yair, No. 40:
The Length of a Cantor's Contract

Question: A cantor was engaged to serve a holy community by twenty-three [men], as is customary, for a period of three years and they liked him. So they wanted to bind him to them by oath and curse not to leave them for another ten years. And they also wanted to stipulate that they would extend [his service] beyond the three years and add to his salary. So he accepted their terms and swore to them. And the *parnasim*[290] also accepted by oath—but not in the presence of the householders—the condition that they would not dismiss [the cantor] within six years. After three years, another holy community that offered him an enormous increase in compensation engaged the cantor. He said that his oath no longer applied because that would cause him to actively violate the rule against hiring one's self out for more than three years[291] since we assert that a workman may back out, as it says in the *Tur* and *Shulhan Arukh*, Hoshen Mishpat 333:3 and also in Yoreh De'ah, end of section 177, with regard to a partnership.

[Answer:] It appears to me that his words are meaningless.[292] There have already been many opinions [expressed] that [an agreement] may be longer than three years. This is what the Tosafists[293] write and Mordekhai[294] [ben Hillel] mentions it without dissent and Rabbi Shabbetai Ha-Kohen endorses it. Further, it is well known that most cantors are neither good businessmen nor men of means. Thus they must hire themselves out as cantors. If so, to hire themselves out long term is allowed.

290. Leaders of the community.

291. Cf. Responsa No. 103; based on Isaiah 16:14.

292. The cantor's contention that he is not bound by any contract more than three years is meaningless.

293. *b. B. Metz.* 10a, *s.v. kil li*, the three-year limit applies to Hebrew slaves, not free men.

294. On *B. Metz*, chapter 6.

Thus wrote [Rabbi] Shabbetai Ha-Kohen there, subparagraph 16. Further, only the workman is subject to the rule of 'no more than three years' since that would make him an indentured servant and [that would violate the principle][295] that we are not servants to men [but to God] . . .

Accordingly, the cantor whose sole role is to fulfill the public obligation [for prayer] and to perform the required ritual and even includes in his compensation what he sings and the like— and thus draws half his salary from the wealthy (as Rabbi Meir of Padua wrote and as cited by [Rabbi Joseph Karo,] *Bet Yosef* in Orah Hayyim 53 and in the gloss by Rabbi Moses Isserles there)—in any case, since he honors God with his voice and the talents with which he is endowed and developed, he is not in the category of a 'servant to servants.'[296] (And further investigation is needed regarding the rabbi and beadle of the synagogue.) . . .

[So] It seems to me,

Y. H. Bachrach

She'elot U'Teshuvot Havat Yair, No. 176: A One-Eyed Cantor

Question: You were astonished that you heard I disapproved of the removal of a one-eyed cantor during the Days of Awe in an unnamed holy community. I never said such a thing and I was shocked to hear it. I surely know, my son, what the sages of blessed memory said, that God uses broken vessels, except that from this there is no proof because that, truthfully, is not a defect. Every broken heart can legitimately be called perfectly righteous, which is not the case with a physical defect, that is, a severe blemish. It never occurred to me that he would be disqualified on the grounds that both the sacrifice and the priestly officiant must be defect-free, as you thought. If what, as you argued is so, why are none of the other qualities and virtues ascribed to a lector in chapter two of *Ta'anit* taken into consideration since these are indisputably applied to a person without any physical deficiency?

In any case, your thoughts are not my thoughts. It is clear [to me] that there is no comparison [between the case of a cantor] and [an] officiating priest for if so, it would apply to everyone, as the *Tur* wrote in [Orah Hayyim] section 98.[297] Fur-

295. See Karo, *Shulhan Arukh*, Hoshen Mishpat 333:3, end.

296. Like workmen.

297. All worshipers—not just cantors—must maintain the proper intent and wear

ther, Rabbenu Asher wrote—and his view is conveyed by the *Tur*, Section 53—that it is wrong to complain against a cantor with a low pedigree since it is better to bring closer those from a distant lineage,[298] refer there, and, accordingly, not to an officiating priest since the sages, of blessed memory, said: "We do not check from the altar and beyond."[299] Even a convert is fit to serve as a prayer leader.

Despite all this, I did object, as you wrote, because it seems to me that in both cases there is reason to surmise that there is someone else who is appropriate and suitable and such. It is well known that the 248 bodily parts are a seat and representation of the 248 supernal lights and the 248 spiritual parts of the soul. Accordingly, in any such case, the seat is blemished and the philosophers wrote that when a sense is partially absent, intellect is partially absent. See *Aqedah*,[300] portion of Shemot, Gate 35, 95b. I wrote along these lines elsewhere that *ab initio* leading the prayer of thanks for food after a meal should not be [a function] given to someone with a severed finger or even someone with a skin disease for they are no better than a person with filthy hands who must wash [before leading] as mentioned in section 121, here too, it is possible for another [cantor to lead] even though this would be a detraction from the dignity of the commandment and even in what is revealed: "When you present a blind animal for sacrifice—it doesn't matter! When you present a lame or sick one—it doesn't matter . . ." (Mal 1:8).

Italy: Seventeenth Century

Leon di Modena (Rabbi Judah Aryeh ben Isaac, 1571–1648) was the precocious offspring of a prominent French family forced to resettle in Venice. His father ensured that he had the broadest education, including singing and dancing. By the age of twelve, he was translating Italian poetry into Hebrew. (He had already mastered rabbinic literature, studied Western classis, and became conversant in mathematics, philosophy, and

---

proper clothing just like any priest officiating over the sacrificial rites.

298. Based on Isaiah 57:19, "It shall be well, well with the far and near . . ." it is better to appoint someone whose lineage is less noble (far) but whose demeanor is superior (near to God). Cf. also Falk, *Bet Yisrael (Perisha and Derisha)*, sec. 53, para. 7.

299. Cf. *b. Pes.* 3b. Should the ancestry of a *kohen* come into question, the courts would investigate his ancestry only until they discovered a priest who sacrificed offerings on the altar. At that point, they would halt the investigation.

300. Rabbi Yitzhak ben Moshe Arama's commentary on the Torah, *Aqedat Yitzhak*.

history.) Rabbi Leon di Modena was a particularly gifted preacher whose sermons attracted non-Jews and Jews alike. He was also religiously progressive, claiming that contemporary rabbis have the power to modify tradition.[301] A series of family misfortunes and a personal predilection to gambling clouded his life. His intellectual brilliance allowed him to successfully argue for the revocation of a decree of ostracism the leaders of the community issued against him. He was also a defender of the musical innovations of the Jewish composer Salomon di Rossi. His responsa appear in two separate collections.

The case before Rabbi Judah Aryeh centers on a fellow who is not the regular cantor, but wants to serve in a cantorial capacity for a part of the High Holidays. His nemesis, however, is intent on his rejection. The Jewish community of Padua sought his expertise in resolving the dispute. Rabbi Judah Aryeh confirms what he considers the well-established law that once a cantor is unanimously appointed or appointed by the vote of a majority (the current Italian practice) any future complaints are to be disregarded. However, he affirms that even a single individual may constrain a cantor from fulfilling his role at his inception. Since the case before him is one of an initial appointment, the aspiring cantor's enemy can constrain him. He also argues that the law is sensible since a cantor must have the unqualified intent to represent all worshipers, and it would be unreasonable to presume that the cantor would be able to include his enemy in his prayers.

Ziknei Yehudah, No. 107:
May an Individual Prevent a Cantor from Leading Prayers?

> Can an individual preclude his enemy from praying as a prayer leader during the Days of Awe? To Padua.
>
> Question: Reuben and Simon, individuals in the synagogue, hate one another and for a number of days could not speak peaceably one with the other. Now Reuben wants to lead one the prayers during Yom Kippur as a cantor in the synagogue and Simon says he does not want him because he is his enemy. Let our teacher guide us: Can Simon alone prevent him [from serving as cantor] or not?
>
> Answer: It is a recurrent topic in the legal literature and with regard to this matter it is obvious that Simon can constrain

301. Cf. Modena, *Bet Yehudah*, Shabbat 1.

Reuben from leading any prayer service during the Days of Awe. Since clearly the same [applies] even for other days of the year: anyone who did not enjoy universal acceptance from the outset or was not appointed by a majority of the congregation—as is the custom today—apart from this [may be constrained from leading prayers]. These are the words of our teacher Rabbi Joseph Colon,[302] Section 44,[303] with regard to a mourner and whether he may lead public prayer. This is what he says: "It all depends on the attitude of the congregation because prayer is their domain and [prayer] is in place of public sacrifice, that is, the daily offerings, that they brought for the public, and it is inappropriate to have as their representative who sacrifices on their behalf someone of whom they do not approve. And for this reason, Rabbenu Simhah ruled that even an individual can control the cantorate by saying 'I don't want so-and-so to be the cantor' unless he had previously agreed to him." This is what Rabbi Joseph Karo,[304] of blessed memory, brings forward,[305] as did his student,[306] author of the *Levushim*,[307] in the section cited below: "There are those who say that an individual may not prevent without good reason even from the outset, and so forth . . . and if it is clear he is his enemy, he may prevent [him from leading prayers] if he had not already agreed to him."[308] Here we see this [authority] affirm that an antagonist certainly may prevent his enemy from being appointed lector throughout the year and, by ineluctable deduction [we conclude] that he [may] prevent him [from serving] on the Days of Awe. By virtue of the fact that the aforementioned teacher and student so wrote in *Orah Hayyim*, Section 582[309] that in these days when we stand in judgment we need great mindfulness, "they must therefore meticulously look for the most worthy prayer leader possible, one who excels in good deeds, who will pray the penitential prayers and the Days of Awe liturgy, who is thirty years old—since then he is of settled mind—and who is also married. However, any Jew is suitable

---

302. Rabbi Joseph Colon ben Solomon Trabotto (ca. 1420–1480) was considered the preeminent Italian authority of his era.

303. Colon, *She'elot U'Teshuvot MaHaRIK*, No. 30, secs. 3 and 4.

304. Author of the *Shulhan Arukh*, published in 1575.

305. Karo, *Shulhan Arukh*, OH 53:19.

306. Not his actual student but a successor.

307. Rabbi Mordekhai ben Abraham Jaffe (*ca.* 1530–1613).

308. Yaffe, *Levush Ha-Tekhelet* 53:20.

309. Yaffe, *Levush Ha-Hur* 582:9.

so long as he is acceptable to the congregation. But if he seizes
[the position] and prays against the will of the congregation, we
do not respond 'Amen' after him. Likewise, he must fulfill the
obligation of all in his prayer. If he has an enemy he intends
to exclude [from his prayer], even his supporters are excluded,
since what applies to one[310] applies to all."[311]

From this we learn three things that apply to our case: 1.
For the Days of Awe one must search for someone who excels
in Torah and good deeds. 2. He must be acceptable to the congregation and not usurp [the position to pray] against their will,
as they wrote as well regarding a lector for the whole year, Section 53, mentioned above, paragraph 20, because then trivial-
ity is especially forbidden. 3. His intent must be to include an
enemy and fulfill his obligation [for prayer]—the listener and
the speaker must share the same intent—and in this case, this
one will surely not intend to fulfill [the obligation for prayer] for
that one. And if this is true throughout the year, it is certainly
true for the Days of Awe. These things are clear and in print in
[the works of] the legal authorities. Nothing here is my own.[312]
I am only satisfying the questioner. It is as if I have copied them.

Signed and sealed,

Yehudah Aryeh mi-Modena, here, Venice.

Israel: Seventeenth Century

Rabbi Yom Tov ben Moshe Zahalon was a preeminent scholar of the
late-sixteenth and early-seventeenth centuries. His place of birth was
assumed by M. Binyahu[313] to be Safed sometime before 1560. His self-
identification of "Ha-Sephardi" suggests he traced his history to Spain.
He was a student of Rabbi Moses of Trani and ordained by Rabbi Moses
Alshikh. By 1584, he was accounted as one of the leaders of the Jewish
community in Israel. Attacks against the city by local Arabs caused him
to flee for a time to Damascus, but after returning to Israel, he took up
residence in the towns of Peki'in and, later, Sidon. After the sack of Safed

310. That is, the exclusion. If his enemies are excluded from his prayers, his friends
are excluded too.

311. Almost the entirety of his quoted passage appears verbatim in Rabbi Moses
Isserles' gloss on Karo, *Shulhan Arukh*, OH 581:1.

312. This is somewhat misleading. While he bases his view on earlier rulings, he extends the precedents. Rabbi Yehudah Aryeh is being more modest than disingenuous.

313. Margaliot, *Encyclopedia L'Toldot Gedolei Yisrael*, 3:735.

by the Druze in 1604, MaHaRYTaZ (as he is known by his acronym) was sent to Italy and Holland to raise money for reconstruction. His travels also took him to Egypt and Turkey. His last dated sighting is 1611. Rabbi Zahalon published a commentary on *Avot D'Rabbi Natan,* as well as on the book of Esther. An initial collection of his responsa was published with a preface by his grandson in Venice in 1694. Machon Yerushalayim published more of his responsa in 1979. Of note is his view that the *Shulhan Arukh*—written by one of his teachers, Rabbi Joseph Karo—was intended for children and simpletons![314]

In the following responsum, Rabbi Yom Tov Zahalon is surprised that the question is even asked since there is a clear precedent from the responsum of Rabbi Isaac bar Sheshet to the judges of Alkolina (probably Alcoy, near Valencia) on an analogous case where a cantor's term of employment was renewed after three years without requiring him to pay taxes even though the renewal did not include this stipulation.[315] The congregation, ruled RIBaSh, must honor the original terms when they can be determined. Otherwise, local custom prevails.[316] He also explains that sharp words spoken during heated negotiations are forgivable. Although the outburst might be perceived as an insult, it is not intended to be so. Rather, it reflects disappointment with the process.

Responsa MaHaRYTaZ, No. 104: Is a Wealthy Cantor Exempt from Taxes?

May our Master instruct us regarding a prayer leader in Andrianople[317] who is a learned elder and God-fearing [man] and serves in the Ashkenazi synagogue. There is a long-standing agreement in the city—valid and binding—that taxes are not collected from the prayer leader. Now this prayer leader [in question] was wealthy, and now that the term of his tenure nears its end, the congregation entered into negotiations and demanded from him that he now pay tax, saying that they never stipulated that he would be exempt and he deceptively began his career in the cantorate so that he would be exempt, and they do

314. Zahalon, *She'elot U'Teshuvot MaHaRYTaZ,* No. 76.

315. *She'elot U'Teshuvot RIBaSh,* No. 476.

316. Cf. *y. Yev.* 12:5; *y. B. Metz.* 7:1 and see also *Sof.* 14.

317. Adrianople (in English) or Hadrianopolis (in Greek) or Edirne (in Turkish) is a city in East Thrace on the western side of the Bosporus, near the Turkish border with Greece. Jews have lived in this important Ottoman administrative center since 1453.

not want to exempt him since he is an extremely wealthy man. He contends that there was no need for specificity since the long-standing rule was undisputed. So he called them 'robbers' since they did not heed the law of the Torah. The congregation wants to punish him for this and collect taxes from him. May our master instruct us: with who is the law? And may his reward be doubled from Heaven.

And the sages of Constantinople and Salonika wrote on this matter and one of the disputants submitted their petition to me, and so forth.

Answer:

... The gist of his words that is relevant to our question that has come before us for judgment is that it is as clear as day that a prayer leader is exempt in all respects since Rabbi Isaac bar Sheshet has written on this matter that even if the custom were to pay cantors, and even if there were no stipulation the second time—it was unspecified—in any case, his intention was on the first [appointment] so that if it were unclear, we rely on the custom, thus here, in our case, when the city custom is predicated on a long-standing agreement where the presumption is indisputable that no taxes are collected from prayer leaders. They cannot deprive him [of the exemption from paying taxes] unless they specifically said to him: 'if you were appointed to be prayer leader, we will not exempt you.' Since they did not so inform him, we judge according to the city custom and its agreement.

Now it is wrong to say that this [case] is different: he is the cantor of one congregation, but all other congregations where he was not the cantor do ask [their cantors] to pay. This cannot be. The agreement includes all cantors in all holy congregations to exempt them [from paying] taxes and this is not written down at all, nor that they would pay the cantor's share for him—as is the custom in our community, Safed, may God protect and defend it. Hence, since they knew he was to be appointed as cantor, it was on them to warn him and say 'We will not exempt you from taxes' or to tell his congregation to warn him accordingly. Since they did not so specify, on this it rests, and they take nothing from him.

Rabbi Yom Tov Zahalon now turns to the issue of the cantor's public disparagement of the congregation.

... I am amazed at the questioner who asks if it is worthy to punish the prayer leader in that he called them 'robbers.' What kind of question is this? By right he called them so, out of exasperation and anger. He certainly did not intend to slander them, meaning they are actually robbers. Rather, he thought they were taking money from him unlawfully. If so, he is not subject to punishment . . .

The principle that emerges from our analysis is that it is improper to punish him for calling the majority 'robbers' because in his view—and based on what he was taught—what was taken from him *was* robbery. And Moses, our teacher, of blessed memory, was not punished for calling Israel 'rebels.'[318] Rather, [he was punished] for insulting their ancestry, as I explained, or because he failed to sanctify God's Name at the waters of contentiousness, but not for calling them 'rebels.' This is simple and clear. My heart tells me—and it is a witness—that this failing did not emanate from the great and good leaders of the illustrious Jewish city of Andrianople whose reputation precedes it and whose residents are supremely virtuous. This can only be a case where their hearts have impelled them, thinking they have acted rightly. But after seeing the response of the judges, they will repent and apologize to the learned cantor who was wronged. And it would be nice of him to forgive them.

And may God grant us righteousness to illumine our eyes with the light of His Torah and show us wonders. May this be His will.

Ukraine: Seventeenth Century

Rabbi Jacob ben Rabbi Joseph Reischer was born into a prominent rabbinical family in Prague around 1661. While he enjoyed productive years as the rabbi of Worms (Germany) and Metz (France), he is remembered best for his first rabbinical position in Rzeszow, Galicia, from which his surname was derived. He died in Metz in 1733. His literary output—with almost all books titled after his given name, "Jacob"—was considerable. His works reveal a sharpness of mind that justifies the high esteem in which his colleagues held him. He wrote novellae on some of the most difficult and arcane sections of the Talmud. His explication of the laws of Passover (*Hok Ya'akov*), first published in Dessau in 1696, became so popular that it was subsequently published in the *Shulhan Arukh*. His commentary *Iyyun Ya'akov* (published in Wilhelmsdorff in 1733) on the midrashic collection *Ein Ya'akov*, shows his mastery of aggadic texts. But it is Rabbi Reischer's *Shevut Ya'akov*, a collection of responsa in three

318. Num 20:10.

parts with supplementary talmudic novellae, which arguably is his greatest legacy.

In his defense of a cantor who reneges on his agreement, Rabbi Jacob Reischer argues that cantors are not essential: there are other competent members of the congregation who can always stand in. The fact that others could fulfill the role of adequately leading prayers attests to the rising level of competency among Jews of this period.

Sefer Shevut Ya'akov, No. 6: May a Cantor Break a Contract?

Question: May a prayer leader who had hired himself out for many years renege on his agreement during its term or not—especially when the community claim that he was contracted to them by an oath?

Answer: The matter is unclear. But [the solution] stands on whether or not the hiring was a binding agreement. If it were not a binding agreement, the worker may simply back out "in the middle [of the day]" as explained in the Talmud and the decisors [of Jewish law]—see Hoshen Mishpat, Section 333[319]—on the grounds that he is not a "servant to servants."[320] With regard to a prayer leader, it is conceivable that this concern does not apply since he is [not a "servant to servants" but] a servant to God because prayer is in place of sacrifices making him (*i.e.* the cantor) an agent of the All Merciful One. If so, the principle of 'servant to servants' does not apply. However, since the congregation or a certain individual wants to prevent him from being a prayer leader in any other congregation but theirs and not go to another place on the grounds that he is their hireling, the principle is surely at work.[321] So he can back out in the middle [of his term].

Based on this reason, even a school teacher or a scribe who also does God's work may, according to the rulings of the decisors of Jewish law, back out of their agreements, as explained in *Shulhan Arukh* [Hoshen Mishpat], Section 333[:3] in the

319. Subparagraph 3. It is the day laborer's prerogative to quit in the middle of the day. If the cantor is comparable to a day laborer, he could quit in the middle of his term of appointment.

320. Cf. Lev 25:55 and *b. B. Kam.* 116b. Without the option to be quit of his employer, the worker would be nothing short of a servant to another person and Jews are servants to God alone.

321. By trying to prevent the cantor from going elsewhere, they are, in effect, claiming he is their servant.

gloss—provided that it is not in the category of "an irrecoverable loss."[322] Here, with regard to a prayer leader, according to the majority opinion, it is not an irrecoverable loss[323] since nowadays everyone is competent to go down to the lectern and pray—although he may not have a [pleasant] singing voice (for further explanation see [*Shulhan Arukh*] Orah Hayim, Section 13, and refer further to *Magen Avraham*,[324] sub-section 20)—and it is also common to authorize others [to serve as temporary cantors].[325] This is easy to understand.

Therefore, it quite simply seems to me that he can back out. Moreover, it is possible that even if the agreement was completely binding, he may also back out, as the unqualified words of the decisors—and Rabbi Isaac ben Sheshet[326] and Rabbi Shabbetai HaKohen in Hoshen Mishpat, Section 33[3][327]—indicate, and not like Rabbi Yom Tov ben Ashbili, see there. And in *Responsa Havat Yair*, No. 140 I saw that, independently [of my opinion], he distinguished between a school teacher and a prayer leader who is not called 'a servant of servants' even though, in the end, he left the matter in doubt. But in my humble opinion, the principle is as I have stated.

Rabbi Reischer goes on to consider an alternative view that states that a cantor may not renege on his agreement.

Now in light of this, it is fair to cite proof that a prayer leader may not be able to back out at all from what the *Shulhan Arukh* rules in Orah Hayim, Section 310[328] that it is forbidden to hire cantors to pray on *Shabbat*.[329] If they (*i.e.* cantors) were hired for [the term of] a year or a month, all agree that it is permitted by reason of "incorporation."[330] But if backing out applied, "incor-

---

322. Hoshen Mishpat 333:5. A worker cannot back out when it would cause the hirer an irrecoverable loss. For example, workers hired to transport musicians for a wedding may not quit during transport since there is no time to hire substitutes. The absence of music would be an irrecoverable loss to the celebrants.

323. An "irrecoverable loss" is grounds for a legal exception from the general rule.

324. Rabbi Abraham Abele ben Rabbi Hayyim Ha-Levi Gumbiner (1637–1683).

325. Others can stand in for the cantor so the cantor is not essential.

326. Rabbi Shabbetai Ha-Kohen in Karo, *Shulhan Arukh, Hoshen Mishpat* 333:5.

327. Subparagraph 14.

328. Should be 306:5.

329. It would seem as if they are being paid for services rendered on Shabbat.

330. *Havla-ah*, in Hebrew. Payment for services performed on Shabbat violates the rabbinic enactment against engaging in commerce. But payment for services

poration" should be forbidden as the Tosafists[331] and Rabbenu Nissim[332] wrote in [the tractate] *Ketubot*, Chapter 'Even though,' *s.v.* "for he would rather be hired on Shabbat": "And should you say hiring on Shabbat by way of incorporation is allowed . . . one can say that here it is forbidden because it is not like incorporation at all since we are not adding to all Sabbaths together what is counted every day because if he broke [the agreement] today or tomorrow mid-week, all of the other days of the week do not join together,"[333] so say the Tosafists[334]—and Rabbenu Asher,[335] *Agudah*,[336] and Rabbenu Nissim there. (The language of Rabbenu Nissim was cited somewhat differently by Rabbi Moses Isserles in *Darkhei Moshe*:[337] "Rabbenu Nissim wrote at the end of the chapter 'Even though' that if he were hired for a month—if they stipulated with him that they will pay him according to the number of days—he is called a 'day worker' and would be a Sabbath hireling since he could back out mid-month and thus he is not called a monthly worker.") And Rabbi Moses Isserles ruled similarly in *Shulhan Arukh* there,[338] Section 306:4 in his gloss. Accordingly, in our case, it is demonstrated that he cannot back out for if this were not so, he would be like a Sabbath hire.

Yet, in truth, the words of Rabbenu Nissim that were copied in *Darkhei Moshe* and *Shulhan Arukh* are perplexing to me. For how can he back out mid-month? After all, they hired him for the entire month except that they would pay him a daily rate.

He goes on to analyze the problem and concludes: "the later authorities erred in this." He adds:

---

performed on Shabbat subsumed (incorporated) under a broader arrangement is permitted (Cf. *b. B. Metz.* 58a) since the compensation received is for the entire service and not specifically for any service performed on Shabbat.

331. *b. Ket.* 64b s.v. *mihazei.*

332. Commentary on al-Fasi, *b. Ket.*, 287, 28a, top.

333. If allowed to back out of an agreement that included services performed on Shabbat, the cantor would appear to be paid only for services performed on Shabbat. Consequently, the entitlement to back out and the principle of incorporation are mutually exclusive. Since the principle of incorporation is accepted as law, the entitlement to back out is refuted.

334. *b. Ket.* 64b s.v. *mihazei.*

335. *Ket.*, chapter 5, sec. 37.

336. A concise compendium of Talmudic principles collected by Rabbi Alexander Ha-Kohen Zuslan of Frankfort (d. 1349), first published in Cracow in 1571.

337. *Tur*, OH, 306, subparagraph 2.

338. Orah Hayim.

In my humble opinion, the truth is as I have stated and in every case the cantor may renege provided that there is no irrecoverable loss [, namely,] there is no one else capable of praying . . .

So it appears to me,

Jacob, the insignificant.[339]

MODERN SOURCES

Germany, Eighteenth Century: Hiring and Firing the Cantor

In 1756, the same year that Frederick the Great of Prussia promulgated his edict for organizing Prussian Jewry in the context of emancipation, two imperial barons imposed a constitution on the obscure Jewish community of Sugenheim, Franconia, numbering a mere twelve households. More than a bureaucratic instrument, the constitution was intended, according to Jacob Rader Marcus, to regulate the life of Jewish subjects, keep them from annoying the local authorities with quarreling, and maintain decorous conduct in the new synagogue built the year before. (Eliminating fisticuffs in the synagogue and quarreling over bookstands were of particular concern.) Since the community was too small to support a rabbi, its chief Jewish functionary—and only paid professional—was the cantor. Among his duties were teaching, calling members to prayer, slaughtering kosher meat, and leading prayer services.

The Sugenheim Constitution consists of thirty-two clauses, of which six directly govern the conduct and compensation of the cantor and six more indirectly impinge on his responsibilities. It appears that cantors were less than reliable in fulfilling their duties and, accordingly, threats of fines or dismissal were included. Of particular note is the need for any applicant to document his qualifications. This may be the first datable requirement for credentials and references in hiring a cantor. Two other points need be mentioned. First, unlike earlier historical periods, the cantor's salary was divided into three parts. One part of his compensation was assessed communally. Another part was determined by ability to pay. And a third part was based on services rendered so that those who had no children to educate paid a lesser share. Second, the cantor is hired and fired by a majority decision. The earlier legal requirement of communal unanimity has been jettisoned in favor of majority rule.

---

339. A self-deprecating description often appears with the signature of many great scholars.

The translation below, based on Max Freudenthal's 1929 publication of the Sugenheim Constitution, is that of Marcus.[340]

The Constitution of the Jewish Community of Sugenheim Town

Inasmuch as the Jews here in our town of Sugenheim are not yet provided with a fixed code of laws—as a result of which much quarreling and confusion have developed among them and both the local lords have been annoyed several times—therefore both of the jointly ruling lords (namely, The Right Honorable Imperial-Immediate Baron, Sir Christopher Friedrich, Baron of Seckendorff, Lord of Sugenheim Town . . . and also the Right Honorable Imperial-Immediate Baron, Sir Christoph Wolfgang Philipp, Baron of Seckendorff, Lord of Sugenheim Town) have deigned to confer the present communal constitution on the local Jewish community. They are to be guided by it in their conduct of their synagogal and other Jewish ceremonies in their newly built communal synagogue, and in the punishment, according to the circumstances, of the malicious and the stubborn. As follows: . . .

III. The Cantor Shall Call [People] to the Synagogue Regularly

Whenever there is to be a religious service the cantor shall call people to the synagogue regularly so that no one may excuse himself because of ignorance. If, however, the cantor forgets this and does not call people on the appointed days, he is to be fined ten *Kreuzer* the first time, and if he blunders frequently he is to be fined fifteen to twenty *Kreuzer*, or mayhap even dismissed. . . .

V. No Householder Is To Lead Prayer on the High Holidays

No householder is to lead in prayer on the High Holidays. A cantor is to conduct the services unless the entire community is content to use a lay leader. . . .

XIX. The Hiring of a Cantor

The majority of the votes of the Jewish residents of the town and of those who have children to teach shall decide in the hiring of the cantor. However, they must select an able person, one who can serve well as the schoolmaster and understands ritual slaughtering thoroughly. He must also be able to account for his

340. Marcus, *Jew in the Medieval World*, 212–18.

origin and for his conduct in the past by means of the proper
documents. . . .

XX. The Wages of a Cantor and the Teaching of the Children

The cantor's wages are to be made up of three parts, namely,
one-third [to be paid] by the pupils, one-third by taxation [of
wealth], and one-third [a fixed sum for all] by the family heads.
He is required to teach a lad till he is thirteen, a girl till she is
eleven. One studying the Five Books of Moses is to be taught
one hour a day; a child studying the prayer book, one half-hour
daily; and one learning the alphabet, a quarter of an hour daily.

XXI. Paying the Cantor

Every householder living here, if he has a child, is expected to
contribute as much to the cantor as he would if he sent a child to
school to begin his studies. This applies even to those who have
children too young to begin their studies.

XXII. Discharging a Cantor

A cantor is not to be discharged immediately at the request of
a few householders who dislike him. Inasmuch as the cantor is
selected by the majority vote of the Jews who live in the place
and of those who send their children to school, he is, therefore,
to be discharged only by these groups. . . .

XXXII. The Publication of This Communal Constitution

In order that no householder may be able to excuse himself
through ignorance, the communal chiefs shall have the cantor read this communal constitution to all the householders,
publicly, word for word, in the synagogue, right now and then
every year at Pentecost and relate its entire contents exactly and
without deviation.

   In witness whereof and for further authentication, the honorable, gracious, baronial rulers have graciously deigned to confirm this communal constitution with their esteemed signature
in their own hand and with the impression of their hereditary
baronial seal.

   Sugenheim Town, 30th of December, in the year 1756.

Alsace: Eighteenth Century

Rabbi Joseph ben Menahem Steinhardt (ca. 1720–1776) was raised in
Bavaria. He studied under Rabbi Jacob Ha-Kohen Poppers, author of the

responsa collection *Shav Ya'akov*, and was later elected rabbi of Nieder-Ehenheim in lower Alsace. In 1755, he was appointed rabbi of Fürth, where he served until his death. Aside from his commentary on the Torah and his novellae on the tractate *Bava Metzia*, his responsa published in Fürth in 1773 serve as the best indicator of his mastery of talmudic literature.

In a lengthy responsum, Rabbi Steinhardt describes a synagogue scandal in Verona in which the outrageous outburst of a synagogue leader in the middle of a festival prayer service becomes the basis on which Rabbi Steinhardt evaluates the merits of incorporating children in the synagogue service as a kind of junior choir working with the cantor along with analyzing the relative standing of competing customs. The situation reveals just how vulnerable the cantor can become when trying to balance satisfying the personal—and misguided—directives of synagogue leaders and fulfilling his responsibilities to the congregation and its rabbi.

Sefer Zikhron Yosef, Orah Hayim, No. 5: *The Vulnerability of the Cantor*

To the illustrious rabbi, our teacher and rabbi Menahem (May the All Merciful protect him and guard him!) head of the rabbinic court of Verona, Italy (May God protect it!).

Question: In a place where it was customary on the festivals and holidays for the congregation to recite *Hallel*[341] together with the cantor[342]—except for "*Hodu*"[343] and "*Ana*"[344] which the prayer leader sings and the congregation responds to him,[345] as it is customary [to do] throughout the lands and districts of Ashkenaz—a new custom was recently introduced[346] (about fifteen years ago) by the synagogue leaders with the approval of the rabbi and teachers at that time, to position two youths

---

341. Literally, *Hallel* means "praise" in Hebrew. It is a prayer consisting of Pss 113–118 with the addition of several scriptural passages and a concluding blessing (Cf. *m. Pes.* 10:7).

342. Although the author uses *sheliah zibbur* (prayer leader), the account that follows suggests that his role and status is more than a random congregant appointed for leading one service.

343. Ps 118:1–4 begins with the Hebrew word *hodu*, meaning "give thanks."

344. Ps 118:25.

345. Cf. *b. Pes.* 118a, 119b.

346. Literally, "new ones who came but lately" (Deut 32:17).

on either side of the cantor to alternately sing Psalm 116:12–19 while the congregation repeats all they say or responds to them in an undertone. This custom has spread widely, even when these youths are not yet *B'nai Mitzvah*.[347]

... On the first day of *Shavu'ot*, the scholarly rabbi of the city led the morning prayer service and when he reached *Hallel*, he noticed that there were no youths who came forward to sing. Since he did not want to stop and wait [for youths to come forward],[348] he began to say the passage aloud with the congregation after him, with no objections to him doing so except from one synagogue officer who, after the conclusion of the service, called over the cantor who was scheduled to lead prayers on the second day [of the festival][349] and, on his own initiative and without consultation, quietly ordered him not to do tomorrow what the rabbi did today. Instead, the cantor was instructed to follow the custom and wait until the youths come forward. [The elder] cautioned him (*i.e.* the cantor) not to tell anything about what he had ordered him to do to anyone else. On the second festival day, when the cantor reached *Hallel* and began to recite it, the entire congregation immediately joined with him[350] aloud and they recited antiphonally. Now when the synagogue officer saw that his advice was not followed, he grew very angry and interrupted the service by shouting out his disapproval of the cantor and then approached the lectern and reprimanded him further, thus casting aspersions on the rabbi [who did the same thing] yesterday. Afterwards, [the elder] heaped sin upon transgression by publicly criticizing his own rabbi and disparaging him, claiming that he changed the old custom and other such things ...

Answer: I am amazed at the teachers back then[351] who agreed to this new custom. I am amazed at how they could justify it. What could possibly have come to them to change long standing custom regarding the recital of "*Hallel*" which is a long-standing custom, fixed by most Jews, and mentioned in *Tur*, Orah Hayim Section 422 and in other earlier and later

347. And thus not yet adults and therefore unable to fulfill the requirement of prayer for others.

348. It seems that the only concern he had was to expedite the service without delay. Delaying the service would be a *tirha d'zibura*, or a burden to the congregation.

349. Apparently the cantor was not expected to lead the prayer service on both days of Shavu'ot.

350. Assuming that children would not be participating.

351. Fifteen years previously.

authorities. The prevailing custom throughout the districts of
the cities of Ashkenaz that the congregation recites it aloud with
the prayer leader except for "*Hodu*" and "*Ana*" which the prayer
leader sings and the congregation answers after him. It is forbidden to change the old and fixed customs of a city, particularly
in matters of prayer, as the decisors ruled in [*Shulhan Arukh*]
Orah Hayim in many places, particularly regarding any specific
custom mentioned by a decisor, as is written in the Responsa of
Rabbi Moses Isserles, No. 21 in the name of Rabbi Joseph Colon and brought forward in *Magen Avraham*,[352] Orah Hayyim,
Section 690, subparagraph 22. Refer there. Moreover, according to the author of Responsa *Sha'arei Efraim*,[353] No. 10, it is
wrong to annul an old custom even when the custom is legally
questionable.[354]

In addition . . . [deduce] from Sukkah 28a That it would
disgrace the congregation when minors lead *Hallel* . . . Similarly,
according to Section 53 of [*Shulhan Arukh*] Orah Hayyim that
we do not appoint a prayer leader unless his beard is full . . . If
so, it is impossible[355] to understand how they decided to allow
two youngsters to sing together, this one a verse and that one
another.

Here Rabbi Steinhardt considers—but rejects—two possible justifi-
cations for allowing minors to lead *Hallel*.[356]

. . . It seems that those teachers calamitously changed a long-
standing custom on tenuous grounds, and he who has the power
should annul this new custom, particularly after we have seen
how the custom was subsequently corrupted . . .

From the good words above, it seems clear that the rabbi
who led prayer on the first day of *Shavu'ot* acted well in beginning Hallel aloud with the congregation without waiting for

352. Rabbi Abraham Abele Gumbiner (*ca.* 1635–1682).

353. Rabbi Efraim Zalman Margolis (Margaliot) (1762–1828).

354. For example, Rabbi David Halevi Segal, *Turei Zahav* on *Shulhan Arukh*, OH,
494, rules that the custom of singing *Akdamut*, a mystical payer extolling God, on
Shavu'ot after the first verse of the Torah reading, should be annulled on the grounds
that it interrupts the Torah reading. But Rabbi Margaliot rules it should nonetheless be
retained because the custom of singing *Akdamut* is old and fixed.

355. Literally, "as hard as lupine," a plant of the pea family whose spiky leaves are
coarse.

356. See Gumbiner, *Magen Avraham*, Section 479, subparagraph 2, and *Hoq
Ya'akov* 479:6, as well as *b. Ber.* 50a: "Rabbi Meir asked: Whence do we know that even
fetuses in the womb joined in the Song at the Sea? etc."

the youngest of children not yet *B'nai Mitzvah* to approach and sing . . .

. . . What transpired is repugnant: something that should never again transpire among Jews. An officer of the synagogue had such impudence that without the agreement of his colleagues and the majority of the congregation (May God protect it!) he ordered the cantor to pray on the second day and not do what the rabbi did on the first. And he insisted that he (*i.e.*, the cantor) not tell his colleagues or anyone else. This man had the haughtiness not to first ask or inquire of the rabbi why he acted thus, since perhaps his explanation might be compelling and reasonable so as not to swiftly cause a quarrel in the future. He heaped sin on transgression by interrupting the prayer service by raising his voice against the cantor twice—and foully—seeing that he had not followed his advice. He assaulted the dignity of the cantor and debased the honor of the rabbi who led prayers on the first day. He added to his wickedness by approaching the rabbi to argue with him "blunt talk like sword thrusts (Prov 12:18)." These are not just one or two indiscretions. He committed despicable and contemptible wrongs: publicly embarrassing a fellow (for which there is no share in the World to Come), insulting a scholar, and insulting a friend in the presence of a scholar. And it is taught at the beginning of chapter 'Portion:' "These have no share in the World to Come," and so forth ". . . and the *apikoros*" about whom it is said in the Talmud, [Sanhedrin] 99, end of side b: "This is he who insults a scholar," *etc.*, ". . . insults his friend in the presence of a scholar." It is also an attack against the dignity due God, May He be praised, because he disturbed prayer and interrupted praise, and the honor due the congregation Adat Yeshurun[357] since he stopped them from celebrating and praying, and he exalted himself above them egotistically as if saying: "There is none but me (Isa 47:8, 10; Zeph 2:15)," putting his will ahead of theirs, and in the height and breadth of his haughtiness his sin is too great to bear, may we be saved from such punishment!

. . . In judgment against this man, he is obliged to pay a hefty fine and be subject to social ostracism.[358] All this is simple and clear.

I am shocked that the [members of the congregation] (May God protect it!) who stood there were silent and did not

---

357. Likely the name of the synagogue or perhaps a term of respect: "the righteous assembly."

358. See *b. Ber.* 19a; *Shulhan Arukh*, Yoreh De'ah, 243:6, 334:45.

act to preserve God's honor and the honor due their rabbi and excoriate that man and smite him with their words and punish him appropriately for disturbing prayer and publicly abusing a scholar.

Therefore, "my thoughts urge me to answer for my feelings (Job 20:2)" that there is no remedy for this man until he fully repents and sincerely regrets what he did and stand on the pulpit from where the Torah is read and, with broken heart, ask forgiveness from God, blessed be He, as well as forgiveness from the congregation, may God protect it, and especially from the scholarly rabbi, may God protect him, and also from the cantor [*Shulhan Arukh*] Yoreh De'ah, Section 243, I have transgressed, *etc.*"[359] I hope that in hearing this, his heart will relent and act accordingly. If, God forbid, he turns a cold shoulder and refuses to do as I say, let the gentleman inform me of his name so that he being there and me being here I will know exactly what to do to him, with God's help, for the honor of God and His holy Torah, may the zeal of the Lord bring this to pass. However, I expect that he will not reject our words and will act on them and repent and be healed, and God's curse will turn to blessing, long and vouchsafed to all. And it shall be peace from the Lord of peace . . .

Shalom, and may his eminence be enthroned securely before God forever, selah, for glory, fame, and praise.

These are the words of he who seeks his wellbeing always,[360] his beloved, the insignificant Joseph from Steinhardt, residing here in the community of Fürth and Agfi.[361]

Hungary: Nineteenth Century

Rabbi Moses ben Joseph Schick (1807–1879), born in Brezove, Slovakia, studied with the strident, archtraditionalist Rabbi Moses Schreiber in Pressburg from the ages of fourteen to twenty. He was appointed the rabbi of Khust[362] in 1861, a position he held for the rest of his life. He is the author of more than 1,000 responsa, published in stages, with the first collection printed in Munkacz (Hungary) in 1880. According to legend,

359. These are the traditional words of the confessional recited on the Day of Atonement.

360. A reference to himself.

361. Possibly: Eggenfelden

362. In present-day Ukraine.

when the Hapsburg Emperor, Joseph II, required Jews to adopt surnames at the end of the eighteenth century, the name "*Schick*" (meaning "fancy" in German) was chosen since it was an acrostic for "The Jewish name is sacred" (*Shem Yisrael Kadosh*).

With increasing frequency, cantors of this era repeated words and phrases in the liturgy for its musical utility, dramatic impact, and emotional effect. In the following responsum, Rabbi Schick considers the propriety of cantors repeating words and phrases in prayer.

She'elot U'Teshuvot MaHaRaM Schick, Orah Hayim, No. 31: May a Cantor Repeat Words?

With God's help, Holy Sabbath Eve, portion of VaYak-hel 5635,[363] Khust, May God protect it!

Life and peace to the rabbi, the great light, the prominent, a crown of Torah, our rabbi and teacher Aaron Wilheim, head of the rabbinic court Poesing,[364] may God protect it!

I received his letter in which he asked me to make my opinion clear on the matter of cantors who sing and repeat the words many times over in their singing to show off their voices. [He wants to know if] this is forbidden by law, since the cantor in his congregation repeats over again the words and phrases (even words in the *Amidah* and *Kedushah*)?

A wise man's question is half the answer. His eminence[365] has written wisely [giving] a number of proofs that even in *Hallel* they [*i.e.* the Rabbis] taught[366] that only in the place where they customarily repeat[367] is [repeating] permitted and also what is written in *Berakhot* regarding "*Shema, Shema*[368]" is like "*Modim, Modim*[369]" which, they taught, is shameful. And even

363. The date corresponds to February 26, 1875.

364. Poesing (sometimes Boesing in German, or Pezinok in Slovak) is located in Slovakia, near Bratislava. At the time of this communication, the population of this Jewish community totaled less than 400 people.

365. That is, the questioner, Rabbi Aaron Wilheim.

366. Cf. *b. Suk.* 38b. The rule to follow local custom in repeating words and phrases in *Hallel* is encoded in the *Shulhan Arukh*, OH, 422:4.

367. The example being *Hallel*.

368. That is, repeating the word *Shema*. *m. Ber.* 5:3 teaches: "Someone who says '*Modim, Modim*' is silenced" since it appears that he is acknowledging two divinities and the Talmud, Berakhot 33b, end, applies the analogy that saying "*Shema, Shema*" is tantamount to saying "*Modim, Modim*."

369. The printed text reads: "*Milta, Milta.*" The emendation is mine.

though they do not silence him while he is in the act [of repeating words], they must reprove him [afterwards] so that he does not do this foul thing again. The men of the Great Assembly, of blessed memory, invest each and every word with a specific mystery and anyone who adds, detracts. This is his opinion in brief.

And all his words are correct. To me this behavior is also bad: new ways introduced lately. And the Ga'on, author of *Tevu'at Shor*, in his book *Bekhor Shor*, in the section on *Rosh Hashanah*, p. 16,[370] explicates the verse and writes extensively there on the shame of these things and how it is the obligation of every rabbi who has the power to eliminate them. This evil—to add and repeat things—is new. According to the law, it appears to me to be forbidden on five grounds.

From "Do not add." For we learn from Rosh Hashanah 28b that a *kohen* who says at the time of the [Priestly] Blessing ["May the God of your fathers] add to you[r numbers] a thousand fold" violates the verse that says: "Do not add to the word." And from the verse that forbids adding we learn that it is also forbidden to add even a letter or refrain . . . and we learn by analogy from this that we have no license to add anything that was not formulated by the Sages, of blessed memory . . .

And in *Abudraham*, and the *Kol Bo* and in *Orhot Hayim* and also in the *Tur* in several places, it is explained that most prayers and blessings totaled a precise number of words and letters (*Cf. Tur*, Orah Hayim 112, 114, 186, 582 and in 51 and 53) . . . And anyone who adds, detracts. Prayers and blessings are all measured out by number, and it is forbidden to change the formula established by the rabbis. And even if this does not fit the scriptural prohibition of "adding," it surely violates the rabbinic prohibition, and all that the rabbis enjoined is tantamount to a scriptural prohibition.

If [words are] added to the *Kedushah* or similar [prayer], it is as if he is speaking falsehoods to God since at the beginning of the *Kedushah* we say: "We sanctify Your Name," and so on, "Just as it is sanctified in the heavens above" yet he is saying other words!

In my humble opinion, [repeating words] is like an interruption: a hiatus in completing the blessing. And we hold according to the ruling in [*Shulhan Arukh*] Orah Hayim 104:5

---

370. The printed text uses the two Hebrew letters, *yod* and *vav*, to numerically represent sixteen. Apparently Rabbi Schick did not worry about the fact that these letters might be seen to represent a name of God.

that if he delayed in completing the blessing, he must go back to the beginning, and certainly if he talked . . . This also applies to those cantors who unnecessarily double words in the middle of prayers. This certainly is an interruption and they must go back and repeat, in my humble opinion.

Regarding those who sing *Kaddish* and *Kedushah*,[371] the sages, of blessed memory, applied to them the midrash that has the Torah complain to God that it[372] has been made into an instrument by his children. See *Turei Zahav*, Orah Hayim 560:5. [What is inappropriate] in the taverns is surely [inappropriate] in holy places[373] during prayer where prayer is made into song.[374] This diminishes holiness and thus ought not to be done.

And further, as the sages of blessed memory noted Malachi's complaint: "Present it now to your governor. Will he be pleased with you?". . . Similarly here: if he makes some petition to God and repeats the words twice or thrice, will God hear his voice or respond to his petition? . . .

If the *hazzan* who sings is God-fearing in his heart and heeds the rebuke and does not abandon what is right and does what is forbidden, he may sing sweetly and with a pleasant voice without repeating words. And it would be proper for his honor[375] to tell the *hazzan* nicely yet directly to stop doing it and to speak to the congregation in a heartfelt way that they should no longer want or desire it. For the defender shall become the prosecutor, God forbid, and it is possibly like the fulfillment of a commandment by a trespass . . .

And it is upon you, members of the congregation of Poesing, May God protect it, not to take notice of other places where something like this is done with no one—in our sinfulness—to prevent them. Since I have already explained to you so that in your hearts you will understand that this is inappropriate to do and there is no allowance to do it. And know, therefore, before whom you stand, said the sages of blessed memory. And those who listen shall be triply blessed and God will be with

371. At a celebratory meal or in a banquet hall.

372. Just as the Torah should not be used for profane purposes, neither should prayer.

373. That is, in synagogues.

374. When cantors repeat words of prayer to fit with a musical scheme and highlight their talents, making prayer much like popular songs, they devalue prayer. Rabbi Schick reasons that if such singing is ruled inappropriate in places where popular songs are usually heard, then such singing is certainly inappropriate in synagogues.

375. That is, Rabbi Aaron Wilheim.

them to sustain the truth as much as is possible and the pleasant words of the wise are heard and may his strength be assured.

The words of the undersigned who seeks his peace, the in-significant[376] Moshe Schick of Brezove.

Hungary: Nineteenth Century

Rabbi Moses ben Samuel Schreiber (1762–1839) was a child prodigy. By the age of thirteen, he was delivering well-received public discourses. His formative years were spent in Frankfurt—the city of his birth—and in the neighboring city of Mainz. His proficiency was in Talmud. Yet he also learned astronomy, geometry, and history. After serving in a series of relatively minor positions, he accepted an appointment as Rabbi of Bratislava (Pozsony, in Hungarian; Pressburg, in German) in 1806. His first wife died childless in 1812, and shortly thereafter married the widowed daughter of Rabbi Akiva Eger. His *yeshiva* in Bratislava attracted as many as five hundred students, many of whom went on to become the rabbinic leaders of central Europe. (That institution continues in its post-Holocaust location of Jerusalem.) Rabbi Schreiber's most important literary legacy is a collection of more than 1,000 responsa published posthumously under the title *Hatam Sofer* (*Seal of the Scribe*), *sofer* being the Hebrew equivalent of Schreiber (scribe). The word Hatam is reputed to be an acronym for *Hiddushei Torat Moshe* (The Torah Novellae of Moses). His children, who were also rabbis, continued to use the surname *Sofer* in all their published works. Negotiations with the Slovak leader Josef Tiso allowed for the construction of a concrete mausoleum that now encases his burial site on the left bank of the Danube River near Bratislava Castle. The Old Cemetery in which he was originally buried was partially destroyed during the construction of a road tunnel and tram station.

Three responsa follow. In the first responsum, Rabbi Schreiber considers a case wherein a local rabbi dismissed a cantor for cause—moral turpitude, including adultery, theft, drunkenness, and bigamy. Each of these charges is amply justified by reliable witnesses as well as the cantor's own admission (after being beaten for his misbehavior). On legal grounds, the *Hatam Sofer* rules that although there were only single witnesses to each sinful act, as a matter of Jewish law, the testimonies combine. Even so, he argues, any one of these acts would have been serious

376. Rabbi Schick is not insignificant at all. He follows the stylistic pattern that requires even the greatest authority to demonstrate a modicum of modesty.

enough for dismissal on the grounds that it violates the mishnaic requirement of good character. Equally important, Rabbi Schreiber affirms that
a cantor may never be dismissed on the basis of unsubstantiated rumors.

The second responsum regarding what clothing is suitable for a cantor actually becomes a question on the relative merits of the Sephardic
and the Ashkenazic modes of prayer. In nineteenth-century Germany,
it was neither remarkable nor confusing for the prayer leader to use one
mode and the congregation another. While the Sephardic mode seems
preferable, Ashkenazi Jews should retain their own tradition. With regard to clothing, it is always good to be careful.

The third responsum supplements the first. It is the curious case of
the cantor's fiancée, who claims that she gave birth to his child, which was
conceived before they were married and while she was living in another
city. This premarital coitus is grounds for his dismissal. Rabbi Schreiber
suspects her motives and bemoans the regrettable trend of sexual loose-
ness. Yet concomitantly, he confirms the custom of a standard three-year
tenure for rabbis and cantors, even though logic suggests longer-term
contracts would be preferred. During the term of tenure, a cantor may
not be dismissed. But once the term expires, the cantor must fulfill all
the requirements of good character or risk renewal. Of particular note
are the disparaging remarks he makes about cantors in general. Reflected
in this responsum is the attitude that all contemporary cantors are essentially alike: moral failures whose egos exceed some limited musical talent.

She'elot U'Teshuvot Hatam Sofer, Orah Hayim, No. 11: Grounds for Dismissing a Cantor

May there be much peace from Heaven and good long life to
my honorable colleague, the great and scholarly rabbi known
everywhere, the crown of Torah, our rabbi and teacher Shalom
Ullman,[377] (May his light shine!) head of the rabbinical court
and head of the holy community of Lachenbach, (May God
protect it!).

In the matter of Yosef Makhov Holtaya[378] who was disqualified from serving as cantor by his honor on the basis of

377. Rabbi Shalom Ullman (1755–1825) was the author of *Divrei Rabbi Shalom*,
published in Vienna in 1826. Both his son and grandson served as rabbis in Lachenbach, now in Austria. Since the eighteenth-century, Jews in Lachenbach have enjoyed
autonomous administration under Prince Esterhazy.

378. It is unusual for respondents to give an actual name. That one is given here is

a letter from three rabbis of the holy communities of Tab,[379] Kemmern,[380] and Zelem.[381] I looked carefully into the reports of the rabbis and their testimony and I reviewed all sides of the complaint and found no grounds to grant a dispensation for him to serve as a prayer leader since, according to them, he committed adultery, stole, committed various other abominations any one of which would have been sufficient to disqualify him let alone in combination.

Rabbi Shreiber goes on to analyze two seemingly conflicting paragraphs in Section 53 of the *Shulhan Arukh*. According to Rabbi Moses Isserles's gloss on paragraph 25, a cantor may not be dismissed on the basis of unsubstantiated claims like being caught with a non-Jewish woman. But according to Rabbi Elijah ben Hayyim,[382] cited in Rabbi Abraham Abele Ha-Levi Gumbiner's commentary[383] on paragraph 4, even an individual can disqualify a cantor if the cantor's malfeasance is persistent. Rabbi Schreiber considers resolving the conflict by reasoning that each deals with a separate case. Paragraph 25 deals with a cantor who is acceptable to the entire congregation who may not be removed on the basis of unsubstantiated claims even if persistent. Paragraph 4 deals with a case where a minority objects to being served by a cantor with a compromised reputation. But Rabbi Schreiber rejects this distinction on the basis of an opinion attributed to Rabbenu Simhah,[384] from which he infers that in a case where the malfeasance was unclear, yet some individual argued for the cantor's removal by virtue of a rumor, the cantor may be removed. Further, Rabbi Schreiber reasons by analogy. In the case of divorce, a rumor is warrant enough to divorce a woman even against her will. The same should be true with a cantor.

> . . . Let us return to the case before us: must we disqualify the above mentioned [cantor] on account of the persistent and serious rumor that he was caught with a woman—even if she were not a married woman (this fact was not specified by the

---

probably a testament to the severity of the scandal.

379. Located in Hungary, approximately 150 kilometers southeast of Pressburg.

380. Located in Germany, fifty kilometers north-northwest of Nürenberg.

381. Perhaps Zell am Main, in Bavaria, is intended here.

382. Rabbi Elijah ben Hayim (1530–1617) was highly regarded by Rabbi Akiva Eiger.

383. Gumbiner, *Magen Avraham*, subparagraph 6.

384. Luria, *She'elot U'Teshuvot MaHaRShaL*, No. 20.

witnesses) . . . and that rumor has persisted since the incident, as explained at length in the letter written by the illustrious rabbi of the holy community of Zeze[385] on what was communicated to him from Tapinara.[386] The rumor that circulated about him [originated] from three men who found him naked and sequestered with a woman (—as is explained in the words of the illustrious rabbi of Tab). There is one valid and righteous witness who testifies before us that he himself was present at the spot where he (*i.e.* the cantor) was caught with the woman. And there is also an admission from [the cantor] himself, as the illustrious rabbi of Zeze[387] said, that when they beat him,[388] he said 'What good will your beating do. I did it and would do again what I want in my heart to do.' Hence, for all these reasons, he is disqualified from being a prayer leader even in the absence of any objector for how can we be silent? And certainly a man like this could be disqualified with even one [objector]. Should he (*i.e.* the cantor) say that he would repent [and reform] from now on, we do not believe him since this is the repentance of a trickster, *Cf. Responsa Rabbenu Asher,*[389] Section 58, No. 4.

But for the case before us, we do not need all this. We uphold [the rule] that 'testimony combines,'[390] even to divorce a woman from her husband, see Bet Samuel, Section 11, sub-section 13, and most certainly here. Do we not have two witnesses to adultery and two witnesses to theft (the illustrious rabbi of the holy community of Tab received [the testimony of] a witness to adultery and the illustrious rabbi of Kemmern added that he frequented brothels there)? These are the witnesses to adultery. And the illustrious rabbi himself attests to the theft in his city of tin ware from the house of one Jew. And the illustrious rabbi of the holy community of Zeze[391] reported at length on several incidents of theft, as [mentioned] in the words of these aforementioned rabbis, aside from other matters: "wine inflamed him and liquor pursued him,"[392] he does not join in the quorum

---

385. Should be Zellem. See above.

386. I have not been able to identify this location.

387. Should be Zellem. See above.

388. The beating was not to extract a confession, but to punish him. See *b. Kid.* 81a.

389. Rabbi Asher ben Yehiel (1250–1328).

390. The aggregate of separate testimony combines to hold a person liable.

391. Should be Zellem. See above.

392. Cf. Isa 5:11. This is an indication that the cantor in question was frequently drunk. Drunkenness, it seems, is not an excuse for other improprieties.

of ten,[393] he violated the edict of Rabbenu Gershom,[394] and he changed his name so that he could marry a second wife. So from each and every [violation of] law he is disqualified [to serve as a cantor]. Should he ascend [the bimah] on his own accord, they must remove him. And his demoted status cannot be altered until he goes far away to a place they do not know him[395] and he no longer works at being a cantor at all and he fully repents in God's name for a year or two so that he may be healed.

What seemed to me in my humble opinion[396] I wrote to honor God and His Torah, an incontrovertibly true ruling, here, city of Pressburg, Sunday evening, 5 Tishri 5581,[397]

Moshe, the insignificant, Sofer.

She'elot U'Teshuvot Hatam Sofer, Orah Hayim, No. 15: Sephardic or Ashkenazic Nusah?

Greetings to the eminent rabbi, our teacher, Rabbi Abraham Zvi Katz,[398] may his light shine forth!

His letter reached me and, although I do not know him personally, from the content of his writing his scholarship is recognizable and his heart is judged from his question. Someone has bothered him: protesting against anyone wearing woolen clothing[399] coming up to the lectern [to lead prayers] saying that the prayers they recite in the Sephardic mode is superior and anyone wearing wool is not worthy of leading [it].[400] My dear friends: won't you both concede that most of Israel wear these kinds of clothes and have no worry that some linen thread was woven together with them? To be sure, the careful [person] should be called "holy." But [to say that] this one [wearing woolen clothing] is not worthy or appropriate to go to the lectern on account of this [suspicion is wrong]. They (*i.e.* Jewish legal authorities)

393. He does not attend the synagogue regularly.

394. He had married a second wife while still married to his first wife, contrary to the *herem* (ban) against polygyny in Ashkenazic countries imposed by Rabbenu Gershom around the year 1000.

395. Cf. Rabbenu Hananel on the statement of Rabbi Ilai the elder, *b. Hag.* 16a.

396. Rabbi Schreiber follows the style of his predecessors in assuming self-deprecation.

397. September 13, 1820.

398. Identity and location unknown.

399. Suspected to have linen thread interwoven, and thus in violation of the scriptural prohibition against *sha'atnez* (Lev 19:19).

400. The claim is that the superior Sephardic mode of prayer requires a superior level of conduct: one that is beyond suspicion or reproach.

never mentioned such a thing. Even the protester concedes this. Rather, he (*i.e.* the protester) offers an esoteric reason: the Sephardic mode does not tolerate it. I do not know what he is talking about. Perhaps if I heard him directly and [he] showed me his sources I would understand them and could judge between you. But being so vague, he mouths empty words.[401]

Now I have already given my opinion to those who stand before me that thus I have received from my rabbis (Blessed be the memory of the righteous!) specifically my teacher, the learned, pious, holy teacher Rabbi Nathan Adler (Blessed be the name of the righteous!) and the learned, rabbi of all Jews in exile, the amazing [one][402] (of blessed memory) from whose waters I drank (Thanks be to God!) and from whose quarry I hewed, that all modes of prayer are equal one to the other and what in in this, is in that. However, what we lack is someone who knows the specific differences in the prayers we recite as formulated in these modes since they are all intended for the same thing. Just as there is the same style for many prophets yet there are no two prophets who prophesy in the same style, for each style is different from the other yet the same: going up to one place. When the Lamp of God, the Ari,[403] (of blessed memory) listened and searched and formulated (since he knew the content of these things) he arranged in his prayer book everything in its place, revealing the mysteries of the Sephardic mode in that he was Sephardic. And had he been Ashkenazi, or if there lived one who was like him in Ashkenaz, he would have done the same thing with the Ashkenazi prayer book.

Now in the latest generations, those who have come to the divine, secret words of the Ari (of blessed memory) [find they] are sufficient. We have no one to extract the same [secrets] from the Ashkenazic mode. Thus it is good for them to pray from a Sephardic prayer book where the laws and meditations of the Ari (of blessed memory) are clearly marked. Those who pray [in the] Ashkenazic [mode]—though there, too, all is hinted—the worshiper . . . will quickly rush through his words. It is a universal truth that is it more comfortable for people to pray [in the mode] they understand . . .

401. Cf. Job 35:16.

402. Name not mentioned. Most likely a reference to Rabbi Michel Schneur of Mainz, in whose seminary the author studied from 1776–77.

403. Acronym for Our Master, Our Teacher Isaac: referring to the mystic Rabbi Isaac Luria (1534–1572), generally credited with developing a popular version of the Sephardic mode of prayer.

And therefore, my teacher, the learned and most pious, our teacher Rabbi Nathan Adler, (May the memory of the righteous be a blessing!) he himself went to the lectern and prayed in the Sephardic mode with the payer book of the Ari (of blessed memory), as [did] my learned and amazing teacher (May the memory of the righteous be a blessing!). However, when they prayed in the mode of Ari, all of the others who joined in the quorum for prayer prayed in the Ashkenazic mode. Even the son of the learned [rabbi], author of *Minhah Levi*, (May the memory of the righteous be a blessing!) never changed from the Ashkenazic mode. And, after the death of his learned father (May the memory of the righteous be a blessing!) he disbanded his synagogue and prayed in the synagogue of the community of Pressburg, which is a well-known and widespread fact. And all this is predicated on the understanding that anyone who lacks a good reason ought not change our mode that is commanded us. (*Cf. Magen Avraham*, beginning of [Orah Hayyim] Section 68, citing the Jerusalem Talmud. And this is what ARI himself wrote.)

The results of our analysis is that those who pray in the Sephardic mode obviously have come to the divine mystery and enter the esoteric level and know what they are saying have acted well. But those who have not yet reached this [state]—like us—what we pray according to the formulators of Ashkenazic prayer, is heard [by God] as well. It is wrong to say that this prayer differs from her partner and does not allow for woolen clothes.[404] This is nonsense.

Note that I have seen the customs of my teacher, the learned Nathan Adler who, on the holiday of *Sukkot*, did not call up to the Torah as *Levi* someone who ate new grain,[405] since at that time the new barley was harvested before the *omer*,[406] and the Levi *aliyah* on the second day of the festival of Sukkot included: "You shall eat no bread nor parched grain or fresh ears until that very same day that you bring [the offering of your God]"[407] so how can he recite Torah blessings and have read before him

404. That is, does not allow one who prays in the Ashkenazic mode to lead the prayer service.

405. The Talmud (*b. Kid.* 36b) leaves unresolved the dispute over whether or not the law prohibiting eating new grain applies in diaspora. Rabbi Adler held with Maimonides, Laws of Forbidden Foods 10:2, and Karo, *Shulhan Arukh*, Yoreh De'ah 293:2, among others, that the law applies outside of Israel.

406. Beginning the second day of Passover.

407. Lev 23:14.

the scriptural passage?![408] And again, when he drinks wine and liquor and eats his bread dipped in wine vinegar,[409] which according to most authorities is still a scriptural prohibition today! And likewise, during a Sabbatical Year, it is inappropriate to call up to the Torah someone who has not effected a *prozbul*[410] on the eve of the previous New Year at the onset of the Sabbatical Year when "Do not charge interest"[411] is read . . .

In the same manner as these [examples], it is worthy for the pious to take care. But not to pray while wearing woolen clothing is nothing to be taken into consideration. If he cannot substantiate his claim or reveal to me his secrets, I must affirm the truth as it is. And He whose name is Truth will guide me along the path to choose.

I sign with a blessing,

Moshe, the insignificant, Sofer, of[412] Frankurt-am-Main.

She'elot U'Teshuvot Hatam Sofer, Orah Hayyim, No. 205: Grounds for Dismissing a Cantor

Greetings and all the best to the great and important, the learned rabbi, the sharp minded, our teacher, Rabbi Solomon, may his name shine forth, head of the rabbinical court of the holy city of Helischtabe,[413] may God protect it!

The seal of his holy hand[414] has reached me and today I am learning,[415] so in short: in the case of the cantor whose fiancée gave birth and she claims she counted the days and the months precisely when he was with her in the city, despite all this, she has no power to remove him from his established position even though she is the source of a persistent rumor—even though

---

408. It would be hypocritical to honor a person who stands in violation of the very words in the Torah being read.

409. Made from the fermentation of the same forbidden grain.

410. From the Greek *pros boule*: a legal procedure enacted by Hillel the Elder (*m. Shev.* 10:3–4) to enable lenders to collect on debts that would otherwise be remitted during the Sabbatical Year (Deut 15:1–6).

411. Deut 15:2.

412. Not "in Frankfurt," since he left that city in 1782, when Rabbi Nathan Adler was still alive, and he refers to his mentor as having died.

413. I have not been able to identify this location.

414. That is, his letter.

415. Preoccupied with his learning, Rabbi Schreiber has little time to devote to a lengthier response.

she counted the days and months perhaps she made herself free
to all[416] because she had her eyes on him since they both were
in the same city,[417] see *Gittin* 89a. Further, if we do not say 'you
will not leave our father Abraham a single son'[418] we would be
lending a hand to all the morally dissolute. If, however, there
are witnesses that when he was in her city he secretly lodged
under her roof—like many of the morally dissolute do today, in
our great sinfulness—then we surely have a good assessment.
And granted there is no warrant to remove him on the basis of
this supposition, there is justification not to hire him in the first
place, which may be deduced from what Rabbi [Joseph Karo]
wrote, [*Shulhan Arukh*,] Orah Hayyim, No. 32, that he removed
him on the basis of an unlawful complaint yet, in any case, since
he was removed, it was as if his contract is restarted and he
would not be hired.

Rabbi Abraham Gumbiner[419] hinted at this in Section 53
[in the case] there [when a cantor was removed] during his
term—though his removal was not according to the law and was
null and void and the original contract was in effect—nevertheless, he ruled that 'once removed, never restored,' which would
certainly be true in this case where his term expired. To hire
him anew would not be right in that he is not a man who others can rely on: he is a disgraced rebel[420] who should go out by
himself.[421]

Indeed, I have already written[422] that it is customary to set
a three-year term for rabbinic contracts and subjugation is not
permanent. For who has ever heard that a rabbi or other such
[professionals] would accept a position far away and uproot his
settled household:[423] his wife and children, and go elsewhere for

416. That is, appear promiscuous.

417. Cf. *b. Mak.* 23b. Although she might have calculated the dates, we have no
reason to presume she did not consort with another man at the same time. So while
her claim is an admission of promiscuity—she had sexual relations before marriage—
it is a denial of infidelity.

418. In *b. Git.* 89a: "a single daughter," that is, deny the efficacy of the report. But
the point is the same: everyone is susceptible to false reports, especially those that
cover up personal misconduct.

419. In *Magen Avraham*, his commentary on the *Shulhan Arukh*.

420. Having violated the rule restricting sexual relations to marriage.

421. Cf. Exod 21:3. That is, without renewal.

422. Schreiber, *She'elot U'Teshuvot Hatam Sofer*, OH, No. 206. The printed order is
not chronological.

423. Literally: "well fed horses." Cf. Jer 5:8.

only three years only afterwards to move again? God forbid to even think of such a thing! But the custom of Israel is law.[424] To the advantage of the rabbi (and subjugates[425]), he has the option if he wants to go elsewhere after three years, even though other workers who are considered irreplaceable do not have the option to back out during their terms [of employment] and this term is perpetual. He, in any other case, may opt out after three years, the reason for this being that he is forbidden for hiring himself out for more than six years—and there are those who say no more than three years—for otherwise he would be [worse off than] a Hebrew slave (Cf. Rabbi Shabbetai Ha-Kohen, [Shulhan Arukh,] Hoshen Mishpat 333, subparagraph 170) . . .

This being the case, here as well, if a cantorial contract is similarly construed, it is like 'during his term' wherein he may not be dismissed. But if they stipulated with him explicitly that his term expires after three years and then either party may back out and a contract with a new term is required, we do not accept him when there are refuting witnesses[426] that he cohabited with her. So it appears to me.

This is all according to the law. But if his eminence[427] sees that this [ruling] would increase controversy—let him relent.[428] Even without this, these days—even during the Days of Awe—one who has put his hand on his chin[429] and shouts with a pleasant voice as if God will hear his prayer does not fulfill the obligation of others, so what difference does it make to us or him or them if they push him aside and take another in his place? They (i.e. cantors) are all alike, in our sinfulness. And in our mishnah at the end of the tractate Kiddushin,[430] it is the mule drivers who are mostly considered [wicked]. And the scholar, our teacher, Rabbi Jabob Emden (of blessed memory) wrote that in his days we should include most bankers. And I say in our day these cantors should be included. One of my teachers, the learned rabbi, Rabbi Mendel Lillig (May the memory of the

424. Thus a three-year employment agreement is standard.

425. That is, those ritual professionals subject to contractual obligations.

426. The witnesses refute the cantor's claim that he did not cohabit with the woman in question.

427. That is, the questioner.

428. Rabbi Schreiber gives the questioner the rabbinical discretion to set aside the ruling if its application would cause dissension in his community.

429. This is a description of a cantor striking a casual pose during prayer.

430. m. Kid. 4:14. In every generation, it seems, there was a class of professionals who were held out for particular disdain.

righteous be a blessing!) a judge and rabbi of the seminary in Frankfort-am-Main, would regularly joke about the old, foolish king who, in his obvious senility was seated on a three-legged chair: one, cantors who conducted all the prayers of Israel to [a place] outside the camp, like disqualified sacrifices (May the Compassionate One protect us!); two, ritual slaughterers who provide the community with non-kosher meat; three, scribes who produce defective *tefillin* and *mezuzot*—yet the king was satisfied.[431] May God take pity on us and establish his peace and peace for all Israel. May the festival of Passover be celebrated with rejoicing!

These are my words with deep affection, Thursday, 13 Nisan 5599,[432]

Moses, the insignificant, of Frankfurt-am-Main

Poland: Nineteenth Century

She'elot U'Teshuvot Avnei Nezer, Orah Hayyim, No. 30: The Extent of a Familial Defect

Born in 1838, Rabbi Abraham Bornsztain of Sochaczew (a suburb of Warsaw) was a close disciple of the Kotzker Rebbe, Rabbi Menahem Mendl Morgenstern, whose daughter he married. He was the founder of the Sochatchover Hasidic dynasty. A scholar of considerable renown who served as the head of the rabbinical court, his written answers to questions on Jewish law were published after his death in 1910 in seven massive volumes.

In this short response, Rabbi Bornsztain acknowledges that the cantor's employability is circumscribed by good character and any assessment of good character extends to consideration of the conduct of family members. In other words, Rabbi Bornsztain accepts the principle that any cantor may be dismissed or rejected on the basis of the bad conduct of a family member. To put it somewhat differently, an indiscretion committed by the family member of a cantor is considered a defect in a cantor himself.

What Rabbi Bornsztain adds to the discussion is that any defect *qua* defect must be one for which there is a broad consensus among Jewish

---

431. Rabbi Lillig bemoans the fact that incompetent cantors, cheating butchers, and fraudulent scribes are undermining Jewish communities, while the rabbis, like the foolish and senile king, remain oblivious.

432. March 28, 1839.

legal authorities that such a defect would be disqualifying. Otherwise, the defect in the family member is not strong enough to bar a cantor from employment, especially when the cantor in question possesses a good voice.

Curiously, the responsum does not consider the worthiness of the cantor whose brother abandoned Judaism.

> To the Holy Community of Blashke,[433] May God protect it!
>
> Regarding the question they have about prayer leaders for Rosh Hashanah:
>
> They have two [cantors][434] who are Torah observant and God fearing and another two who are equally observant and God fearing with better voices but [each] with a family defect. The father of one was a ritual slaughterer in two towns and two rabbis dismissed him because his knives did not meet their approval. He went to another town in the province of Friesen and slaughtered there. The second has a full biological brother who became an apostate (May God protect us!). Whom should they take for the Days of Awe?
>
> It seems to me that they should take the one with the better voices. To be sure, the prayer of a righteous man who is the son of a righteous man is better heard [by God].[435] However, there is a plausible argument that can be made for the one who slaughtered in Friesen. It is well known that the matter of sharpening knives varies from one community to its neighbor and the knives [used] in Lithuania we would not permit *ab initio*. And I have heard that in Friesen they slaughter with thick [bladed] knives and it is conceivable that in Friesen his knife was good. What to us is considered a defect is not a defect there. His son should not be penalized for that.

Ukraine: Nineteenth Century

The Kossover Rebbe, Rabbi Menahem Mendel Hager, established his dynasty in Galicia (today, Ukraine). He wrote a well-known commentary on the Torah entitled *Ahavat Shalom*, from which the following passage

---

433. Blashke is located in Moravia, what is now the northeast part of the Czech Republic.

434. Apparently, the cantorial duties were divided between a pair of professionals. The exact division of responsibilities is not indicated.

435. Cf. *b. Yev.* 64a.

is taken. His descendants established a dynasty in Vizhnitz. Rabbi Hager died in 1825.

Ahavat Shalom, Va-ethanan (cited by Rabbi Gedaliah Felder, Yesodei Yeshurun, Volume 1, p. 42): The Power of the Cantor

> The cantor is the conduit through which pass all influences. Therefore, the rabbis (of blessed memory) use the expression "he who passes before the lectern" (*b. Ber.* 34) and not "he who stands by the lectern" because "to pass" signifies the passage of influences. Thus the cantor must be filled with the best of all kinds of spiritual qualities: [knowledge of] Torah, prayer, good deeds, repentance, and a broken heart. With these he remains in constant connection with God, who receives prayer. The cantor must reciprocally connect with the collective [fellowship of] Israel so that he becomes the mediator between Israel and its heavenly Father and binds them together. For his reason, the cantor has the power to fulfill the religious obligations of the congregation for the entire congregation is invested in him and he is invested in them.

Belarus: Nineteenth Century

Rabbi Yekhiel Mikhel ben Rabbi Aaron Ha-Levi Epstein (1829–1908) was born in Belarus. He was the brother-in-law of Rabbi Naftali Tzvi Yehudah Berlin, of the famous *yeshiva* in Volozhin. After studying locally, he took his first rabbinic position in 1854. Nine years later, he was appointed the rabbi of Navahrudak (formerly, Nowogrodek) where he served as a congregational rabbi until his death. His magnum opus was the *Arukh Ha-Shulhan*—intended to update the *Shulhan Arukh* published three hundred years earlier—which was published serially beginning in 1884. His rulings were particularly valued because of his intimate familiarity with "Jews in the pews."

Rabbi Epstein faithfully transmits the rules regarding the cantor, but with an admitted resignation to the fact that the earlier rules have been largely ignored because of changed circumstances and general disinterest. The role of the cantor has transmuted from that of prayer expert who led prayers every day to a musical functionary and entertainer with far fewer pulpit duties. Note the contradiction in Paragraph 5 in which Rabbi Epstein claims that a cantor is unnecessary because of the high

THE CANTOR IN JEWISH LAW

level of competence of Jews who no longer need someone to fulfill their obligation while, at the same time, he bemoans the fact that most contemporary congregants are incompetent. His ambivalence toward cantors is matched by his depreciation of the Jewish community acting on what Jews think rather than on what Jewish law demands, and exceeded by his acknowledgment of rabbinic impotence. Noteworthy is his minimalism: the only qualification of any importance today is a cantor's piety

Arukh Ha-Shulhan, Orah Hayyim 53:5:
The Changing Role of the Cantor

In this section, both the *Tur* and the *Shulhan Arukh* wrote the laws regarding a prayer leader. It is the fact that in the days of our ancestors there was a permanent prayer leader for weekdays, Sabbaths, and festivals. And this was very good because he knew well the order of prayer, he did not elongate [the time of the prayer service], he did not mispronounce, and he was a God-fearing man. But nowadays, in our sinfulness, in all our lands [of residence] there is no permanent daily prayer leader at all. Rather, random individuals go to the lectern as they wish— especially since the custom has spread that someone mourning the death of a father or mother or someone commemorating a *yahrzeit* leads prayers—even when he is an ignoramus and cannot distinguish between his right hand and his left and does not know the meaning of the words and is unfit to lead prayers and the prayers are all distorted: one mispronouncing, another skipping. This is great darkness and chaos! But this has spread even generations earlier and we have no power to eradicate it. Yet even from the very nature of prayer itself: we no longer have a need for a cantor since we are all experts and we no longer need a cantor to fulfill our obligation [for prayer] when each of us prays individually.

Paragraph 6

After listing the ideal qualifications of a prayer leader,[436] Rabbi Epstein concedes the rule that absent the person who epitomizes all the virtues "let them choose the best available congregant," adding:

and if there was a choice between an elderly ignoramus with a good voice who is favored by the congregation and a

436. Cf. *b. Ta'an.* 17b.

thirteen-year-old who understands what he is saying but lacks a good voice, the minor is preferred. But, in our great sinfulness, in these times, public opinion holds sway, especially in canto-rial[437] matters, there is no power to constrain them (it), and may our God Who is merciful pardon our iniquity and not destroy us.[438]

Paragraph 13

After stating the laws governing the proper conduct of services by the cantor and following the rule that "anyone who prolongs the prayer service acts wrongfully in that this is an imposition on the congregation," he comments:

> And there is much to say about cantors[439] today, in our vast sinfulness, however "just as one is commanded to say [that which will be obeyed, one is commanded not to say that which will not be obeyed]."[440] And it is forbidden to repeat words.

Paragraph 21

But these days when everyone prays individually and there is no community cantor at all who leads prayers on weekdays and even on Sabbaths the cantor prays only occasionally, and only on *Rosh Hashanah* and *Yom Kippur* and the festivals does the cantor pray and his purpose is [only] musical, and many of the city's residents do not pray at all in the synagogue when the cantor prays, and the cantor is obligated to serenade the bride and groom before the wedding ceremony and to entertain at a circumcision and perform other such functions, it is obvious that an individual has no power to dismiss [the cantor], not even a minority of the congregation has the power to dismiss. But when the majority of the community wants to dismiss the cantor, the minority cannot prevent them [from doing so]. And they pay him from the community chest. And these individuals must bear the financial responsibility [should the cantor be dismissed wrongfully] unless the minority can bring proof that the cantor is unacceptable for then the law is on their side.

Paragraph 32

---

437. *Hazzanut*, in Hebrew.

438. Ps 20:10.

439. *Hazzanim*, in Hebrew.

440. *b. Yeb.* 65b, based on Leviticus 19:17.

... and we find the title *"hazzan"* [mentioned] in the *Mishnah* with regard to several matters. In the first chapter of *Shabbat*,[441] Rabbi Ovadiah mi-Bertinoro defined *"hazzan"* as "teacher of small children," and in chapter three of *Makkot*[442] he defined [*"hazzan"*] as "a functionary, a marshal of the court." And in the fifth chapter of *Tamid*,[443] he also defined [it] as "functionaries," see there. And the *Arukh*, under the heading *"hazzan,"* defined *"hazzan"* as public prayer leader,[444] derived from the root 'hozeh,' [meaning,] that he must see how he is to read the Torah." Nowadays, the title *"hazzan"* and "public prayer leader" are one and the same; he is the one exclusively appointed to pray and sing on some Sabbaths and Festivals and Rosh Hashanah and Yom Kippur and the congregation prays individually without them needing him to fulfill their obligation [to pray]. Therefore, we need not be too particular with them.[445] In any case, it is an imperative that he be God-fearing, and if not, his prayer is an abomination that provokes accusers, may God protect us!

Russia: Twentieth Century

Modern Liturgy in Russian Synagogues: Rules for a Proper Cantor

Pinchas Minkowsky was born in the Ukraine in 1859. His mother was a descendant of the great scholar, Rabbi Yom Tov Lippman Heller. Minkowsky studied the cantorial arts informally with his father—a noted cantor in his own right—and formally in Vienna. He married at sixteen, and at the age of eighteen he was appointed the successor to Cantor Nissen Spivak in Kishinev. In 1880, he ascended to the position of primary cantor of the prestigious Choral Synagogue. He also spent three years as the celebrated cantor of New York's Kahal Adat Jeshurun synagogue. But his longest tenure was in the Broder Shul in Odessa where he served as cantor for thirty years. He died in Boston in 1924, and is buried in Philadelphia.

---

441. Mishnah 3.
442. Mishnah 12.
443. Mishnah 3.
444. *Sheli'ah zibbur*, in Hebrew.
445. That is, in holding them to the accepted standards or qualifications.

Despite his personal success, Minkowsky was concerned about what he perceived to be a decline in the position of the cantorate as well as his colleagues' lack of professionalism and religious authenticity. Thus, chapter 25 of his multivolume Yiddish work rendered *Modern Liturgy in Russian Synagogues,* published in 1910, includes eighteen steps (*Takkanot*) intended to raise the standards of cantors in tsarist Russia just prior to the October Revolution. Of the eighteen *Takkanot,* some focused on the organization of cantors as well the establishment of a placement office through a centralized cantors' union. Others focused on an educational curriculum to win over youth to the appreciation of liturgical music. But most of the eighteen *Takkanot* dealt with the conduct of the cantor within the synagogue and community.

Minkowsky was not the first cantor to posit rules for cantors. Rabbi Judah Lieb Minden of Zelichow, Poland, served as a cantor for the German and Dutch communities of Minden and Aptrud. In his *Shirei Yehudah* (*Songs of Judah*), 27b, published in 1696, he criticizes cantors who perform in a theatrical and operatic manner, making "the sound of great waters" (Ps 93:4). In his *Te'udat Shlomo* (*The Attestation of Solomon,* Offenbach, 1718) Cantor Solomon Lipschutz was averse to the artificial techniques cantors grew accustomed to use in order to achieve their desired vocal effects. And in his ethical will, *Yesh Nohlin* (*There Are Those Who Bequeath,* Lvov, 1849) 16b, Cantor Abraham ben Shabbetai Horowitz writes:

> And on Sabbaths and Festivals those cantors who are accustomed to adding many tunes and lengthen words and letters until they become unrecognizable and meaningless are not behaving well . . . extending the melodies is reason to talk and this is unworthy, it also may result in reciting *Shema* after the correct time . . . it is a practice that ought to be arrested . . .

There are three factors that make Minkowsky's rules historically unusual and noteworthy. First, a cantor of international renown and considerable influence generated these rules. Second, they are more expansive and extensive than the critiques of Minden, Lipschutz, and Horowitz. And third, Minkowsky intended the rules he formulated to be widely disseminated.

The eleven rules that follow are translated—with slight modification—from the 1910 Yiddish original by Rabbi Solomon F. Rybak and published in the *Journal of Jewish Music and Literature,* Volume VI, 1983.

Section 1

The person who carries the responsibility of leading the liturgical service is firstly a prayer leader[446] and afterwards an artist. He can be the greatest performer but his art must be treated with secondary importance. Primarily, he must remain a prayer leader.

Section 2

In order to enrich the service, cantors must set aside their provincialism. They must begin to educate themselves in learning and music. They must study Hebrew[447] and musical literature at least two hours each day. Since little of the music is written in Hebrew, a cantor must study one of the modern languages in order to develop in it musical expertise.

Section 3

A cantor who desires to become a distinguished prayer leader must know all the laws pertaining to the service. For this purpose he must study the *Shulhan Arukh*[448] before each holiday and for all the various religious occasions during the year. He will, thereby, know all the laws relating to the prayers for that particular day. He will by this preparation avoid being openly ridiculed[449] for errors and no disputes will occur in the community because of his actions.

Section 4

The cantor must realize that he isn't only a performer but also a worshiper. He should, therefore, when not singing, pray carefully by pronouncing the words with the precise accent and by not slurring or swallowing the silent sections of prayer before the musical composition begins.

Section 5[450]

446. Rybak prefers to leave the Hebrew *shel'iah zibbur*—rendered here and elsewhere as "prayer leader"—untranslated. The meaning is clear: the cantor is a religious functionary who fulfills the ritual duties of the congregation in prayer.

447. Minkowsky describes a situation in which even synagogue professionals were functionally deficient, thus challenging the idea that European Jewry of this historical period were generally learned.

448. Popularly called the "Code of Jewish Law," the *Shulhan Arukh* was written by Rabbi Joseph Karo and published in 1565.

449. No doubt a circumstance of which he was aware, if not personally subject to.

450. Minkowsky notes that when the cantor's ego inflates, two conditions result.

The cantor must always be the first and last at prayer. He must wait for the public—never allowing the public to wait for him. When [on *Shabbat*] the first cantor concludes [with the words] "on a high and exalted throne," the senior cantor with the choir must be ready to begin [with the words] "He who abides eternally." And if he allows the public to wait, he is not a worthy person and even less of a distinguished cantor. The cantor must also not rush to leave the podium for his seat following the repetition of the *Amidah* in order to accept the congregation's handshakes of approval for his concert. The synagogue will only become a public square. It is not proper to acknowledge the public's gestures of approval until the conclusion of the entire service.

Section 6

A distinguished cantor should not wave his hands or head nor practice any theatrical mimicking during the service.[451] These special effects belong in a circus or theater, but not in the synagogue. It is appropriate to refer to the talmudic ruling: "Whoever lifts a hand is considered wicked"[452] or as the Bible teaches us: "The voice is the voice of Jacob and the hands are the hands of Esau."[453] Our power is in our mouths. The cantor should not talk to nor joke with the choir. He must remain diligent at all times. Dr. Nightingale[454] in Vienna used to say: "A good doctor must first be a good person." I will tell you that a distinguished cantor must first be a distinguished person. If a cantor wants to be received by the community as a distinguished cantor and not

First, the cantor sees himself as a person of privilege to whom special allowances apply. Second, the cantor sees himself as a prima donna who basks in the adulations of the public. Punctuality, humility, and propriety, however, are the appropriate Jewish values that ought to be cultivated, particularly in religious leaders.

451. Rabbi Abraham Yitzhaq Sperling (*Sefer Ta'amei Ha-Minhagim*, 53) justifies the custom of many cantors who place both hands at the sides of their face when praying.

452. *b. San.* 58b: "Whoever raises his hand against his neighbor even though he did not strike him is considered wicked." Minkowsky deliberately takes this statement out of context transforming a teaching that condemns making threatening gestures into a rule against making any gesture in prayer.

453. Minkowsky applies Genesis 27:22 that speaks of Jacob's subterfuge in claiming the principal blessing that should have gone to his brother. Minkowsky's intent is to suggest that gesticulation in prayer is inappropriate, linking gesticulation with the "hands" of the wicked Esav. Cantorial gesticulation must have been common enough to warrant Minkowsky's harsh condemnation.

454. Identity uncertain. Perhaps this is a reference to the German physician and explorer Dr. Gustav Nachtigal (d. 1885).

as an itinerant singer, he must first honor himself. Setting the note (on which he is to begin the prayer) must also be as quick as possible.

Section 7

A cantor must not repeat any words or complete phrases. It is against Jewish law and contrary to aesthetics. The cantor must get used to saying the word once. Oh, how much Jewish feeling and musical art can be demonstrated together in one word! Our prayers are rich in words and even sometimes too rich. Just as in our daily lives it isn't proper to repeat the same word, how much more distasteful it is to turn a whole liturgy into a babbling presentation.

Section 8

. . . Cantors imitate mainly those who have popular appeal although ignorant and not musical. A little sweetness of voice is sufficient to make anyone a star among the people . . . Whoever truly loves our people must wage war with them by fighting for standards.[455] Be assured that the people will later thank you. . . .[456]

Section 10

Respect each other's position. When there is a dispute in the community concerning a cantor or if they want to discharge an old, weak cantor before the community has provided for him, don't rush to officiate. "Do not profit by the blood of your brother!"[457] Don't take advantage of your friend in his moment of anguish . . .

Section 11

Do not record synagogue compositions on the gramophone.[458] Flee from that terrible development. Take a holy oath not to introduce into the liturgy any melody heard from that modern

455. Surely a daunting task.

456. Minkowsky offers no proof that this is so. Perhaps it is more a hope than an assurance.

457. Lev 19:16, New JPS translation.

458. Minkowsky takes issue with his more famous colleague, Cantor Joseph ("Yossele") Rosenblatt (d. 1933) who, while refusing to appear on stage in operatic love scenes, nonetheless made records of Jewish liturgical music for various American companies that sold in the tens of thousands. His recording career began in 1913 and continued until his death. Rosenblatt also appeared on screen as Al Jolson's dying father in *The Jazz Singer*.

desecration.[459] Do not sing the immoral compositions of Warsaw and Vilna.[460] We are not like the other nations. We have
only prayer and song in the service of our synagogues. Don't
introduce them into the cabarets. . . . [461]

Section 15

Songs from the theater and concerts and all profane modern
songs must be—under all circumstances—kept out of the synagogue service. We must guard the traditional modes of prayer
likes the eyes in our heads for only the traditional prayer modes
unify us in all synagogues. A singer who is not thoroughly
versed in all the synagogue prayer modes,[462] under no circumstances, should be recommended as a cantor in the community.

Belarus: Twentieth Century

Rabbi Yisrael Meir Ha-Kohen Kagan (1839–1933) was born and died
in modern-day Belarus. His mother moved with him to Radin after the
death of her husband and his father. It was in Radin at the age of seventeen that he married the daughter of his stepfather. And, except for a
period of five years when he taught Talmud in Minsk and Washilishok,
it was Radin that became his residence and the site of his world-famous
yeshiva. In addition to his mastery of Talmud and Jewish law, he was an
advocate of ethical living and leader in the (Orthodox) Agudat Israel
movement. He was widely known as the *Hafetz Hayim*, a name derived
from Psalm 34:13 and the title of his ethical tract, first published in 1873,
on the avoidance of gossip and slanderous talk. *Mishnah Berurah*, the
first volume of which was published in 1884, is his contribution to Jewish
legal literature. Both books are avidly studied to this day.

    In this passage, Rabbi Kagan, referring to the responsum of Rab-
benu Asher (Section 6, Number 1)[463] stands it on its head. Rabbenu
Asher rules that when a community has limited funds, a cantor should
be hired ahead of a rabbi unless the rabbi is an exceptional scholar. Rabbi

---

459. Literally, "a desecration of God's name." Cf. Lev 22:32.

460. While contemporary readers assign religious piety to these centers of Jewish
life in Poland, Minkowsky sees them as urban breeding grounds of assimilation.

461. It seems that cantors were regularly performing in secular venues, much to
Minkowsky's dismay.

462. *Nusha-ot* in Hebrew.

463. See above, p. 107.

Joseph Karo accepts this ruling of Rabbenu Asher as normative law.[464] Rather than inferring that the role a cantor performs is so essential to a community that hiring a cantor takes precedence over hiring a rabbi, Rabbi Kagan claims that Rabbenu Asher is actually arguing that a Torah scholar takes precedence over a cantor. Rabbi Kagan's interpretation correlates with the diminished role of trained cantors in smaller Polish Jewish communities in the first third of the twentieth century, along with the increased role of laypeople in leading prayer services. It also corresponds with Rabbi Kagan's perception that in times of general religious decline, the rabbi takes on a more critical role in Jewish communal life.

Mishnah Berurah, Orah Hayyim 53, Bi'ur Halakhah, s.v. Sheliah Zibbur: A Rabbi Over a Cantor

Stemming from a responsum of Rabbenu Asher, a great obligation falls on every community to engage a rabbi who will instruct them in the mitzvot of the Torah and its statutes on how to conduct themselves, so they should not be like the blind groping in the dark. Even if this means that the obligation of prayer will have to be set aside completely for them (because they will be unable to hire anyone to lead them in prayer) the obligation [to hire a rabbi surely] takes precedence, especially when the townspeople are able to pray by themselves. Let those few outlying towns that have no rabbi and proper guide quake and fear in their great sinfulness.[465] For though they hire a ritual slaughterer for their poultry and animals, they still need a proper guide who will instruct them in the laws of the Sabbath and festivals, the difficult and demanding laws of Passover, the laws of ritual immersion . . . and the other laws of the Torah . . .

Of course, this criticism does not apply if the ritual slaughterer is [also] an exceptional scholar, well versed in the Torah, someone who is ordained by the renowned authorities of the land to rule on questions of Jewish law. But [the criticism] certainly does apply to those communities or congregations that engage for hundreds or rubles a cantor renowned as a fine singer so that he should sing for them in a mellifluous voice, when they could hire for the same money both a rabbi and a competent

464. Karo, *Shulhan Arukh*, OH 53:24.

465. These towns that fail to hire a rabbi should fear the punishment that awaits them.

prayer leader[466] who can lead them in prayer on the Sabbath and festivals as is the norm in our land. By so doing, their prayer would be accepted in the heavenly realm on high, unlike now when their engagement of a cantor is not really for Heaven's sake.[467] To this the scriptural verse (Jer 12:8) applies: "She raised her voice against Me, therefore I have rejected her."

Ultimately, [without a rabbi, Jewish life in] the town will deteriorate. Since it has no spiritual guide to lead the people in the ways of God, they will decline in degrees: leading to violating the Sabbath and holy days and eating food on Passover that is not absolutely kosher. They will do who knows how many other forbidden things that are punishable offenses (May God protect us from such people!).

United States: Twentieth Century

The attraction of the operatic stage proved too tempting for some very fine cantors, despite Minkowsky's adamant protestations. Rabbi Israel H. Levinthal (1888–1982), a descendant of a line of illustrious rabbis, a master preacher, author, ardent Zionist, community leader, and rabbi of the Brooklyn Jewish Center for more than sixty years, sent a letter of inquiry to several well-known scholars of Jewish law. He requested guidance on how to respond to the invitation his cantor, Richard Tucker (born Reuben Ticker), received in 1944 to appear with the Metropolitan Opera Company of New York City. Rabbi Levinthal's query and two responses appear below. The first response[468] is that of Rabbi Dr. Solomon Goldman (1893–1953). Like his colleague, Rabbi Levinthal, Rabbi Goldman was a Zionist activist. He served as president of the Zionist Organization of America. He was also a recognized scholar of Jewish law—and a personal friend of Rabbi Levinthal. The second response is that of Rabbi Louis Ginzberg. Rabbi Ginzberg was a renowned talmudic scholar, a descendant of the Vilna Gaon. Born in Kaunas, Lithuania, in 1873, he immigrated to the United States in 1899. Three years later, he was appointed to the faculty of the Jewish Theological Seminary of America, where he taught until his death in 1953. He was the author of seminal works on Talmud, Midrash, and Jewish history.

466. But not a trained cantor.

467. That is, for justifiable religious reasons.

468. I am grateful to Rabbi Elliot Gertel for providing me a copy of the original letter and Rabbi Dr. Goldman's response.

Correspondence between Rabbi Israel Levinthal and
Rabbi Solomon Goldman: May a Cantor Join an Opera Company?

October 12, 1944
Dr. Solomon Goldman
Anshe Emet Synagogue
Pine Grove at Grace
Chicago, Illinois

Dear Sol:[469]
    I know how very precious your time is and I really hate to trouble you with matters of this sort. I have, however, a "she'elah"[470] that I would like to put to you and would very much appreciate your opinion. As a matter of fact, I am writing to a few of our colleagues[471] so that their views may help me formulate my own opinion in this matter.[472]
    The Cantor of our Center has received an offer to appear in important roles at the Metropolitan Opera House. He has been with us now, the second year, and has made a splendid impression upon our congregation. He is an excellent cantor[473] and has done much to improve our services.[474] The members would regret exceedingly his leaving us and they feel that it would be a distinct loss to our synagogue. On the other hand, the question arose, could he in keeping with Jewish law and tradition, serve as cantor and at the same time appear in the opera.[475] If this were an appearance on the theatrical stage, there would, of course, be no question as to their refusal to permit him. Many,

469. Rabbi Levinthal dispenses with the flowery language and protocol typical of earlier response and instead uses a familiar and informal name.

470. *She'elah* is the Hebrew term for "question." More specifically in rabbinic circles, it is a question on religious practice.

471. It is far more usual for a questioner to direct his query to one scholar.

472. This is somewhat disingenuous since it seems that Rabbi Levinthal has already developed an opinion on what is appropriate, as indicated in the next paragraph regarding Sabbath violation.

473. Other than his musical abilities, which must be significant enough to earn an invitation to join an opera company, Rabbi Levinthal does not say wherein lies his excellence.

474. Rabbi Levinthal offers no specific indication on what constitutes that "improvement" to services.

475. Interestingly for the synagogue membership, the question was not whether he must choose between the cantorate and the opera, but whether he could do both simultaneously.

however, feel that the opera itself, is such a high form of art, that it should not be placed on the same plane as the ordinary stage. It is, of course, understood that he would not appear on the Sabbath or that he would do anything that would directly be in violation of Jewish law. The trustees are discussing this matter at the present time but I imagine that I will be approached for my opinion.[476] Before I formulate an opinion, I would like to get your own views on the subject.

Is there, to your knowledge, a direct legal prohibition to a cantor serving in such a capacity?

Would it be contrary to Jewish tradition?

If you feel that it is contrary to Jewish tradition, would you regard this as such a serious breach that would necessitate the rabbi taking a definite stand in this matter?[477]

If I may put to you a personal question—suppose you were faced with such an issue, how would you meet it?

I hope you will forgive me for putting you to this trouble, but I am sure that you can realize how much I need help in such a matter.

The letter continues with some personal pleasantries.

With kindest greetings and all good wishes to you, your wife and children from May and myself,

Cordially yours,

Israel

October 18, 1944
Dr. Israel H. Levinthal
The Brooklyn Jewish Center
667 Eastern Parkway
Brooklyn 13, New York

Dear Israel:

I regret exceedingly that I cannot, at present, give the question you ask in your letter of October 12th the time and thought it merits, particularly from the point of view of Halachah.[478] Briefly, let me say this:

476. As is often the case in congregational life, the rabbi is consulted last rather than first, if at all.

477. Rabbis who take a stand on any matter become vulnerable to criticism and might jeopardize contractual renewal. Thus, avoidance of taking a stand would be to the rabbi's advantage.

478. *Halachah* is the popular term for that which is in accordance with Jewish law.

You are, of course, acquainted with the Shulchan Aruch, 53, 25 where it is enjoined that a cantor be removed from his post if he is singing shirei nacherim. There is a difference of opinion as to the reading there and the meaning of the term. Later authorities concluded that it referred to idolatrous songs (church music). That is the opinion of the Bach.[479] A very late authority interprets it to mean shirei elilim[480] and actually adds if the songs are not specifically devoted to them, namely, the idols, the cantor may sing them, meaning of course that he is not to be removed for doing so. I do not recall, except for some vague impression that Adret[481] does deal with the matter, an early responsum on the question, but then my knowledge of the literature is very limited. I remember having read somewhere that the question arose many years ago in Odessa when the Yiddish theater was first organized. In those days the plays produced were for the most part what we would entitle musical comedies and the Rabbonim would not allow cantors to take part in them. In recent years you undoubtedly recall the decision rendered in the case of the late Cantor Rosenblatt.[482] He was granted special permission to sing in the opera house because of his economic embarrassment at the time. I do not, however, know whether the Rabbis whom he consulted wrote a responsum.

It is hard to say whether a cantor's regular participation in opera would be contrary to Jewish tradition. In talmudic times all art was intimately associated with paganism and in later centuries with the Christian Church. The separation of art from paganism never happened and from Christianity only in the Middle Ages. We can, therefore, understand why the Rabbis frowned on the attendance at theatres and circuses. You will recall that in connection with the latter, some permitted it because it might occasionally afford a Jew the opportunity to

---

479. Rabbi Yoel Sirkis (Poland, 1561–1640) is known by the acronym of his commentary on the *Tur: Bayyit Hadash.*

480. Meaning: idolatrous songs.

481. Rabbi Solomon ben Abraham. See above.

482. According to his son (S. Rosenblatt, *Yossele Rosenblatt: The Story of His Life*, 1954), Rosenblatt saved little, invested unwisely, and spent extravagantly. In a desperate attempt to pay back his creditors for a failed project in 1925, he exhausted himself on the vaudevillian stage. He was offered the lead role as the cantor in *The Jazz Singer,* but refused it on the grounds that he did not want to be filmed singing liturgical pieces in a popular film.

save a human life.[483] Maimonides in his Moreh[484] and in a responsum is as charitable toward singing as was Plato to poets. He ruled it out. On the other hand, I am inclined to believe that the Rabbis of all ages would have prohibited a cantor from making the public rendition of secular music his regular occupation. They looked upon the *sheliah zibbur*[485] as the emissary of the people who was offering their prayer to God. They even gave him precedence over the Rabbi, except where the latter was a recognized scholar.

My personal feeling is that even though the tradition might be said to be indefinite, I would, in our age and environment, rule *le-humra*[486] and if the question were raised in my congregation, I would ask for the resignation of the cantor.

I expect functionaries of the Synagogue to be completely absorbed in Jewish life and thought. If they are gifted with any talent, they should zealously use it for the furtherance of Judaism. The opera has so much to offer by way of popular appeal and applause, and I am apprehensive that the Synagogue would very soon take second place.

The line of demarcation between opera and refined vaudeville has become attenuated in our day and may altogether disappear in a decade or two. At any rate our successors may not be as troubled as we are and extend the heter to suit their day and their whims.

Wagnerian opera is idolatry and Nazism[487] and in this connection I would say about the voice of the cantor what the Rabbis said about the ear of the slave.

There are too many cantors today who have degraded the vocation and made of it vaudeville.[488] Most of them are in the Orthodox Synagogue[489] and if we allow our cantors to go into the opera, I am very much afraid that in a short time these men will contribute to the further degrading of their calling.[490]

---

483. See Rabbi Natan in *Tosef. A. Z.* 2:2.

484. This is a reference to *Moreh Nevukhim*, the *Guide of the Perplexed*. The correct reference is *She'elot U'Teshuvot HaRaMBaM*, No. 224.

485. See introduction for meaning and derivation of this term for cantor.

486. This means "stringently."

487. Writing in 1944, Rabbi Levinthal has vivid and antithetical associations of Richard Wagner and his support for Nazism.

488. It is a standard complaint against cantors in many ages.

489. This is an interesting observation, if true.

490. How exactly this would happen goes unsaid.

If the cantor goes into the opera in one decade, then in the next decade, the Rabbi will allow himself to go on the radio as a commentator or generally for commercial reasons.[491] Allow me to add parenthetically that a number of years ago I turned down quite a substantial offer from a business firm.

I have dictated in haste and not with the serenity and con-secration that *she'elah* deserves, but this, too, is in itself evidence of the degradation of the Rabbinate.

Here some pleasantries in kind are offered.

With kindest regards to you and your dear family, in which Alice joins me, I remain,
Cordially yours,
[Sol]

The Responsa of Professor Louis Ginzberg,[492] No 1: May a Cantor Appear in Major Roles at an Opera House?

October 16, 1944

Dear Doctor Levinthal:

I am in receipt of your letter of October 12, in which you ask my advice whether it would be proper for your Congrega-tion to have its Cantor appear in important roles at the Metro-politan Opera House

There is, of course, no special law incumbent upon a can-tor.[493] He is to be a good Jew, but so also are his Congregants. Yet, while there is no specific prohibition in Jewish law which would prevent a cantor from serving in that synagogue while at the same time appearing in the opera, I do not think that combina-

491. Today rabbis will regularly appear as commentators on television and radio, making their congregants proud rather than upset.

492. This collection was edited by Rabbi David Golinkin and published by the Jew-ish Theological Seminary of America in 1996. The actual responsum appears on p. 75.

493. Rabbi Golinkin understatedly writes: "This is not entirely accurate" (*Responsa of Professor Louis Ginzberg*, 76n2). In fact, it is inconceivable that a scholar of Rabbi Ginzberg's caliber would overlook or be unaware of the many rabbinic sources that circumscribe the cantor's behavior and list his qualifications. See extensively above. It is more likely that Rabbi Ginzberg understood *y. Ta'an.* 2:2, 65b that states: "If they do not have [someone with all these qualities], they appoint whomever they want" to mean that the congregation has the ultimate authority to choose a cantor on any basis they think matters. Accordingly, there are no disqualifying rules. In fact, it is as if there are no rules at all.

tion of a cantor and an opera singer is a very healthy one. There is no law prohibiting a rabbi from appearing in a cabaret, but do you think that any congregation would seriously consider having a cabaret singer as a rabbi? Of course, I am quite aware of the fact that certain music may serve very high cultural purposes. Yet, I am, at the same time, sure that people would find it quite strange to see their cantor one day recite the Neilah prayer and the following day sing a love duet with some lady. My advice is therefore that you try your utmost to prevent your Cantor from accepting the offer made to him by the Metropolitan.

With kindest regards to you, Mrs. Levinthal, and to the children in which Mrs. Ginzberg joins me, I am

Very sincerely yours,

Louis Ginzberg

Postscript to the Correspondence:

According to Darryl Lyman, "Tucker wanted to remain as cantor at the Brooklyn Jewish Center. But, on the recommendation of a panel of five rabbis (by a vote of three to two), he resigned his post there."[494] Rabbi Golinkin[495] writes that: "Louis Ginzberg was apparently one of the five rabbis asked." Rabbi Goldman was another. After only two years of service Cantor Richard Tucker (1913–1975) left the Brooklyn Jewish Center and went on to have a distinguished operatic career.

Current Reform Responsa, No. 52, Section 12, 214:
Is a Cantor Necessary?

Rabbi Solomon B. Freehoff was a descendant of Rabbi Shneur Zalman of Liady, the Alter Rebbe of Chabad-Lubavitch. Born in London, England, in 1892, he came to the United States in 1903. He graduated from the University of Cincinnati in 1914, ordained by Hebrew Union College one year later, and went on to serve on its faculty. He served as the chairman of the rabbinical advisory committee of the Jewish Welfare Board, where his acumen, broad knowledge, and authority were universally recognized. The size of his personal library was legendary. He also served as president of the Central Conference of American Rabbis and the World Union for

---

494. Lyman, *Great Jews in Music*, 229–30.

495. Golinkin, *Responsa of Professor Louis Ginzberg*, 76n3.

Progressive Judaism. Rabbi Freehof was able to make his scholarship accessible to a popular audience, attracting hundreds of Jews and non-Jews to his Pittsburgh synagogue's book review series. Among other works, he wrote nine books of responsa (in English). He died in 1990.

The collection of responsa from which the passage below is taken was published in 1969. It reflects a remarkable change from the reputed Golden Age of Cantors of only several decades earlier. It represents a new wave of congregational life in which a cantor is considered nonessential.

> Question: Is it essential in Judaism that religious services or any portion thereof be conducted by a cantor, or may any individual competent to read the prayers, equally do so?
>
> Answer: The services must be read aloud, usually with the traditional chant. The basic purpose of the audible reading is to fulfill the duty of worship for those who are unable to read the service themselves, but this reader need not be a cantor. Any member of the congregation can read the service aloud for the congregation. In fact, during most of the year, a member of the congregation (anyone, usually, who is commemorating the anniversary [of death] of a close relative) conducts the service. Some Reform congregations, therefore, do not have any cantor at all. The rabbi reads the service.

Sefer Mishneh Halakhot, Part 7, No. 15: May an Old and Infirm Cantor Sit While Leading Prayers?

A descendant of Rabbi Yom Tov Lipmann Heller and Rabbi Judah Loew of Prague, Rabbi Menashe Klein (1924–2011), also known as the "Ungvarer Rav," was a Holocaust survivor. Born in Irlyava, Czechoslovakia, he studied in the *yeshiva* of the nearby city of Ungvar under the tutelage of Rabbi Joseph Elimelekh Kahane. The Nazis deported him to Auschwitz in 1944 and transferred him to Buchenwald, from which he and 426 other youths (including Elie Wiesel) were liberated in 1945 and evacuated to a French sanitarium. After a brief time in France, he immigrated to the United States in 1947. It was in New York that he studied with Rabbi Aaron Kotler and Rabbi Israel Kanievsky, and especially with Rabbi Yekutiel Halbertsam, from whom he received rabbinic ordination. In 1964, he founded his own *yeshiva* in Brooklyn. He established the new community of Kiryat Ungvar in a Jerusalem neighborhood in 1983 in memory of his hometown. His last years were spent in Israel and he is buried in Safed. Rabbi Klein's literary output was substantial. He published twenty-five books and eighteen volumes of responsa, entitled *Mishneh Halakhot*, over fifty years.

The responsum that follows addresses the case of a cantor who is no longer able to stand throughout the entire Mussaf service on *Yom Kippur*. The questioner asks for confirmation of the allowance he made for the cantor to sit, provided that he remained stationary. Rabbi Klein proceeds by considering the fundamental assumption that the *Amidah* must be recited standing. He rejects the initial inference that the *Amidah* requires standing and, if recited while seated, would require repetition. However, Rabbi Klein injects the principle that a sitting cantor impugns the dignity of the congregation. Therefore, the cantor must stand or be replaced by someone who can. However, two exceptions are in order. First, if no suitable replacement is available, a sitting cantor may lead. The principle of "the best person available" is a recurrent one in the literature. And second, if the cantor in question is long tenured, serving the congregation from his youth, he is entitled to a special dispensation. Recognizing the special status of a cantor of distinguished service appears in writing of several earlier authorities.

Rabbi Klein concludes with two interesting side notes. Nothing may be learned on a [any?] topic from the behavior of noted rabbis from whose exceptionality no extrapolation is possible. Second, the same rules for a cantor do not apply to a private (non-synagogue) *minyan*.

> Praised be God, eleventh [day] of the month of mercy[496] 5732,[497] in New York (May God protect and redeem it,[498] amen!). To my dear friend, the honorable rabbi and scholar, venerable and pious, *etc.* Efraim Greenblatt[499] (May he live many good days, amen!) [of] Memphis, Tennessee.

496. That is, Elul.

497. August 21, 1972.

498. The reference here is to the city of New York. Jeremiah 29:7 urges Jewish exiles to pray for the city in which they live. And Rabbi Hanina (Avot 3:2) teaches: "Pray for the welfare of the government . . ."

499. All the honorifics are not *pro forma*. Rabbi Efraim Greenblatt (1932–2014) was born in Jerusalem to a rabbinic family. In 1951, he moved to New York, ostensibly to take up a post to help support his family. But Rabbi Moses Feinstein, who ordained him as a rabbi, sent him to Memphis, Tennessee, to serve as rabbi there—a position he held for fifty-eight years. He attracted many students, established educational institutions, and published eight volumes of his own responsa (one volume remained unpublished) under the title *Rivevot Efraim*.

After greeting the scholar, with regard to his question about a prayer leader who found it difficult to stand during the Additional Service on *Yom Kippur*, is he permitted during the repetition of the *Amidah* to sit and rest a bit on a chair, his feet not moving from his place?[500]

It initially appears that someone else who can stand throughout the prayer should be honored as the prayer leader. Is it not [the case] that in previous times all reputable people would stand [during] the entire Day of Atonement, with some standing from the night before and until the ensuing night—unless they could not find a suitable prayer leader except someone who is physically weak and cannot stand through the [duration of the] entire prayer? Let us look into the matter.

Note that in the Tur, *Shulhan Arukh*, Orah Hayyim, Section 94,[501] [it says] "an ailing person prays even when lying on his side"[502] and the *Kessef Mishneh*,[503] Chapter 5 in the Laws of Prayer, paragraph 2, wrote that: "an elderly man who cannot stand, sits in his place and prays. And if he can stand at the point where bowing is required, let him stand and bow." See further *Turei Zahav*[504] there: the reason for standing while praying is so that "the awe of Divine immanence is upon him."[505] But, the author of the *Shulhan Arukh*, there in paragraph 9 ruled that he who must pray sitting must, when possible, revert to praying when standing, indicating that it[506] invalidates. So it appears that he rules like Rav Ashi [in] *Berakhot* 50,[507] who says: "He prays by himself with the congregation while sitting and when he returns to his home he prays while standing" and he,[508] of blessed memory, explains that he must be of the opinion that even after the fact, he must go back and pray later, and if so, it is certainly the case that a prayer leader must not pray while sitting. However, the *Turei Zahav*, among other later authorities, was amazed by the author of the *Shulhan Arukh* and interpreted

500. Cf. Karo, *Shulhan Arukh*, OH 95:1.

501. Para. 6.

502. "Provided that he can focus his thoughts."

503. Rabbi Joseph Karo's commentary on Maimonides' *Mishneh Torah*.

504. Commentary of Rabbi David Ha-Levi.

505. OH 94, subparagraph 4.

506. I.e., sitting ordinarily invalidates the efficacy of the *Amidah* recited in that position

507. The text must be emended to 30a.

508. i.e., Rav Ashi.

Rav Ashi [to mean that] his prayer while standing was a [mere] additional supplication and not as Maimonides interpreted. And after RaShI[509] and the Tosafists[510] and Rabbenu Hananel[511] and Rabbenu Asher[512] and [the author of the] Tur[513] are all of the opinion that there is no need to go back and pray, the essential legal principle is that the prayer of someone sitting is [valid] prayer for all (refer there and enough).

However, to be a sitting prayer leader—even though we say that there is no legal prohibition—there is the prohibition based on 'the dignity due the congregation.' It is surely the case that their prayer leader sitting before them and praying to the Omnipresent does them no honor.

That he (*i.e.*, the prayer leader) should sit and rest for a while and not pray while the congregation waits for him until he rests a bit and regains his strength, would still be prohibited as explained in the Gemara of *Yoma* (70a) with regard to the High Priest who, when reading the Torah,[514] as stated,[515] ". . . 'and on the tenth day' which is in the book of Numbers, he recited by heart," [implying that] he was not allowed to roll [the Torah scroll] from place to place in the presence of the congregation. In the Gemara they gave the reason 'because of the dignity due the congregation.' RaShi[516] interpreted 'dignity due the congregation' [to mean] that they would be waiting all the while in silence. See Tosafot there[517] who posed a question on the basis of the Gemara in *Gittin*[518] [which states] that "things in writing are not authorized to be read by heart," which they strained to explain. They also cited the Jerusalem Talmud there.

Rabbi Klein draws an analogy: if it is improper to make the congregation wait in the case of Torah reading, it is similarly improper to make the congregation wait for a recuperating cantor.

509. *b. Ber.* 30a, s.v. *la hazinan.*

510. *b. Ber.* 30a, s.v. *m'samekh.*

511. *b. Ber.* 30a.

512. *Ber.*, section 20.

513. ben Asher, *Arba'ah Turim*, OH 94.

514. As the supplementary portion, *maftir.*

515. In the Mishnah, Yoma 7:1.

516. *b. Yoma* 70a, s.v. *mipnei k'vod tzibbur.*

517. *Tos. Y.*, s.v. u-v'assor.

518. 60b.

The explanation that emerges is that permission to read aloud what is written is preferable to rolling the Torah from place to place before the congregation on account of the 'dignity due the congregation,' making the congregation sit quietly and wait until the Torah is rolled and can be read. If so, [the same rule ought to apply] more in this case where the prayer leader would sit by himself to rest and the congregation would sit silently. This certainly is not dignified for the congregation.

Therefore, in my humble opinion,[519] it is surely improper to allow it *ab initio*. Rather, the prayer leader should strengthen himself—even if it pains him it is worthy—or they should appoint a different prayer leader. However, where it is impossible to [find] another who is suitable as he or he has been established in this position since his youth and now has [grown weak as he has] aged, there is, in my humble opinion, a suggestion I can make to the sage. That is: during the [recital of the] pietistic poems that are customarily sung, like "*Am Pifiyot*" and the like, let them honor one of the congregants to sing it while the prayer leader sits and rests on a chair. Or, when the congregation recites any poem, it is permitted [to let him sit] in this manner provided that the congregation doesn't mind it nor will it cause them distress. And so long as—it is understood—it is done with the condition that his intention is for the sake of Heaven.

In just this way we observed our senior rabbis who, in their old age, sometimes sat in the middle of prayer—and they were truly righteous and holy men who sacrificed their lives in the sanctification of God's name (May it be blessed!)—and how could we criticize them (God Forbid!). However, there is no proof from them since who can compare to them? Not everyone can claim the same status. And further, we have already brought up elsewhere in the name of Rabbi Meir of Rothenberg with regard to one who sets up his own prayer quorum in which others join that in such a case [the worry about causing] distress and other like things does not apply since they come to his house to pray in accordance with his[520] intentions, which is not the case for those who attend a community synagogue.

And with this I wholeheartedly give my trusted friend the blessings of a good inscription,[521]

---

519. Rabbi Klein employs the standard, self-deprecating expression used by most rabbinic scholars when making a ruling.

520. That is, the one who set up his own prayer quorum.

521. Such a wish—that a fellow Jew would be inscribed for a blessing in the Book of Life—is standard from the beginning of Elul through Yom Kippur.

Menashe, the insignificant.[522]

Poland: Twentieth Century

Born in Kupiskis (Kupishok), Lithuania, in 1914, Rabbi Ephraim Oshry
survived the Holocaust in the Kaunas (Kovno) ghetto. After liberation
in 1944, he retrieved his buried notes and published his answers to the
many questions posed to him in a five-volume Hebrew series (from 1959
to 1979) entitled *Responsa from Out of the Depths*. An abridged English
version (translated by Y. Leiman), from which the responsum below was
taken, appeared in 1983 under the title *Responsa from the Holocaust*. After living in Rome and Montreal for a short time after the war, he settled
in New York where he served in a major Orthodox congregation and
founded two *yeshivot*. He died in 2003.

Noteworthy is the fact that Rabbi Oshry does not rely on the Jerusalem Talmud's exception to allow the best available man to lead rather
than requiring only the fully qualified to lead. He seems to rely on the
ruling in *Or Zaru'a*[523] requiring a demonstration of repentance for an
incidental homicide before leading prayers.[524] Also interesting to note is
the remarkable readiness of the questioner and the community to search
dutifully for the ideal candidate even in desperate times.

Responsa From the Holocaust, No. 110: May a Mercy Killer Lead Prayers?

Question: On an ice-cold winter day, during our long imprisonment, the Germans were beating the slave laborers to move
more quickly. But they could not. Dressed in the poorest of rags,
which barely covered them, let alone provide any warmth, the
unfortunate and miserable Jews were suffering from horrible
pain. Their feet had swollen from the intense cold. Every step
was torture. From time to time they stumbled. Many of those
who fell ill never rose again.

After seeing scores of his fellow prisoners fall and die on the
spot, one of those marchers, unable to walk any longer because

522. Self-deprecation and humility are the hallmarks of many of the great
authorities.

523. Cited above.

524. Cf. also *Responsa Teshuvot V'hanhagot*, below.

of his own unbearable suffering, said to his friend struggling right behind him, "Please do me a favor. Give me a push so that I will fall. If I rise, push me down again. And again. Eventually my strength will give out and I will not be able to rise again. I cannot bear the pain and suffering. I would prefer to be dead."

Unable to convince his stronger friend to carry out his act, he had to beg him repeatedly. Finally the man took pity on the broken Jew, saying to himself, "What difference does it make if he dies now or later? He is better off dead than living in so much pain. How can I not do what he asks when he begs me with his very last ounce of strength?"

So the stronger friend pushed his friend down. When the weaker friend rose up again, he pushed him down again. Although the man was able to get up each time, when he arrived at his place of work he was so weak that he simply collapsed and died.

After our liberation in 1944, when we were blessed by G-d to see the end of Nazi power, we began to arrange the High Holidays prayers. As is customary in Jewish communities, we sought a man who would meet all the requirements for leading the prayer on such an awesome and holy day. After an exhaustive search, we found a suitable man. However, a number of people identified him as the man who had pushed his friend to death. They claimed that a murderer was unfit to lead our prayers on *Rosh Hashanah* and *Yom Kippur*. The questions I had to answer were the following: Was the man considered a murderer? Did he have to accept special penance—generally a personalized program of self-denial, study, and sometimes affliction—for his sin? And would the penance suffice to allow him to lead the public prayers?

Since it was difficult to find a suitable replacement and time was extremely short, I was asked to seek some way, following the law of the Torah, to permit him to lead the prayers for the surviving Jews.

Response: The man who pushed his friend is not to be regarded as an outright murderer but rather as someone who brought about the death of a fellow Jew. For the victim did not die immediately after being pushed, but rather continued to walk until he reached his place of work, where he finally collapsed and died. In fact, there is no evidence that his friend had died as a result of being pushed; it may very well be that he would have died anyway. To atone, it is enough that this man do penance.

But the penance should be severe, because Maimonides[525] considered someone who brings about the death of another, a murderer. Even though he may be innocent in the eyes of the Torah, it cannot be forgotten that he may have brought about the death of his fellow Jew: He must therefore accept upon himself full penance, and only after he carries it out could he lead the community in prayer. I also instructed him, after penance, to immerse himself in a *mikveh* as part of the purification process, after which God would erase his sins and heed his prayers.

Once the man had carried out the entire sequence of penance, he led the prayers on the High Holy Days with profound emotion, sighing, and weeping. Many Jewish Russian soldiers from the front joined us, and they too were deeply inspired and stirred by this man's sincere, broken-hearted cries.

Israel: Twentieth Century

Rabbi Benzion Meir Hai Uziel was born in Jerusalem—where his father, Rabbi Joseph Raphael, served as head of the rabbinical court—in 1880. By the age of twenty, he founded and taught in a Jerusalem *yeshiva* dedicated to training Sephardic youth. In 1921, he was called to serve as the rabbi in Salonika, returning to Israel in 1923, where he took the position of rabbi of the city of Tel Aviv. He was named as the Sephardic chief rabbi of Mandate Palestine in 1939, and served until the establishment of the state of Israel when he was elected Sephardic chief rabbi of the new state. He served in that post until his death in 1953. He authored seven volumes of responsa from 1935 to 1964, published under the title *Mishpatei Uziel* (*The Judgments of Uziel*).

Evident from the passage that follows, Rabbi Uziel held cantors in high esteem. Earlier respondents considered the cantor to be an employee with or without certain special privileges. But at the beginning of the twentieth century, the cantor was valued by at least this authority as one who fulfills a role different from that of anyone else: representative of the Jewish people—not merely the prayer leader of a congregation—in mediating its prayers to God.

---

525. Cf. Maimonides, *Mishneh Torah*, Laws of a Murderer and Protection of Life, 2:2.

Mishpatei Uziel, Volume 3, Addendum No. 1:
The Value of a Cantor

The prayer leader who is agreeable to the public and goes to the lectern according to Jewish practice is not like any other working craftsman who does his job with pay or without pay according to the will of those who engage him. Rather, he is the agent of Israel, each congregation being a microcosm of the collective. So every prayer leader in his place is no less than the agent of all Israel to pray and recite holy words before the Holy One of Israel Who is esteemed in holiness.

She'elot U'Teshuvot Teshuvot V'Hanhagot,
Volume I, Orah Hayim, No. 99: May a Penitent be a Cantor?

Rabbi Moses Sternbuch was born in London, England, in 1926. After completing his studies, he served for a time in Johannesburg, South Africa, before settling in Israel, where he rose to become the rabbinic leader of the *Edah Haredit*.[526] A prolific author, he published a multivolume commentary on the Jewish holidays, as well as commentaries on the Torah, Maimonides, the Passover Haggadah, and repentance. He also authored compendia on the laws of the home, customs pertaining to the writing of a Torah scroll, *tefillin*, and *mezuzot*. He published a compilation of the customs of the *Vilna Ga'on*—an illustrious ancestor of his—and he continues to serve as the rabbi of the Vilna Gaon Synagogue in Har Nof. His frequent public lectures have also been collected and published. His responsa continue to be published under the title of *T'shuvot V'Hanhagot*.

In the responsum translated below, Rabbi Sternbuch considers whether a penitent is suitable to serve as a cantor, considering the fact that while repentance is a virtue, it reveals a prior state of sinfulness, which could be construed as a disqualification under the parameters set out by the Talmud.

> Question: Is a penitent allowed to be a cantor in a synagogue? There are those who object and say that it is inappropriate to appoint him.
>
> *Ta'anit* 16a says it is forbidden to appoint as a prayer leader one whose reputation was fouled in his youth. And this is what the *Shulhan Arukh*, [Orah Hayyim,] Section 53, paragraph 4

---

526. Commonly dubbed the "ultra-Orthodox community."

ruled. The decisors there wrote that even if it is clear that he repented, it is inappropriate to appoint him. Based on this, Rabbi
Moses Isserles writes[527] that if he trespassed unwittingly, that
he committed accidental homicide, for instance, he is permitted to be a prayer leader. But if he trespassed intentionally [he]
may not because his reputation was ruined before repentance.
The *Magen Avraham* was astonished [by Rabbi Isserles, ruling
instead] that even [if he trespassed] intentionally he could be
a prayer leader if he repented. He did not exclude him on the
basis of a compromised reputation except to lead prayers on
fast days (see there). In his commentary, the *Vilna Gaon* (*ad
loc.*) explained the words of Rabbi Moses Isserles to mean that
a penitent is preferred over a saint occasionally but not permanently, meaning that he concedes to Rabbi Moses Isserles that it
is forbidden to take a penitent as a permanent prayer leader if he
had sinned with regularity.

The *Mishnah Berurah*[528] rules the gist of the law to be that
if he repented—even if he trespassed intentionally—he is suitable on all other days of the year except public fast days and the
Days of Awe, but he mentions additionally that many decisors
disagree [saying] that the intentional trespasser is forbidden [to
lead prayers] even if he repented, as Rabbi Moses Isserles [ruled].
It seems simple that he who did not receive a Torah education
and was in the category of 'a baby taken captive' and he now is
a penitent, to all opinions he is fully righteous. The decisors deal
only with someone who received Torah education and strayed
and is called 'intentional violator.' Even if he repented, in any
case, according to some decisors, it is inappropriate to appoint
him since he has a bad reputation in that he knew the rules but
failed to follow them. But a penitent who was never educated in
Torah, yet now he adheres to the Torah, [the concept of] 'had a
bad reputation from his youth' does not apply. To the contrary,
he has an advantage to be a prayer leader: his prayer is accepted
by and acceptable to the Omnipresent since he sanctified God's
name through his repentance.

Therefore, it seems clear that current behavior trumps past
misconduct so although he lacks the merit of his ancestors to
aid him, he enjoys the merit that he returned to his Creator and
(God forbid!) he should be suspected or reminded that he is a
penitent. There is no greater sin than shaming him in this way.

527. Karo, *Shulhan Arukh*, OH 53:5.

528. Rabbi Israel Meir ben Aryeh Zev Ha-Kohen Kagan (1839–1933), *Mishnah
Berurah*, OH 53, subparagraph 22.

In our day, close to Messianic times in the Final Generation, the light of repentance is glimmering. We must bring [Jews] near, not distance them (God forbid!). In his Torah commentary, RaShI explains at the beginning of the portion Toldot, that the prayer of the righteous who is the son of the righteous is more acceptable. Nevertheless, this applies only when both adhere to the same values. In such a case, we prefer the righteous man who is the son of a righteous man. But where one's conduct is superior to the second, we certainly do not prefer the inferior on account of ancestral merits.

And with regard to what they said "righteous son of righteous [man]"—it is not merely someone who keeps Torah and mitzvot but as we[529] explained in Ta'am V'da-at on the Torah that it means a righteous man who constantly repents and grows daily in achieving the virtues of [divine] service. A righteous man is defined as a person whose [good] conduct today surpasses that of yesterday. But to us and to the questioner, the most important thing is that the prayer leader arouse the congregation to repent. We only judge a person by his current behavior. If we see in him that he is not merely "returning" in repentance, but is actually a "master of repentance," that is, he has completely repented and [is] governed by penitence and will remain so, God forbid that we should prevent him from being a permanent prayer leader, as I wrote.

She'elot U'Teshuvot Miyam HaHalakhah, Vol. 1, No. 23: Are Short Sleeves Appropriate Dress for a Cantor?

Rabbi Yonah Metzger was born in Haifa in 1952. He served with distinction as a chaplain in the Israel Defense Forces. He was appointed district rabbi of North Tel Aviv and was subsequently elected in 2003 as chief Ashkenazic rabbi of Israel, serving until his resignation in disgrace in 2013. (He was tried and convicted of fraud and corruption. As of May 2017, he is serving a three-and-a-half-year prison sentence.) He has authored ten books, one of which was awarded a special prize from the president of Israel.

From the responsum that follows, it appears that Rabbi Metzger makes no distinction between the ages of prayer leaders or the service being led.

---

529. Rabbi Sternbuch uses the royal "we" in referring to himself.

The *Mishnah* (Megillah 4:6) teaches that one whose clothes are torn (*po-he-ah*) "may not go to the lectern." According to Rabbi Isaac al-Fasi,[530] the meaning of *po-he-ah* is someone whose clothes are torn and his shoulders and arms are exposed so that his clothes appear as if they are missing from the joint and downwards. The *Vilna Gaon* (on Orah Hayyim 53:13) accordingly concludes that both arms and shoulders must be exposed for a person to be disqualified as a prayer leader. It is in this context that Rabbi Metzger considers the case of short sleeves. Rabbi Metzger relies on a relatively obscure respondent to establish that the arm above the bicep is the area that must be covered as a matter of modesty. Sleeves that cover this area are sufficient to qualify for proper clothing in prayer. But the stricter approach—and the one he favors—that is based on the dignity due the congregation requires covering the arms before leading prayers. A personal testimony supports the stricter view.

> Question: May a young man lead the afternoon service on *Shabbat* at a *Bnei Akiva*[531] branch when he is wearing short sleeves?
>
> Answer: There are those who allow a prayer leader to wear a short sleeve shirt since the spot [on the arm] where *tefillin* are worn and upwards are covered by a sleeve while below this spot, uncovered, since this spot does not fall into the definition of "covered places" that are forbidden to be revealed (*Responsa Yitzhaq Yeranen*,[532] Part 2, No. 3), although there are some decisors who are concerned with this because of 'the dignity due the congregation.' I saw that Rabbi Tzvi Yehudah Kook,[533] may the memory of the righteous be a blessing, who was concerned when, in his house, a young man stood up to pray while wearing short sleeves and he asked him to drape a *tallit* over his uncovered arms on account of the 'dignity due the congregation.' And blessings to those who are strict.

---

530. *Megillah*, 1143, 16a.

531. B'nei Akiva is the largest religious Zionist youth movement in the world. It was established in Mandate Palestine in 1929 as the youth division of Mizrachi.

532. Authored by Rabbi Isaac ben Joshua of Djerba (Tunisia), born ca. 1870.

533. The son of the lionized first chief Ashkenazi rabbi of mandate Palestine, Rabbi Abraham Isaac Kook, and a scholar and influential teacher in his own right as head of Mercaz HaRav Kook. He was born in Lithuania in 1891, and died in Jerusalem in 1982.

Sha'arei Halakhah, No. 5, p. 20:
Dismissing a Cantor Whose Voice and Strength Have Weakened

Born in 1935, Rabbi Zalman Druck studied in the Ponevez Yeshivah in Israel, the land of his birth. He was appointed the Rabbi of Rehavia, and then in 1982 became the first rabbi of the Great Synagogue in Jerusalem, where he served until his death at the age of 75, on December 12, 2009. He published several important books, including *Sha'arei Tefillah* on the laws of prayer, *Mikra'ei Kodesh*, and *Mikdash Me'at*. The passage that follows appears in his work on Jewish law, *Sha'arei Halakhah*, published in 1992.

A Prayer Leader Whose Voice and Strength Have Weakened

What is the law regarding someone who had regularly served as a cantor in a community over many years, and over time had aged and grown vocally weak, and the public wants to dismiss him from his position or hire an assistant and he objects?

In the *Shulhan Arukh*, Orah Hayim 53:25, the author ruled that a cantor may not be dismissed from his position unless some disqualifying fault was found in him. Indeed, that "his voice be pleasant" is a virtue for a prayer leader as explained there, but this does not fall under the heading of a disqualifying factor for which he may be dismissed, even though it is a fundamental prerequisite for a prayer leader.

In the ensuing sections, Rabbi Druck explains with appropriate citations that, analogous to a rabbi, there is a presumption of a contractual relationship even with no formal contract. Hence, the congregation cannot unilaterally renege. The only exception would be a failure to perform. But in this case, the cantor performed as well as he could. Further, there is a distinction between unspecified and specified terms of employment. Specified terms of employment come with no automatic renewal. Thus, if a cantor were appointed without any specified time, it is treated as an indefinite appointment for which the congregation is required to pay him fully even though his skills diminish with age. So if they want to hire an assistant cantor, it would be at their own expense.

And if they no longer wish to engage him and after the congregation made a plausible determination that he can no longer serve them, they must pay him severance as is customary. The source for the custom of compensation is advanced in *Sefer Ha-Hinukh*, Commandment 482. Even though this mitzvah applied only to a Hebrew slave when the Jubilee Year was observed, nowadays, "let the wise man hear and increase in learning (Prov 1:5)" that a Jew who is hired for a long or even a short time ought to be generously compensated when he departs from that which God, may His Name be blessed, blessed him. Some found a hint for the custom of severance from the verse, "so that you walk on the right path (Prov 2:20)" and "follow the paths of the righteous (*ibid.*)." as explained in the *Gemara*, Bava Metzia 83. They already remarked on this from what is stated by Rabbi Moses Isserles, [*Shulhan Arukh,*] Hoshen Mishpat 12 [2], that one may not impose supererogatory rules.

Similarly, the author of Responsa *Imre Esh*,[534] Part 1, Yoreh De'ah, No. 92 wrote about the case of a cantor who was dismissed by the congregation for good cause (he disappeared from town for eighteen weeks) who by law could be dismissed without any compensation. Nevertheless, they were required to pay him in accordance with the local custom. As explained in the Mishnah Bava Metzia 83, when it comes to hiring workers, "all follows the local custom." The author of Responsa *Tzitz Eliezer*,[535] Part 7, No. 48, Chapter 10 similarly wrote about an employee who was absent for many workdays and was dismissed for cause. However, since local custom required it, the institution [for whom he worked] was obligated to pay him severance. And there is no difference between full-time and part-time employees.

Indeed, Mordekhai [ben Hillel] on *Bava Metzia* there[536] writes that custom preempts law only when it is a venerable custom. A custom that has no source in the Torah is nothing more than an error in reasoning. However, in accordance with *Sefer Ha-Hinukh* mentioned above, there is a basis and an allusion in the Torah [for severance pay] that we legitimate following local custom.

And in our case, there is an explicit, sincere, and truthful warrant that the officers—without the authorization of the congregation—may dismiss the cantor—if there is no less harsh way of satisfying him, provided that they pay him severance. And thus wrote the author of *Responsa Bigdei Shesh*,[537] No. 33.

---

534. Rabbi Meir ben Judah Leib Eisenstat (1786–1842).

535. Rabbi Eliezer Yehudah Waldenberg (1915–2006).

536. 83a, 366.

537. Rabbi Raphael Shalom Saul ben Meir HaKohen Munk. Responsa were published in Jerusalem, 1973.

She'elot U'Teshuvot B'mar'eh Ha-Bazaq,[538] *Volume 3, No. 6, p. 10:*
May Sabbath Violators be Cantors?

When the students and colleagues of the distinguished, Belarus-born rabbi Saul Yisraeli (1909–1995) began to collect the questions sent to their esteemed master by fax and e-mail from all over the world—and then respond quickly by committee—they chose a name suited to modern correspondence. *Bazaq* is the Hebrew word for "lightning." (Bezeq, incidentally, was Israel's largest telecommunications company.)

The general laxity of Jewish religious observance is hardly unique to Jewish life in the United States at the turn of the twenty-first century. Earlier respondents, directly or obliquely, have made this observation. The number of Jews suitable for leading prayer services is in decline. But what has changed is the sense of entitlement. Jews have every expectation that they are entitled to the opportunity to honor their dead, whether or not they are suitable or even competent. Congregants whose expectations go unmet are liable to resign from their synagogues or worse: lobby for a change in policy or a change in leadership.

The answer that follows shows how contemporary authorities face this challenge. Strict adherence to Jewish law would be counterproductive. So in the name of preserving Judaism at a time of spiritual crisis, a reluctant accommodation needs to be made. Yet, there is a line beyond which even the most lenient may not cross: intermarriage.

> New Jersey,[539] U. S. A.
>
> Tammuz 5752[540]
>
> Question: May a rabbi who serves a very small number of worshipers who are Sabbath observant give permission to a Sabbath violator to be a cantor? What should be taken into account is that should the rabbi refuse, it is likely to cause a fracture in the congregation when the right to pray will be left in the hands of two or three men (and sometimes in the hands of the rabbi alone) and thus the Sabbath violators will not be able to lead prayers even on the *yahrzeits*[541] of their parents!
>
> Answer: Strictly according to law, no permission should be given to Sabbath violators—and even to persistent violators of other commandments—to go to the lectern even occasionally.

538. Following the publisher's transliteration.

539. No more specific location is given.

540. August 1992.

541. *Yahrzeit*, from the Yiddish "time of year," refers to the anniversary of death.

Indeed, because of the situation of 'spiritual endangerment' to the community described, one should not prevent the congregation that allows Sabbath violators to go to the lectern from doing so. Rather, one ought to rely on the lenient opinions.[542] Certainly, it is preferable that these people lead only the introductory service. In any case, no permission ought to be given to one who intermarries to go to the lectern.

Israel/United States: Twenty-first Century

The Status of Women in Jewish Law: Responsa, Chapter 3, Section IV, 111f.: Women Cantors

Historically, leading prayer services was an exclusively male domain. The main purpose of the prayer leader was to fulfill the obligation of prayer for others. Since women are exempt from the *mitzvah* of public prayer, they cannot lead public prayer since only one who is under obligation can perform a *mitzvah* for others also under obligation.[543] However, just as the traditional role of women in Western society was being questioned during the last third of the twentieth century, so was the traditional role of women in Judaism. By and large, Orthodox Judaism has remained faithful to traditional practice. And, unbound by the strictures of Jewish law, the Reform Movement has accepted women cantors since 1955. However, conservative Judaism struggled to maintain a loyalty to tradition while adapting to changing attitudes.

Women had been admitted to the degree-granting program of the Cantor's Institute of the Jewish Theological Seminary of America since the Cantor's Institute's inception in 1952. In 1987, Rabbi Ismar Schorsch, Chancellor of the Seminary, announced that henceforth women would be conferred the diploma of *hazzan*. Rabbi Schorsch's explanation for this decision was twofold. First, in accepting the paper presented to the faculty by Rabbi Joel Roth justifying the ordination of women as rabbis, the principle adopted was that women could become self-obligated for *mitzvot*

---

542. In footnote No. 4 of this work, the authors refer specifically to the view that allows for appointment as a cantor the best available person (as determined by the congregation). Further, the opinion of Rabbi Hayim ben Rav Israel Benveniste (1603–1673) in his *Shayarei Kenesset Ha-Gedolah* on *Tur*, OH 53:2 is cited as support: "Nowadays, in our sinfulness . . . we pursue [cantors] with sweet and pleasant voices even if sinners . . ."

543. Cf. *b. R.H.* 29a.

from which they had traditionally been exempted and were thus equal to men.[544] In other words, approving women as cantors was an implicit, logical extension of approving women as rabbis. Second, Rabbi Schorsch hoped to avoid the same divisive public debate concerning women as cantors as there was on women as rabbis. (The prospect of women as cantors was initially considered only as an obstacle to the ordination of women as rabbis.) Rabbi Schorsch's hope was dashed when the Cantors Assembly, the international organization of cantors in the Conservative Movement, voiced its disapproval by failing to admit women as members over three successive years, from 1988 to 1990. Only an *in camera* vote of the executive council of the Cantor's Assembly in 1990 led to the membership of women.

The Committee on Jewish Law and Standards of the [Conservative] Rabbinical Assembly adopted two earlier—and conflicting—decisions on women as cantors. In June of 1974, the majority voted that women should not serve as cantors with a minority voting that women may. That the seminary's move to invest women as cantors stood in opposition to the majority position of the body assigned the task of settling matters of Jewish law for the Conservative Movement was never formally explained. It was left to others to make the case.

A 1984 paper[545] by Rabbi Philip Sigal of Grand Rapids, Michigan, was the first formal attempt to deal with the question of women serving as cantors—among other roles—in the Conservative Movement. Rabbi Sigal argued that extrapolating from the implication that women may blow *shofar* and the opinion that women may read *Megillah*, one might legitimately deduce that women can serve as prayer leaders. In addition, the widespread practice of women being counted in the prayer quorum (as a result of the vote of the Committee on Jewish Law and Standards) is tantamount to custom. As custom, it holds the force of law. Hence, if women are legally equal to men in the prayer quorum, women can fulfill the obligation of prayer for men. Rabbi Sigal's paper was not adopted.

What follows is another attempt to legitimate women as cantors by Rabbi Dr. David Golinkin, president and professor of Jewish Law at the Schechter Institute of Jewish Studies in Jerusalem. For twenty years he served as Chair of the *Va'ad Halakhah* (Law Committee) of the Rabbinical Assembly that writes responsa and gives halakhic guidance to the

---

544. A position refuted by both Professors Israel Francus and David Weiss Halivni in their faculty papers based on *b. Kid.* 31a, *Ber.* 20b, and *Pes.* 116b.

545. Cf. Sigal, "Responsum on the Status," 269–96.

Masorti (Conservative) Movement in Israel. He is the founder and director of the Institute of Applied Halakhah at The Schechter Institute, whose goal is to publish a library of halakhic literature for the Conservative and Masorti Movements. His support for women as cantors is also part of a larger project that includes support for counting women in the quorum for prayer. Noteworthy is that he makes no reference whatsoever to the 1987 justification offered by Rabbi Schorsch, or to the 1984 Sigal paper. Rabbi Golinkin's responsa collection was published in English in 2012.

The Status of Women in Jewish Law: Responsa, No. 3, Part IV, pp. 111–112: May Women Serve as shelihot[546] tzibbur?

The basic principle allowing someone to fulfill another's obligation is found in Mishnah Rosh Hashanah 3:8:

A deaf-mute, a lunatic [sic] and a minor cannot fulfill a religious duty on behalf of a congregation. This is the general principle: one who is not obligated to perform a religious duty cannot fulfill it on behalf of a congregation.

We have shown above that women are obligated to recite the *Amidah* in every service, including *Mussaf* and *Ne'ilah*, and to sanctify God's name. Therefore, according to the general principle above, it is permissible for them to serve as *shelihot tzibbur* for *barekhu*, *kaddish*, *hazzarat hashatz*, and *kedushah*.

The only objection that could have been raised would be with regard to reciting the *Shema* because we have learned in Mishnah *Berakhot* 3:3 cited above that women are exempt from reciting the *Shema*. If so, how can they fulfill the congregation's obligation to hear the *Shema*? Our reply is that this would indeed be an obstacle if we still recited *Shema* in public responsively (porsim al shema), *i.e.*, that the *hazzan* would read the *Shema* aloud to the congregation responsively. But that ancient practice disappeared 1,500 years ago and our reciting the *Shema* (Keriyat Shema) requires neither a minyan nor a *sheliah tzibbur*. If so, it makes no difference whether the *sheliah tzibbur* for *ketriyat shema* is obligated or not. Therefore, it is permissible for a woman to be the *shelihat tzibbur* for all of the above services, as explained above.

---

546. Author's spelling.

2

The Cantor in Jewish Lore

LAW AND LORE ARE both accumulated bodies of knowledge reflecting the norms of a given group. Nonetheless, there are significant differences between them. Law is the domain of experts whose rulings, in literate traditions, are preserved in writing. Lore, in contrast, is the domain of the common folk whose views and attitudes are transmitted orally. Law is accumulated in books and codes, while lore is accumulated in a variety of popular media, including stories, songs, sayings, and jokes. Legal scholars have the advantage of easily researching specific texts. Folklorists, on the other hand, must collect material from the common people, often by way of interviews. Law remains fixed until intentionally amended. Lore remains fluid and will reflect changing cultural views. Whether or not folklore is the product of a group or can be the output of an individual is subject to scholarly dispute.[1] But for the purpose of this chapter it is irrelevant.

The folkloric traditions regarding the cantor serve as an important balance to the legal tradition. Jewish law is the output of rabbinic debate. Jewish lore represents common perceptions that persist outside the texts that serve as the fodder for rabbinic debate. Jewish lore is another tool for assessing the office of the cantor.

---

1. Cf., e.g., Hafstein, "Politics of Origins," 300–15.

THE CANTOR IN THE MYSTICAL
AND HASIDIC TRADITIONS

The mystical tradition beginning with the *Zohar* is more concerned with the valence of prayer than those who lead it. Accordingly, the sources have little to offer explicitly on the office of the cantor. Since, however, the cantor served as the mediator of public prayer, and since the Kabbalists imagined prayer as a potent instrument in communing with God and securing God's blessings, it would be fair to infer that the cantor played an important role for the community. Since, moreover, the mystics endowed song with special power and effectiveness, the cantor—indubitably the expert in song—becomes a valuable asset. However, the status that the cantor enjoyed as a master of prayer did not give him license to alter the formulae of prayer that had been validated by authority and imbued with cosmic significance. The very efficacy of prayer was dependent upon fidelity to the text.

Of further concern to the mystics was mindfulness. The daily regimen of prayer requires a wholeheartedness that extends beyond the special circumstances of fast-days. The *Zohar* supports the view implied in the Mishnah and articulated by the Geonim that mindfulness is essential in prayer at all times. The kabbalistic antidote to formalism is devout attentiveness. Hence, many of the mystical manuals composed by students describing the positions their mentors took while praying emphasize concentration and contemplation. Even the cantor is subject to this concern.

The valuable role filled by the cantor was appreciated from the outset of Hasidism,[2] although within its third generation the very position of cantor was in dispute. The earliest Hasidic traditions depict cantors as uniquely gifted and blessed with transformative powers that are welcome even in heaven. But, at least in the Hasidic communities of Ukraine in the early nineteenth century, cantors were being replaced with untrained prayers leaders, and congregational prayer aloud was preferred over cantorial *recitative*. Partly to blame was the behavior of cantors themselves, as some exhibited bad character or served their egos rather than their

2. In contrast to Abraham Millgram who writes (*Jewish Worship*, 511): "The Hasidim refused to be a passive audience. So they did away with cantors altogether." Both the Ba'al Shem Tov and Rabbi Nahman of Breslov thought highly of cantors and endorsed them. See below. See also Meir Shimon Geshuri on "Rabbi Ya'akov Prager," 153–56, who describes how thousands of acolytes would come to Aleksandrów Lodzki, Poland to listen to him lead prayer services with his choir.

mandate. But it is also reflective of two trends identified by many of the respondents mentioned above: a growing populism and a decline in cantorial expertise.

Spain: Thirteenth Century

The pioneering work of Gershom Scholem[3] helped establish the fact that the *Zohar* (*Book of Splendor*), attributed to the first-century *tanna*, Rabbi Simon bar Yohai, was actually a thirteenth-century work by a Spaniard, Moses de Leon. The false attribution of earlier times, however, neither diminishes the influence of this text nor repudiates the fact that a kind of Jewish mysticism—known as Heikhalot and Merkavah mysticism—goes back to the talmudic period. However, according to Joseph Dan,[4] reliance on prayer as part of the Jewish mystical experience did not emerge until the second half of the twelfth century.

The passages below are taken, with minor revisions, from the 1934 Soncino edition of *The Zohar*.[5]

Zohar, Beshallah 63a-b: Praying from the Depths

The cosmic picture suggested by the following passage features a deep chasm at the base on which a reservoir (cistern) sits, while above the reservoir sits the earth with the heavens above. Blessings and other of God's gifts (like grace) travel from the heavens above to the depths below. Human prayer has the capacity to draw those blessings up from the depths into the reservoir from which they may be dispensed to all. But the capacity of prayer to affect this process is contingent on its efficacy, and that is linked to mindfulness. Hence, mindfulness is more than just the posture of attentiveness or concentration. It is the essential vehicle through which God's gifts may be received. Everything that fosters mindfulness is a virtue, and that which inhibits mindfulness is a vice:

> Rabbi Hezekiah discoursed on the verse: "A song of degrees. Out of the depth I have cried unto you" (Psalm 130:1, 2). 'This Psalm,' he said, 'is anonymous, because all men can apply it to themselves in all generations. Whoever prays before the Holy

3. See Scholem, *Major Trends in Jewish Mysticism.*
4. Dan, "Emergence of Mystical Prayer," 85.
5. Sperling et al., *The Zohar*, 3:197–98, 377–78; 5:378.

King must do so from the depths of his soul so that his heart may be wholly turned to God and his whole mind be concentrated upon his prayer. David[6] had already said, "I seek you with my whole heart" (Ps 119:10). Why, then, should he now go further and say "out of the depths?" The reason is that when a man prays before the King he should concentrate his mind and heart on the source of all sources, in order to draw blessings from the depth of the "Cistern," from the source of all life, from the "stream coming out of Eden" (Gen 2:19), which "makes the city of God rejoice" (Ps 46:5). Prayer is the drawing of this blessing from above to below; for when the Ancient One, the All-Hidden,[7] wishes to bless the universe, He lets His gifts of Grace congregate in that supernal depth, from where they are to be drawn, through human prayer, into the "Cistern," so that all the streams and brooks may be filled therefrom.'

Zohar, Terumah 131b: 132a: Song to Awaken Love and Joy

The passage below is the first part of a disquisition on the order and significance of the elements in the Sabbath Morning prayer service, especially music and song. Music, in general, Heschel claims, "is the soul of language."[8] And religious music in particular "is an attempt to convey that which is within our reach but beyond our grasp." Although a cantor is not specifically mentioned, the purpose of the cantor is intimated. The text asserts that analogous to the Levitical choir in temple times, the singing of the congregation awakens love and joy. And as the congregation sings in the synagogue, three angelic choruses join in heaven above. The instrument to lead the congregation in prayer is the cantor:

'When morning comes and the congregation is assembled in the synagogue, service must begin with hymns and psalms of David. We have already made clear that the purpose of the liturgy is to stir up Mercy and Loving kindness both in the higher and lower range, to bring into being redemptive acts, and to awaken joy; and this was the essential significance of the Levitic service, namely, to awaken love and joy above by means of song and praise. Woe unto him who engages in conversation

---

6. King David was traditionally considered the author of the book of Psalms.

7. "Ancient One" and "All-Hidden" are mystical synonyms for God. Cf. Dan 7:9, 13, 22.

8. Heschel, *Insecurity of Freedom*, 248.

of a secular nature in the synagogue, for he causes separation, he weakens the faith. Woe unto him, for he has no part in the God of Israel, since by his lack of awe before the Divine Presence he as much as denies the reality thereof, showing contempt toward the influence of the power which comes from above. For when Israel is occupied with the singing of psalms and hymns of praise and with prayer, three groups of supernal angels also assemble . . . the most supreme groups of angels . . . join the worshipers in their singing of the Psalms of King David . . . At the hour when the Song of the Sea is recited the Community of Israel is crowned with the crown with which the Holy One, in the time that is to be, will crown the King Messiah. That crown is engraved with Holy Names, those same names which glittered as crowns of fire upon the head of the Holy One Himself on the day when Israel crossed the sea and Pharaoh and his hosts were drowned therein. Therefore that song must be recited with special devotion, and he who is able to recite this hymn in the present world will be found worthy to behold King Messiah in the hour of His crowning and to sing then the song of redemption. All this is beyond dispute.

Zohar, Ha'azinu 287a-b: Song Links People to God

The Torah is called a "song" (Deut 32:44). In explaining why this is the case, this passage extols the aim of song to link people to God. Here again, while the cantor is unmentioned, the importance of the cantor is implied. Music, says Heschel,[9] is the language of mystery. It is the task of music, he goes on to say, to bring together the words in the liturgy with the reverence in human hearts.[10] And it is the task of the cantor to make that connection:

> Rabbi Yosi asked: 'Why is this discourse called "song?" Rabbi Isaac answered: 'Just as a song is drawn from heaven to earth by the holy spirit, so these words were drawn from heaven to earth by the holy spirit.

---

9. Heschel, *Insecurity of Freedom*, 250.

10. Heschel, *Insecurity of Freedom*, 250.

Germany: Thirteenth Century

An unidentified disciple of Rabbi Elazar ben Judah of Worms (ca. 1176–1238), author of *Sefer Ha-Rokeah*, compiled a treatise aimed at preserving Rabbi Judah the Pious's extant quotations on the liturgy. His actual commentary was lost. The treatise was disseminated in several manuscripts under the title *Sodot Ha-Tefilah* (*Secrets of Prayer*). Mostly a polemical work, its aim was to canonize the liturgical tradition of Ashkenazic Jewry by claiming that any change in the precise wording of the prayers would have cosmic consequences. According to mystical theory, the words and letters from which the ancient rabbis composed prayers reflect a heavenly harmony: what Joseph Dan, professor of Jewish Thought at the Hebrew University, calls "a sacred divine rhythm."[11]

The legitimate worry that cantors would change the liturgy willy-nilly persisted for hundreds of years.[12] Rabbi Joel ben Samuel Sirkis, a Polish authority who bridged the sixteenth and seventeenth centuries, complains about those cantors who added a verse to the evening service for the Sabbath on the grounds that it is contrary to the *Sefer Minhagim* of Rabbi Isaac Tirna,[13] and contrary to "what our predecessors were accustomed to say according to what we heard and learned from our rabbis." Rabbi Sirkis adds: "But in today's generations, people are accustomed to say it and we do not know how it happened that they do the opposite of the words of the rabbis and *Minhagim*."[14] He goes on to speculate on the reason for the unauthorized interpolation:

> My heart tells me that in this and similar matters, what happened is that unsuitable cantors—who are now accepted widely in congregations because they sing mellifluously even though they are not learned and do not know the laws of prayer, and the power of the wealthy has imposed itself on the scholars of this generation—have brought them to us. But what is proper is to revert to the original custom, as already done by some of the

---

11. Dan and Talmage, *Studies in Jewish Mysticism*, 91.

12. Maimonides, for example, discouraged the practice of cantors (*hazzanim*) interpolating songs and religious poetry into the liturgy—in order to enhance the service or to celebrate a circumcision or wedding (Cf. Maimon, *Teshuvot Ha-RaMBaM*, No. 207, p. 2:365, and also note 3, where Blau lists other authorities who opposed additional religious poetry in the prayer service).

13. A popular compilation of Polish customs first published in Krakow in 1597.

14. *Bayyit Hadash* on *Tur, OH* 267, *s.v. v'ein lomar*.

proper cantors who know and most of the learned who admit
to the truth.[15]

But the difference between Rabbi Sirkis—even though he was reputed to be a mystic as well—and the author of the passage that follows
is that Rabbi Sirkis determines valid practice to be a function of long-
standing practice rather than supernatural characteristics of the words of
prayer themselves.

Though the cantor is not specifically mentioned, this source helps
explain why the cantor, according to the legal authorities of the same period and earlier, must be a fluent and expert reader who is mindful of the
text. The cantor was expected to be the guardian of the integrity of prayer.

The two passages that follow are, with minor variations, the translation by Joseph Dan.

Sodot Ha-Tefilah: Keeping to the Exact Words

The people [Jews] in France made it a custom to add [in the
morning prayer] the words: "Happy are those whose ways are
righteous,"[16] and our Rabbi, the Pious,[17] of blessed memory,
wrote that they were completely and utterly wrong. It is all
gross falsehood, because there are only nineteen times that
the Holy Name is mentioned [in that portion of the morning
prayer] . . . and similarly you find the word 'Elohim nineteen
times in the pericope[18] of "These are the names . . ."[19] Similarly, you find that Israel were called "sons" nineteen times and
there are many other examples. All these sets of nineteen are
intricately intertwined, and they contain many secrets and esoteric meanings, which are contained in more than eight large
volumes.[20] Therefore, anyone who has any fear of God in him
will not listen to the words of the Frenchmen who add the verse
"Happy are those whose ways . . .," and blessed are the righteous

---

15. *Bayyit Hadash* on *Tur,* OH 267.

16. Ps 119:1. Probably added as a proem to Ps 145.

17. The reference is to Rabbi Judah ben Samuel, "The Pious" (1150–1217), a leader
of German Jewry.

18. That is, the first portion of Exodus, chs 1:1—6:1. A pericope is a short, passage.

19. Exod 1.

20. An indication of the vast literature on mystical prayer.

who walk in the path of God's Torah for according to their additions the Holy Name is mentioned twenty times . . . and this is a great mistake.

Furthermore, in this section[21] there are 152 words, but if you add "Happy are those who walk . . ." there are 158 words. This is nonsense, for it is a great and hidden secret why there should be 152 words . . . but it cannot be explained in a short treatise.

Furthermore, according to the words of the Frenchmen who add "Happy are those whose ways . . .," "Happy" appears four times: "Happy are those whose ways . . .," "Happy are those who dwell in Your House . . .,"[22] "Happy is the people who know . . .,"[23] "Happy is the people whose God is the Lord . . ."[24] This is a mistake and a gross lie, for there are only three occurrences of "Happy,"[25] in keeping with the three occurrences of Yom Kippurim in the Torah,[26] and in keeping with the three occurrences of [the words] "God the Lord of Abraham, Isaac, and Israel,"[27] and in keeping with the three occurrences of [the phrase] "God the Lord of Israel" in the book of Psalms . . . and in keeping with the three thousand year length of the Garden of Eden,[28] and in keeping with the three times that we say "holy"[29] every day. All these are intricately intertwined, and they are connected with grand and great mysteries, written in several volumes. Therefore, everyone who fears God should always pray and say: May my soul never be together with that of the Frenchmen, and may I never be part of their congregation, for they invent things out of their own imagination and add in their

21. Of prayer.

22. Ps 84:5.

23. Ps 89:16.

24. Ps 144:15.

25. In fact, the word "Happy" appears 24 times in the book of Psalms. Thus the precise intent of the author here is obscure.

26. In Leviticus 23 and 25, and Numbers 29.

27. This precise locution appearing only in 1 Kings 18:36, 2 Chronicles 30:6, and probably 1 Chronicles 29:18.

28. Early source for this claim is unknown. Cf. Dan and Talmage, *Studies in Jewish Mysticism*, 117n25.

29. Either a reference to the *Kedushah*—recited twice daily in the morning and afternoon *Amidah* along with the *Kedushah D'Sidra,* recited near the end of morning service—or to the word "holy" that appears three times in the morning and afternoon *Kedushah.*

prayers several words which are not needed. Thus they cause exile to themselves and their children until the end of time . . . [30]

Give heed, you inhabitants of France and the Islands of the Sea,[31] who err utterly and completely, for you invent lies and add several words in your prayers, of which the early sages who formulated the prayers never dreamed,[32] when they commanded us to say the prayers in place of the sacrifices in the Temple.[33] Every blessing that they formulated is measured exactly in its numbers of words and letters, for if it were not so, our prayer would be like the song of the uncircumcised non-Jews. Therefore, give heed and repent, and do not go on doing this evil thing, adding and omitting letters and words from the prayers.[34]

Israel: Sixteenth Century

The mystics of Safed, much like their European predecessors, were concerned with inculcating mindfulness in prayer. To achieve total concentration, all extraneous activities had to be eliminated. The disciples of many of the mystical masters kept a record of the practices of their mentors, leaving behind practical manuals that would be useful in training.

Elijah de Vidas (d. ca. 1593) was an important student of Rabbi Moses Cordevero. His family origins were Spanish, although he claims to have been born in Safed. Aside from expressing his own influential ideas in *Reshit Hokhmah (The Beginning of Wisdom)*[35] he has also preserved some of the practices of Rabbi Isaac Luria,[36] the engine driving Safed spirituality, a figure he knew personally. These practices were extracted and abridged by an Italian scholar, Jacob ben Mordechai Poyetto, in 1580:

30. Dan, MS Jerusalem, Jewish National and University Library, 8° 3 296, fol. 2, cited in Dan, "Emergence of Mystical Prayer," 88–89.

31. According to Dan, England is intended here. Jews were not expelled from England until the Edict of King Edward I, July 18, 1290.

32. Cf. *y. Ber.* 9:1, 12d.

33. Cf. *b. Ber.* 26a.

34. Dan, MS Jerusalem, Jewish National and University Library, 8° 3 296, fol. 7r, cited in Dan, "Emergence of Mystical Prayer," 88–89.

35. First published in Venice, 1579.

36. Rabbi Isaac Ha-Levi Luria (1534–1572) is the founder of practical Kabbalah and remains one of the most widely revered mystical authorities.

Reshit Hokhmah HaKatzar:
The Gate of Awe, Chapter 15: On Devotion

A person shall also be conscientious when reciting his prayers and blessings to make certain that they are spoken with genuine devotion of the heart, that they not be uttered merely out of habit. For Scripture teaches: "And the Lord said: 'Forasmuch as this people draw near, and with their mouth and with their lips do honor Me, but have removed their heart from Me . . .'" (Isa 29:13)[37]

Hanhagot of Moses Cordevero: Leave the Cantor Undisturbed

Probably collected by the brotherhood of mystics that surrounded him, these *Hanhagot* (that is, *Practices*) represent the pious customs of Rabbi Moses ben Jacob Cordevero (1522–1570), a student of Rabbi Joseph Karo in Safed, and brother-in-law of Solomon Alkabetz. In his *Palm Tree of Deborah*, Cordevero made one of the first attempts to synthesize mysticism with traditional Jewish ethics:

> 6. A person should not spend his time thinking about idle concerns during the hour of prayer, but only about Torah, the fulfillment of the commandments and sacred matters . . .
>
> 16. One ought to pray the *Amidah* in a contemplative way to the degree that he is able; at the very least concentrate meditatively during the three opening blessings . . . For with respect to one who fails to concentrate, the Shekhinah cries out: "The Lord has delivered me into their hands against whom I am not able to stand" (Lam 1:14).
>
> 27. One should listen attentively, as is proper, to the reading of the Torah without disturbing the prayer leader in any way.[38]

Ukraine: Eighteenth Century

Born in Podolia, Rabbi Israel ben Eliezer Ba'al Shem Tov (1698–1760) was orphaned at an early age. According to his many disciples, he demonstrated a profound grasp of talmudic study at an early age, but was pulled toward secret Kabbalistic writings. After his second marriage, he

---

37. Fine, *Safed Spirituality*, 134.
38. Fine, *Safed Spirituality*, 35, 36, 37.

went into seclusion, emerging at the age of thirty-six with what was to become the message of Hasidism.

The passages that follow were published in Martin Buber's two-volume *Tales of the Hasidim*, in 1947.

The Cantor of the Baal Shem Tov: Buber, Vol. 1, 61

This passage begins with the elevation of an otherwise undistinguished disciple with limited prospects of financial success to the position of cantor. It ends with the assertion that cantors officiate in heaven as they do on earth. The transformation from jobless disciple to eminent cantor requires a miracle. Ordinary men or fortune seekers, it seems, cannot attain such an esteemed position on their own. The story is also evidence that the founder of Hasidism greatly valued the institution of the cantorate. It includes the astounding contention that there is an angel assigned to each musical verse.

> One of the Baal Shem's disciples once asked him: "How shall I make a living in the world?"
>
> "You shall be a cantor," said the master.[39]
>
> "But I can't even sing!" the other objected.
>
> "I shall bind you to the world of music," said the zaddik.
>
> This man became a singer without peer, and far and wide they called him the cantor of the Ba'al Shem Tov.
>
> After many years he arrived in Lizhensk in the company of his bass singer, who was always with him, and visited Rabbi Elimelekh,[40] the disciple of the disciple of the Ba'al Shem Tov. For a long time, the rabbi and his son Eleazar could not make up their minds to let these two sing with the chorus in the House of Prayer on the sabbath [sic], for Rabbi Elimelekh feared that the artistry of their singing might disturb his devotions. But Rabbi Eleazar argued that because of the holiness of the Ba'al Shem Tov, it would not be right to withhold the honor from the man, and so it was agreed that he should sing at the inauguration of the sabbath [sic]. But when he began, Rabbi Elimelekh noticed that the great fervor of his singing flowed into his own, and

39. As from what may be inferred from the continuation, the Ba'al Shem Tov did not direct this man to the cantorate as an easy way to earn a living, but to serve in a capacity that suited his soul.

40. D. 1787. Known more for his saintliness than his book *No'am Elimelekh*, he is reputed to be the mentor of many disciples.

threatened to drive him out of his mind, and so he had to retract his invitation. But he kept the cantor with him over the Sabbath, and paid him many honors.

After the conclusion of the sabbath [sic], the rabbi invited him to his house again and asked him to tell him about the holy Ba'al Shem Tov, the light of Israel. Then the eyes of the man kindled with new life, and it was clear that there was new life in his throat and in his heart as well. He began to speak and it became manifest that now, since he had not been allowed to sing, all the fervor in his heart, which he usually poured into his song, flowed into his spoken word. He told how, in the great sequence of the songs of praise, the master never recited a verse until he had seen the angel of this verse and heard his special strain. He told of the hours in which the soul of the master rose to Heaven, while his body remained behind as if dead, and that there his soul spoke with whomever it would, with Moses the faithful shepherd, and with the Messiah, and asked and was answered. He told that the master could speak to each creature on earth in its own language. He told that, the moment the master saw an implement, he at once knew the character of the man who had made it, and what he had thought about, while making it. And then the cantor rose and testified that once he and his companions had received the Torah through the mouth of the master as Israel had once received it at Mount Sinai through the sound of thunder and trumpets, and that the voice of God was not yet silenced on earth, but endured and could still be heard.

Some time after his visit in Lizhensk, the cantor lay down and died. Thirty days after that, and again on a Friday, the bass singer came from the bath of purification and said to his wife: "Summon the holy brotherhood quickly to see to my burial, for in paradise they have commissioned my cantor to sing for the inauguration of the sabbath [sic], and he does not want to do that without me." He lay down and died.

Rabbi Nahman ben Rabbi Simhah (1772–1810) was born in Mezhybizh in the house that had once belonged to his great-grandfather, the Ba'al Shem Tov. He married at the age of thirteen. He combined a thoroughgoing intellectualism with spirituality, especially advocating the practice of secluded reflection. He traveled to the land of Israel in 1798, and remained there for a year, returning to Breslov, the seat of his community. A fire forced him to leave Breslov for Uman, where he died a short time later. An early disciple collected many of the stories related to his life, as well as his teachings that were published in separate volumes.

Unlike his contemporary, the "Alter Rebbe," Rabbi Nahman has a favorable view of cantors despite the fact that not all cantors enjoy good reputations (third and fourth selections). The first selection shows that Rabbi Nahman favored the musical abilities of a cantor over the minimal abilities of an ordinary prayer leader. Music in general, and song in particular—teaches the *Zohar*—can be a powerful force in connecting with the divine presence. Consequently, the cantor can serve as a vehicle for achieving communion with God. Of course, as demonstrated by the second passage, cantors must be acceptable not just to the congregants he leads. Cantors must epitomize the virtues that would make him acceptable to God. The challenge is to find a cantor who epitomizes those virtues and not one who takes on the position to boost his image (final selection).

Bi'ur HaLikutim, Introduction, trans. Kaplan, ed. Shapiro, 79: The Value of a Cantor

> When the Rebbe came to Breslov, the cantor asked him if he should sing like a cantor or like a prayer leader, and the Rebbe answered, "like a cantor." The Rebbe later invited Rabbi Chaikel[41] to Breslov to be cantor, for he said that Rabbi Chaikel could draw song from its roots on high. Although Reb Chaikel did not agree to be permanent cantor, he would often lead the services.

Sihot V'Sippurim, p. 138, No. 48: The Cantor's Good Voice

> One of the three things that the Rebbe desired was a cantor with a good voice,[42] who would be acceptable both below and on high.[43]

---

41. According to Rabbi Aryeh Kaplan's manuscript (without citation) Reb Chaikel "was a wonderful singer and the Rebbe asked him to become his regular cantor" (*Until the Mashiach*, 16).

42. Cf. *b. Sof.* 3:10.

43. That is, acceptable to the earthly congregation and the heavenly hosts.

Tovot Zikronot 3: Holy and Profane Song

The Rebbe stayed in Ladizin[44] for the Sabbath on the way to Breslov.[45] There was an incident involving the cantor. The Rebbe spoke on the sources of holy and profane song.[46]

Hayyei MoHaRaN 27b, No. 11 and No. 114: Who Should be Impressed?

A certain man led the Minchah service [on Yom Kippur]. His son-in-law then began to lead the Ne'ilah prayer. The Rebbe, however, did not approve, and the man lost his voice in the middle of the prayers. The Rebbe wanted to pray for the retraction of the Russian decrees endangering Jewish distillery rights . . . but the way the man prayed caused much opposition on High. That night, the Rebbe made a joke about these men, and said that they were praying to impress their wives.

The following story appears in *Tovot Zichronot*, No. 3, 104f, first published in Jerusalem in 1951, translated into English under the title *Likutey MoHaRaN* and published by the Breslove Research Institute, 1995, p. 88–89:

While living in Zlatipolia, Rabbi Nachman had encountered unrelenting opposition, particularly from the Shpola Zeida and his followers. Ladizin, some several hundred kilometers to the west, was very different. There he was received with considerable honor from the local inhabitants. As it happened, that Friday night one of the locals, a follower of the Rebbe, was making a *sholom zokhor* (the customary celebration in honor of a newborn son). Many of the townsfolk were present, including Ladizin's cantor who was expected to lead the singing at the celebration. However, being a follower of Rebbe Nachman's opponents, the *chazzan* had taken a seat at the far end of the table and showed no intention of initiating the singing. The Rebbe sent his host out to find out why. "I just don't have a voice right now," the *chazzan* insisted. Even the threat of losing the customary financial remuneration made no difference. He kept insisting he had lost his voice. "The I'll just have to give him a voice," the

44. A neighboring town, some thirty kilometers away.

45. The event is dated 7 Elul 5562, Friday, September 4, 1802.

46. Cf. Likkutei MoHaRaN 3.

Rebbe countered when told the cantor's excuse. Others began to sing instead. Later, as the celebration was about to conclude, Rebbe Nachman made a comment that left everyone perplexed. Quoting from Proverbs (29:3) he remarked, "Doesn't Scripture teach that anyone 'who keeps company with prostitutes loses his wealth'—his voice?" The next day, Shabbat, Rebbe Nachman taught this lesson, and left for Breslov early the following week.

The following Shabbat one of the poorer residents of Ladizin also made a *sholom zochor*. This time the *chazzan* didn't even show up. This callousness incensed several members of the community and they sent a delegation to bring the cantor, so that the poor man would not be embarrassed. But when they arrived at the cantor's home, they were surprised to find only his wife there. The cantor had gone out, telling her that he was on his way to the *sholom zochor*. On their way back, the delegation decided to look for the *chazzan* in the home of his best friend. When they got there, however, they were again disappointed. The house was dark and no one responded to their knocking. They were about to leave when they spotted the cantor running out of the back door. For some time, there had been talk about the cantor and his best friend's wife. But the rumor had never been substantiated. The cantor's friend had birds nesting near his house, and the cantor attributed his frequent visits there to his desire to hear their melodious chirping. Now, however, the truth was out. The news spread fast and the cantor fled from Ladizin in shame.

After this incident, it was clear to the residents of Ladizin what the Rebbe had meant when he said "Then I'll just have to give him a voice," and why the Rebb___ ___d the verse about associating with prostitutes. The t___ ___ants were awed by Rebbe Nachman's prophetic ___ ___ became his followers and, inspired by this lesso___ ___med ___roups to study Mishnah and Talmud nightly.

Russia: Eighteenth Century

Born in Shklov in 1728 into a distinguished rabbinical family, Rabbi Pinhas ben Abraham Abba, was—according to legend—immediately transformed when he met Rabbi Israel Ba'al Shem Tov in Volhynia. Theirs was a mutual admiration. The Ba'al Shem Tov believed Rabbi Pinhas to be a soul that comes down into this world once every five hundred years. At the behest of the Ba'al Shem Tov, he settled in Koretz and remained there for twenty years, raising many Hasidic disciples. He died in Shipitovka in 1790 while on his way to Safed.

Rabbi Pinhas implies that a cantor's role is to assist the congregant in lifting up his voice. The role of the cantor is as much supportive as it is musical.

Buber, Vol. 1, 126—When Two Sing

> Rabbi Pinhas said: "When a man is singing and cannot lift his voice, and another comes along and sings with him, another who can lift his voice, the first will be able to lift his voice too. That is the secret of the bond between spirit and spirit."

Galicia: Eighteenth Century

Rabbi Levi Isaac ben Rabbi Meir (1740–1809) was born into a distinguished rabbinical family in Husakov. His impressive academic skills earned him the title of "Ilui (Prodigy) of Yaroslav." Married at age seventeen, he was drawn to Hasidism under the tutelage of Rabbi Dov Ber, the Maggid of Mezeritch, and is credited with spreading Hasidism to Poland. He finally settled in Berdychiv, Ukraine, and become known as the rabbi of the city in which he served. His passionate defense of the Jewish people earned him accolades. *Kedushat Levi*—his mystical commentary on the Torah—remains a classic in Hasidic literature.

Buber, Vol. 1, 213: Two Kinds of Praying

Lifting the hearts of congregants is the role of the cantor, who must always be cognizant of his own needs as well as theirs. Lengthening the service is not a cantorial flaw if its purpose is engendering heightened spirituality among the worshipers. This contrasts Rabbi Levi Yitzhak with ibn Migash.

> Once, on the eve of the sabbath [sic], Rabbi Levi Yitzhak prayed before the congregation of a town in which he was stopping as a guest. As always, now too he drew out the prayer far beyond its usual length through the many exclamations and gestures not provided for in any liturgy. When he had finished, the rav[47] of

---

47. That is, rabbi.

that town went up to him, proffered the sabbath [sic] greeting, and asked: "Why are you not careful not to tire the congregation? Do not our sages relate of Rabbi Akiba that, whenever he prayed *with* the congregation, he did so quickly, but that when he prayed alone, he yielded himself to his transports, so that frequently he began in one corner of the room and ended up in another." The rabbi of Berditchev replied: "How is it possible to assume that Rabbi Akiba with his countless disciples hastened his prayer in order not to tire the congregation! For surely every member of it was more than happy to listen to his master hour after hour! The meaning of this talmudic story is more likely this: When Rabbi Akiba really prayed with the congregation, that is to say, when the congregation felt at heart the same fervor as he, his prayer could well afford to be short, for he had to pray only for himself. But when he prayed alone, that is to say, when he prayed with his congregation, but his was the only heart fervent among them, he had to draw out his prayer to lift their hearts to the level of his."

Buber, Vol. 1, 214: The Hoarse Reader

Rabbi Levi Yitzhak's *bon mot* emphasizes the requirement of proper intent. Cantors who lack the awareness of the One before whom they pray are silenced.

> In the congregation of Rabbi Levi Yitzhak there was a reader who had grown hoarse. The rabbi asked him: "How is it that you are hoarse?"
>
> "Because I prayed before the pulpit," answered the other.
>
> "Quite right," said the rabbi. "If one prays before the pulpit, one grows hoarse, but if one prays before the living God, then one does not grow hoarse."

Belarus: Eighteenth Century

Rabbi Schneur Zalman ben Baruch (1745–1812) was born in Liady. He was a child prodigy. By the age of eight he wrote a super-commentary on RaShI's interpretation of the Torah. His Bar Mitzvah lecture manifested such a deep and comprehensive understanding of Talmud and rabbinic literature that the townspeople called him "Rav." He studied Talmud with Rabbi Issakhar Ber in Lyubavici (Lubavitch) until there was nothing left to learn. With the aid of certain "enlightened" Jews he studied philosophy, mathematics, and astronomy. He also studied Kabbalah. At the age of twenty-two, he was appointed the "Maggid" of Liozna, a position he held for thirty-four years. He became a disciple of Dov Ber of Mezerich and entered into the Hasidic universe. His literary legacy includes a multivolume compendium on Jewish law (*Shulhan Arukh Ha-Rav*) and a treatise on Hasidic philosophy of "mind ruling over the emotions"[48] (*Tanya*). In the Chabad-Lubavitch community he is often called "Alter Rebbe," Yiddish for "old rabbi," referring to his status as the founder of the Lubavitch dynasty.

The persistent problem about which Rabbi Schneur Zalman was concerned is the disorganized way in which the leaders of communal prayer took on that role. But his solution of relying on a lottery system or congregational consensus overlooks the obvious solution of simply having a permanent and competent cantor. That this solution is not even contemplated is an indication that in his day and place, the professional cantor was no longer retained. And while some[49]—but not all—of the earlier qualifications for a cantor are advocated, the respondent promotes a style of prayer that is rarely seen outside of some Yemenite and Sephardic congregations where all the worshipers recite the entire service aloud together.

The passage from his responsa that follows was published in a 2004 collection. Although this responsum is properly a source of law, I have included it in the chapter on lore in order to group it with other sources in the mystical and Hasidic tradition.

She'elot U'Teshuvot Ha-Rav, No. 6: Qualifications of a Cantor

Fixing the qualifications of a prayer leader

"Surely rebuke your fellow,"[50] even one hundred times.[51] Regarding this [issue] I cannot keep [my feelings] in[side] or be silent and not to complain further against the "sound of the tune of defeat."[52] I pray (com)passionately that you will have

48. Which gave rise to the acronym CHABAD, standing for "Hokhmah" (wisdom), "Bina" (understanding), and "Da'at" (knowledge).

49. Mindfulness, correct pronunciation, deliberate speed.

50. Lev 19:17.

51. *b. B. Metz.* 31a.

52. Cf. Exod 32:18. The pun works in Hebrew as well.

mercy on your souls. And beware and take good care regarding the Torah and "service of the heart"[53] which is mindful prayer, to all begin [to pray] together as one, word for word, and not this one this way, and that one that way, this one silent, and that one talking idly (May God protect us!). The essential reason [for this ruling] and the cause of the damage [that necessitates it] is that [the process governing] those who go to lead [prayers] is chaotic: anyone who roams about can snatch it or that there is no one who wants it, and so forth.

On account of this, here is the advice given and the fixed rule "without exception"[54]—(God forbid!): Choose qualified men to lead on a permanent basis by way of a lottery or with the approval of the majority, so that they pray word for word, in a moderate pace and aloud, and not stretch out [prayers] excessively, nor shorten nor elide [the words] (God forbid!). They are obligated to lead, each one on his predetermined day, and gather around him all the worshipers who will pray audibly and not elide [the words] (God forbid!) as outlined in the old communal enactments[55] in a number of towns . . . *Gevalt*! *Gevalt*! "How long must this be a snare to us?"[56] Is it not sufficient for us [to have endured] all the chastisements and troubles that have befallen us? (May God protect us and comfort us doubly in consolation and purify our hearts to serve Him in truth.) Be strong and of good courage all who hope in God!

Ukraine/Galicia/United States: Twentieth Century

Born in Warsaw, Rabbi Abraham Joshua ben Moses Heschel (1907–1972) was the great-great-grandson of the Hasidic master, Rabbi Abraham Joshua of Apt. Following a traditional, intensive Jewish education, Heschel went on to earn a doctorate from the University of Berlin. Arrested by the Gestapo in his rented room in Frankfurt, he was deported to Poland in 1938. With the help of the president of the Hebrew Union College in Cincinnati, Heschel was able to immigrate to the United States six weeks prior to the German invasion of Poland. He remained on the faculty of HUC for five years until he accepted a position with the Jewish

53. Cf. *b. Ta'an.* 2a.

54. Cf. Ps 148:6.

55. None are indicated.

56. See Exod 10:7. How long must communities suffer being led in prayer by those who are incompetent?

Theological Seminary of America in New York, where he served as Professor of Mysticism and Jewish Ethics until his death. He was a political and social activist who marched with Dr. Martin Luther King Jr., and served as the representative of American Jews to Vatican Council II. A popular author and personality, Heschel's "depth theology" was beautifully articulated in sublime English prose.

The two stories below were featured at the end of his address to the members of the Cantors Assembly of America at their tenth annual convention in 1957. That address was subsequently printed in the Assembly's 1958 Proceedings, and reproduced in the 1972 collection of some of Heschel's essays published under the title *The Insecurity of Freedom*.[57] Many of Heschel's Hasidic stories are not mentioned elsewhere, but being raised in the Hasidic tradition, their reliability is assured. The first story is not datable. The second story is likely one regarding Rabbi Yisrael ben Rabbi Mordekhai Shraga Feivish, who served as the Rebbe of Husiatyn until 1912, when political events forced him to move to Vienna.

"The Vocation of the Cantor," 252: Proper Preparation

Heschel intended this story to convey to cantors that as much as they should be vocally and textually prepared—the latter a cantorial requirement since the time of the Mishnah—cantors ought also to be spiritually prepared. Intimated, as well, is that when cantors perform their task well, the prayers they offer will prove effective in earning divine acceptance.

> [There was once] a Hasidic rabbi in Galicia, among whose adherents were many *hazzanim*. Their custom was to gather at the rabbi's court for the Sabbath which precedes Rosh Hashanah. At the end of their stay they would enter the rabbi's chamber and ask for his blessing that their prayers on Rosh Hashanah would be accepted in heaven. Once . . . one of the *hazzanim* entered the rabbi's chamber immediately after the Sabbath to take leave of the rabbi. When the rabbi asked him, why he was in a hurry to leave, the *hazzan* replied, "I must return home in order to go through the *Mahzor* (The Liturgy for the Days of Awe) and to take a look at the notes." Thereupon the rabbi replied, "why should you go through the *Mahzor* or the notes; they are the same as last year. It is more important to go through your own

---

57. Heschel, *Insecurity of Freedom*, 242–53.

life, to take a look at your own deeds. For you are not the same as you were a year ago."

"The Vocation of the Cantor," 252–53: The Right Attitude

The motif of the ordinary Jew in financial distress who is encouraged to become a cantor—a motif that first appears with the Ba'al Shem Tov—appears again. In this telling, the very fear of being unworthy is praised as the correct cantorial attitude.

> A learned man lost all his sources of income and was looking for a way to earn a living. The members of his community, who admired him for his learning and piety, suggested to him to serve as their Cantor on the Days of Awe. But he considered himself unworthy of serving as the messenger of the community, as the one who should bring the prayers of his fellow men to the Almighty. He went to the rabbi of Husiatin, and told him of his sad plight, of the invitation to serve as a Cantor for the Days of Awe, and of his being afraid to pray for his congregation. "Be afraid—and pray," was the answer of the rabbi.

THE CANTOR IN JEWISH LITERATURE, FOLK SAYINGS, AND SONG

Cantors appear as minor characters in Jewish literature. The cantor's use of a tuning fork, for example, is a memorable scene in one of Harry Kellerman's popular Rabbi Small detective books, *Saturday the Rabbi Went Hungry* (1966). On rare occasions, cantors occupy a central role. Two such examples follow. The first selection is part of a larger project by Rabbi Judah ben Solomon al-Harizi written around the end of the twelfth century. The second selection is a short story written by one of the premier Yiddish writers in Poland some seven centuries later. Together, they are indicative of the historical ambivalence toward the cantor. On the one hand, cantors were susceptible to buffoonery and ignorance, cultivating their egos at the expense of the prayer service. On the other hand, cantors could redeem human beings from the depths of depredation through the emotive and inspiring power of their voices. The ambivalence is sometimes reflected even in the same story. Isaac Leib Peretz's imaginative tale most certainly reflected a reality of his day: cantors with magnificent voices but of questionable character. But when that vocal talent is harnessed for the greater good—the good of the Jewish people, even the sinners—all personal failings are forgotten. The cantor can be motivated by revenge and even violate Jewish law, but still be heroic. Peretz writes an admiring paean to the cantor in contrast to Rabbi Judah ben Solomon al-Harizi's sharp denunciation.

Spain: Twelfth/Thirteenth Century

Probably born in Toledo, Rabbi Judah ben Solomon al-Harizi (1165–1225)—translator and traveler—is the epitome of the courtly style of Hebrew writing of the period, intensified by the influence of Arabic *maqama*, or rhymed prose narrative. In his introduction (as well as the opening chapter, or "Gate") the author makes clear that, in the name of pure and sacred wisdom and with the intent of remediating the errors into which Israel has fallen, he will reestablish the primacy of the Hebrew language. His work itself becomes the exemplar of his intent. Al-harizi's themes vary. But in exposing those who have violated the sacrosanct status of Hebrew, he chooses as example the boorish and incompetent cantor who, though highly acclaimed, is a veritable dunce. The satire works because, no doubt in his day, Jews were well familiar with the typology he skewers. Not to be overlooked or understated, al-Haziri's writing is as much a parody of the congregations served by such a cantor as the cantor himself.

The passage below follows directly the translation of David Simha Segal.[58]

The Book of Tahkemoni, Gate 24: Of a Jolly Cantor and Folly Instanter[59]

The chapter opens with the author describing his arrival in the beautiful and expansive fictional city of Ashur, where the Jews live well and act in accordance with Jewish law. It was Friday afternoon and, without lodging arranged, the visitor makes his way to the magnificent and well-attended synagogue. He asks the two rotund synagogue officials he

58. Segal, *Book of Tahkemoni*, 215–23.

59. Segal coins some neologisms in order to fit the rhyming pattern suggestive of the original. Here, "instanter" means one who instantiates. The jolly cantor is an example of folly.

chances to sit between to tell him about the community. With profound pride they speak highly of the membership and the rabbis. But they reserve the most glowing compliments for their cantor. The virtuous cantor is a great teacher but even a greater singer. "For holy company seek no better choice. And what a voice! Stranger, attend and rejoice! And what he captains us upon Tradition's seas, unraveling the Torah's mysteries, and the Prophets' and Writings', if you please! To boot, he is Poesy's very flute—a master of liturgic verse, to wit, *piyut*."[60]

The author is anxious to hear this great cantor, a divine gift to the Jewish people, but his first impression is curiosity. The cantor is immense. His long beard is unkempt. But the cantor's ignorance is worse than his appearance. He enters wearing his *tefillin*—forbidden on Shabbat[61]—and stepping all over his prayer shawl. Yet despite these failings, the author-visitor joins the rush forward to listen to the great cantor.

Surprised and disappointed, the author-visitor detects numerous mistakes but is willing to give the highly recommended cantor the benefit of the doubt. (Of course, any Jew familiar with the Shabbat evening prayers service would know that it is among the shortest of prayer services.)

> He opened his mouth as we tendered rapt attention; and lo: our ears imbibed one hundred crystal-clear mistakes—and others not worthy of mention. But I breathed not a word; why do him the disservice? This was the Sabbath; perhaps he was tired, or nervous, or distraught by the demands of the longer service.

Wherever the author-visitor arranged to lodge (details are absent), he returns to the synagogue early Shabbat morning with every expectation that the cantor's art would be impressive.

> The next day, when dawn broke, I swiftly woke, donned Piety's cloak, and sought God's house once more with my holy folk. Lo, the cantor entered and took his honoured seat, and in tones

---

60. *Piyyut* was a form of liturgical poetry introduced as early as the Geonic period. The placement as well as the very acceptability of *piyyutim* was controversial (Cf. Mill-gram, *Jewish Worship*, 168–77). Among the proponents of *piyyutim* could be counted Rav Sa'adiah Gaon (who composed some), Rav Natronai Gaon, Rabbenu Gershom, Rabbi Jacob Moellin, RaShI, Rabbenu Tam, and Rabbi Meir of Rothenberg (who also composed some *piyyutim*) (Cf. Hurwitz, *Mahzor Vitry*, 325–26). Opponents included Maimonides, Rabbi Abraham Ibn Ezra, Rabbi Solomon di Medina, and particularly Rabbi Jacob Emden.

61. Cf. *b. Eruv.* 96a–b; Karo, *Shulhan Arukh*, OH 31:1.

dulcet sweet began the daily blessings as is meet. According to the practice of our nation, he begged God's lamination, thundering, *Make the words of Thy Torah pheasant in our mouth*, rather than *pleasant in our mouth*; and *May the Lord flavor you and grant you peas*, instead of *May the Lord favour you and grant you peace*.[62]

In the next section of the service, his zeal mounting, he made errors beyond counting. For *It is our duty to bless and hallow Thy name* he said *It is our duty to blast and hollow Thy name*, for *Exalt the Lord our God*, he said *Assault he Lord our God*; for *Praise the Lord, O my soul*, he said *Prize the Lard, O my soul*; for *Thine, O Lord, is the greatness and the power*, he said, *Thine, O Lord, is the gratings and the flour*; for *Thou rulest over all*, he said, *Thou droolest over all*; and on he went until I grieved that I had ever seen that place; a-a-rgh, the disgrace! I pressed my palms against my burning face.

The author-visitor was even further appalled by this cantor's repertoire:

He showed us his own, his original *piyutim*—a foul dream, a madman's scheme, a limping, misyoked team, a parade no ear could halt of the blind and the halt; rank crime without metre or rhyme, splume and splatter without form or matter.

The drone went on for hours, leaving asleep the few congregants who remained.

Later, a debate ensues between men of the community who, though not present, had strong feelings about this cantor. The cantor's critic was "of pious extraction, a man of godly action" who takes issue with the cantor sending "the congregation packing with the Amidah lacking." The cantor's priorities are misplaced. The cantor's defender argues that "the essence of adoration is laudation; song, sir, before supplication!" *Piyyutim*, he claims, are universally accepted by all Jewish communities as an essential part of the service. In response, the critic claims that what was once true in temple times is no longer the case. But the real issue, adds the critic, is not the inclusion of *piyyut*, but possession of expertise—a characteristic absent in congregations as well as cantors: "While the cantor goes on squawling, belching, and bawling in wild pretence, no one

---

62. Admittedly, David Simha Segal takes "considerable liberties" in his translation. Nevertheless, it well represents the severity (and hilarity) of the mistakes made by the cantor. The literal rendition of the Hebrew appears in *Book of Takhkemoni*, 535.

knows if he makes sense, if he praises or laments; no, no one can say if he prays—or brays."

The cantor's defender says that this congregation is no different than any other. If other places in Greece and Spain have no objections to *piyyutim* and *kerovot*[63] and tolerate bad cantors, why should this synagogue be any different? But the cantor's critic has none of it. He claims this synagogue is unique in its complete ineptitude:

> See here: in every congregation you will find some ghost of thought a-glimmer—a glint, a glow, a shimmer, some comprehension of the Hebrew word, some eardrums stirred, such that when the cantor sounds the convocation to offer adoration, they at least have an inkling of what he is saying and can begin praying.
>
> But here, no such luck: sooner milk a duck! Here none are ready, none able, for this is a stable! Here ox and ass give wisdom to the coup de grace; here the cantor is a knock-kneed horse who cannot walk his course. He neither sees nor comprehends, he knows not where the service starts or ends; and the mob about him knows even less: they cannot tell if he curse or bless.

The author continues with a short account of another man in another city who tried to defend the emphasis on penitential prayers to the diminution of the essential parts of the liturgy established by the rabbis: "And as for the rabbinic interpretation, Thou shalt serve the Lord thy God—serve meaning the reciting of the Amidah—this he held a bogus explication, a fabrication." But, the author retorts, "anyone who maintains that penitential prayers have pentateuchal backing, while Torah authority for the Amidah is lacking, does more than bray and plod: his sin cannot be atoned, for he blasphemes the great, the mighty, the awesome God."

Gate 24 ends with a summative rhyme, concluding with a prayer:

> God save us from heresy, schisms, and fools, and preserve and protect our lucidity. Oh, grant that we ever cleave fast to Thy Will, and not the fouled skirts of Stupidity.

---

63. *Kerovot* were another form of pietistic poetry inserted in the section of the prayer leader's repetition of the *Amidah*.

Poland: Nineteenth Century

Isaac Leib Peretz (1851–1915) bridged the world of Hasidic pietism he inherited and the world of intellectual rigor and progressivism characteristic of the modern period. Born in Zamosc, Poland, he tried his hand at business and then law before turning to writing. His first book—a poetry collection—was published when he was twenty-seven. Peretz wrote in Yiddish and in Hebrew on a wide range of subjects, both in fiction and non-fiction. He remained very active in the Jewish community throughout his adult life.

"Ne'ilah in Gehenna" gives expression to the power of the cantor in altering fate. The story begins with a description of the sudden death of a hated informer as he arrived in the mythical town of Ladam[64] in his horse-drawn wagon. The death of the informer confounded the bureaucrats in hell where his soul was to reside since there were no extant records of anyone ever having died in that town. The subsequent investigation shows that there was neither omission nor mistake. It seems that the cantor's heartfelt pleas for life had protected all the inhabitants from death. Resolved to change this state of affairs, Satan sets to sabotaging the cantor by silencing him, with unanticipated results.

The following English translation by the Canadian poet A. M. Klein appears in *A Treasury of Yiddish Stories.*[65]

From "Ne'ilah[66] in Gehenna":[67] The Power of the Cantor's Prayer

Why, then, have there never been any candidates for Gehenna from Ladam?

64. Though the pronunciation of the name is elided throughout most of the story, it is clear from the question of the "fiend of reception" that the name ought to be Lahadam. This name is a cleverly disguised acronym for the Hebrew: *Lo Hayu Devarim Me'olam*, meaning, these things never occurred. In other words, it is a fictional town in a fictional account. Cf. *b. Ket.* 108b; *b. B. Metz.* 5a.

65. Peretz, "Ne'ilah in Gehenna," 213–19.

66. *Ne'ilah* ("Locking") is the fifth and final prayer service on the Day of Atonement. Its importance lies in the impression that the gates of heaven will soon be locked, preventing any prayers of repentance from reaching God.

67. "Gehenna" is a rabbinic term for hell. Jeremiah mentions the Valley ("Gei," in Hebrew) of Hinom as a site of Molokh worship that involved immolation (Jer 7:32). According to legend, Gehenna is the lowest level of hell, possibly located in the center of earth, and formed on the first day of creation. It is the place where the wicked are eternally punished with fire after death (Cf. Ginzberg, *Legends of the Jews*, 1:10, 15,

Because Ladam has a cantor! There lies the explanation! And what a cantor! But his voice! A voice for singing, so sweet, so poignant-sweet, that when it weeps it penetrates right into hearts of iron, through and through; it melts them to wax! He has but to ascend the prayer stand, this cantor, and lift his voice in prayer, and behold, the entire congregation of Ladam is made one mass of repentance, wholehearted repentance, all its officers and members reduced, as if one person, to singlehearted contrition! With what result? With the result that, Up There, Ladam's sins are nullified, voided, made of no effect! With the result that the gates of Paradise—because of this cantor—are forthwith flung apart! When somebody comes before those gates and says he is from Ladam—no further questions asked!

It was easy to see that with such a cantor in the vicinity, Gehenna would have to operate in Ladam at a loss. Accordingly the matter was taken over by That Certain Party Himself![68] Head of Hell would deal with the cantor personally.

Satan then curses the cantor so that he loses his voice: "Smitten in the throat. Couldn't bring out a note." Significantly, Peretz adds: "Now, had the cantor himself been a man of good deeds, worth, and piety, one might perhaps have interceded for him, hammered at the gates of Heaven, clamored against injustice, but when the cantor was, as all knew, a man of insignificant merit, a trifle in the scales, a nothing, why, then . . ."[69] So the cantor solicited the help of the great rabbis, imploring their intervention before God but to no avail. It was the *zadik*[70] of Apt[71] who reluctantly decided to tell the cantor the whole story, adding, "but know also that when, at the hour of your death, you come to say the Prayer of Repentance,[72] you will say it with a voice so clear, you will sing it with a voice so musical, that it will resound through all the corridors of Heaven." Dissatisfied, the cantor insists he will get his revenge. A few days later, fishermen retrieve the cantor's dead body from the river. He had com-

---

114; 3:20, 101; 5:14, 143, 184, 417; Fox, *Hell in Jewish Literature*; Schwartz, *Tree of Souls*, 232–43). Even the righteous must pass through Gehenna.

68. Any direct mention of Satan is avoided. It is a name that is too terrible to say.

69. The ellipsis is Peretz's.

70. One who is saintly and pious.

71. Likely a reference to Rabbi Abraham Joshua Heschel of Apt, known as the Apter Rebbe (1748–1825).

72. Peretz is referring to the *Vidui* (Confessional) Prayer that includes a plea to God that if life is truly at an end, may the death serve as atonement for any of the wrongs committed in life.

mitted suicide! About to be tortured in the boiling cauldrons of Hell, the cantor, at last, sings:

> Clear and ringing he sings it forth: "*Yis-ga-da-al . . .*"
> The *Kaddish of Ne'ilah*!
> He intones it, he sings it, and in singing his voice grows bolder, stronger . . . melts away . . . revives . . . is rapturous . . . glorious as in the world aforetime . . . no, better . . . sweeter . . . in the heart, deeper . . . from the depths . . . clamorous . . . resurgent . . .
> Hushed are all the boiling caldrons from which up to now there had issued a continual sound of weeping and wailing; hushed, until, after a while, from these same caldrons, and answering hum is heard. The caldron lids are lifted, heads peer out, burned lips murmur accompaniment.

The cantor continues with his *Ne'ilah*:

> The cantor sings on, and the congregation in Hell in undertone accompanies him, prays with him; and passage by passage, as the prayer is rendered, hurt bodies are healed, become whole, torn flesh unites, skin is renewed, the condemned dead grow pure.
> Yes, when the cantor comes to verse where he cries out, "Who quickeneth[73] the dead," and Hell's poor souls respond, "Amen, Amen," it is as if a resurrection, there and then, is taking place!
> For such a clamor arises at this Amen that the heavens above are opened,[74] and the repentance of the wicked reaches to the Heaven of Heavens, to the Seventh Heaven, and comes before The Throne[75] itself! And, it being a moment of grace and favor, the sinners, now saints, suddenly grow wings! One after the other out of Gehenna they fly . . . to the very gates of Paradise.

United States: Nineteenth Century

Hazzan Chaim Weinshel (1834–1901) was a beneficiary of the "Cantor Wars"—the competition among many New York congregations to attract members from the burgeoning immigrant population at the end of the

---

73. That is, "revives."

74. Cf. *b. Sab.* 119b: "The gates of heaven (Garden of Eden) are opened to anyone who says 'Amen' with all his strength."

75. Of God.

nineteenth century by hiring cantorial "stars." Contemporary reports tell that on the first Shabbat at which he officiated in the Anshei Suwalk synagogue, crowds filled the adjoining streets jostling to enter to hear him. Weinshel was happy to accept the then-astounding sum of $1,000 per year in salary, but he was also disappointed by the general boorishness and ignorance of American Jews. In 1891, he published in Hebrew a scathing poem giving an account of his observations, including how easy it is for an unskilled Polish émigré to become a cantor in America. It also implies that many of his colleagues are frauds, taking advantage of the ignorance of American Jews. The translation that follows is that of the rabbi and scholar, Abraham J. Karp:[76]

> There [in Suvalk][77] they bang with hammers like their fathers. Here they become instant hazzanim praying for the well-being of their brethren.
>
> In a language he has not mastered, he lifts his voice in prayer. An ignorant person, how can he pray well?
>
> And there is one who never thought to lead in prayer until a friend calculatedly, declared him one—and he became ordained and led! . . .
>
> When his uncle found no work for him, he said: "I'll make you a hazzan. You'll pray for your people. You'll live in comfort, eat your bread with dignity."
>
> He objected: "How can I be a hazzan? I shouted at the millstones, but I don't know any Hebrew—how can I be a hazzan, a master of prayer?"
>
> The uncle answered: "My son, calm yourself. I am the master here, head of the congregation. I'll call a meeting of my herd, my sheep and donkeys. Then you'll see my power, how my flock fears me . . . I have spoken—who will question my words? You are the chief cantor of my synagogue, so cease your foolish idle words. You are the hazzan, and your salary is five hundred a year."
>
> The mill worker opened his mouth, roared and shouted in a gravelly voice that grated on the ears like an owl's shrieking.
>
> "Is there a better hazzan?" the uncle stated. "He is the best of all: musical, sweet-voiced, hazzan, the one we'll choose."
>
> The miller became a hazzan and informed his wife in the Old Country; the poor woman went into shock and ran to the

76. Slobin, *Chosen Voices*, 53.

77. Weinshel's parody is made even more delicious by using as an example the Polish town whose emigrants founded the synagogue in which he served.

rabbi: "Save me from my demented husband. He claims to be a hazzan—he must have lost his mind!"

At the rabbi's behest, the wife sent a letter imploring her husband to return home, where there are doctors who could cure him . . . but there, the miller, now a noted hazzan, was singing at weddings, circumcisions, and at gravesides, and money was pouring in from all directions.

The women carried him on their fingertips. He received a new tallit with a large, silver embroidery as a present . . .

The hazzan sent an answer to his wife: ". . . Weep not, my sweet one, fear not that your husband has lost his mind. My mind is clear—it's the congregation that's gone crazy!"

THE CANTOR IN YIDDISH
FOLK SAYINGS AND SONG

Here again, the attitude toward the cantor was markedly ambivalent. Folk wisdom could prove to be studiously neutral, but it typically ran the gamut from supportively defensive to critically offensive.

The folk saying cited by Shirley Kumove, "A cantor should be married; he should be able to pray with a broken heart," is a variant on Mishnah *Ta'anit* 2:2 that assumes that a cantor with dependent children will pray wholeheartedly.[78] But it does not have anything to say about the nature of the office or the qualities of the person who holds it.

Supportive of the cantor is the saying cited by Kumove[79] that "One is an expert in simple things and another is an expert in pig bristles. But all are experts on a cantor." Criticism of the cantor, it seems, is not dependent on any real evaluative tools. Everyone has an opinion on cantors whether or not it is based on evidence, experience, or compliance with any set of standards. Thus the cantor is exceptionally vulnerable. The implication here is that the cantor merits some degree of latitude. An ambivalent defense of the cantor is expressed by the saying: "No matter how well the cantor sings, there will be criticism: Oy! Is that a cantor? He pleads to God like he would plead to a robber."[80] The first part is clear enough. Disapproval of the cantor is independent of his vocal skill. This ought

---

78. A married cantor was required for the high holidays. Cf. Ganzfried, *Kitzur Shulhan Arukh*, 128:7.

79. Kumove and Newfeld, *Words Like Arrows*, 27.

80. Kumove and Newfeld, *Words Like Arrows*, 28.

to elicit some degree of sympathy. Yet the second part—an example of undeserved criticism—describes the cantor as overly theatrical, turning his praying into braying; appealing to God in tones a potential victim would use to deter a robber. (Of course it does not occur to the coiners of this folk saying that a Jew very well ought to pray to God in such a way.) What should not be overlooked, however, is the underlying assumption that the cantor's worth is solely dependent on his vocal skills, an assumption challenged by many legal authorities, but reflective of the Central and Eastern European milieu after the seventeenth century. Similarly, the saying that, "All cantors are fools; but not all fools can sing,"[81] is a tepid defense of the cantor. It grants that cantors as a class are deficient in judgment and understanding, but that is not all that is important. In the area of vocal abilities, however, cantors excel; and that itself is worthwhile. These vocal abilities make the cantor unique, despite people who think otherwise. Leo Rosten[82] cites the folk saying: "Any Jew can sing better than the cantor—only at the moment he has a cold." The first clause of this saying ("Any Jew can sing better than the cantor") sounds much like a casual dismissal of the cantor's talent. But the subsequent clause turns that initial claim on its head. The idea that all Jews will have colds all the time is preposterous, thus exposing the falsity of the initial claim. So what starts out as a scornful belittling of the cantor's talent as pedestrian, ends up a tacit recognition of the cantor's exceptionality.

Just as commonly, folk wisdom takes a critical view of cantors. A saying Rosten[83] ascribes to Joseph Zabara takes the concession that a cantor is a fool and adds to it the vice of arrogance: "A *khazen* is a fool: he stands on a platform and thinks he's on a pedestal." In this saying, even the cantor's musical talent cannot save him from disparagement. The saying cleverly builds on the fact that cantors lead prayer services in the synagogue from the *bimah*, an elevated platform. But rather than see that platform as a boost in height, the cantor takes it to mean a boost in ego. Even the musical talent of the cantor is questioned. Kumove cites the folk saying that, "A cantor takes money for screaming, and a rabbi for his silence."[84] That rabbis and cantors are popularly viewed in a kind of competition for the approval of the congregation underlies this saying.

81. Kumove and Newfeld, *Words Like Arrows*, 27.

82. Rosten, *Hooray for Yiddish*, 177.

83. Rosten, *Hooray for Yiddish*, 177.

84. Kumove and Newfeld, *Words Like Arrows*, 28.

That the cantor's ministrations are described as "screaming" ("*shreien*," in Yiddish) is not complimentary. In contrast to the rabbi's purportedly serene and thoughtful demeanor, the cantor comes across as histrionic. The theatricality of the cantor suggests a manufactured piety that critics of cantors view as fraudulent.

Despite the implicit popular criticism of cantors—or perhaps merely an understanding of the people who held the position—cantors were still thought to have transformative power. Cantors had the tools to inspire the masses—particularly the struggling underclass—and offer them some relief from their toils. The folk song (composer and lyricist unknown) of "*A Chanzndl Oyf Shabbes*" ("A Cantor for the Sabbath") extols the itinerant cantor who visits a small Jewish town for the Sabbath and evokes glorious religious feeling in each of the congregants, who express their delight in the terms most familiar to them.

> Once a cantor came to a small town to chant the Sabbath prayers.
> Three prominent men of the village came to hear him:
> One was a tailor, the second was a blacksmith, and the third was a wagon driver.
> The tailor spoke up: "Oy! How he did chant! The way that a needle could give a quick stitch, or the hot iron a good press.
> Then the blacksmith spoke up: "Oy! How he did chant! The way that a hammer would give a sharp blow or the bellows a hard squeeze. Oy! How he did chant!
> Then the driver spoke up: "Oy! How he did chant! How he did chant! The same way that a driver would pull on the reins or crack his whip hard in the air! Oy! How he did chant!

Each perceives the same performance interpreted through their individual experiences, but the common report was that the cantor had succeeded in inspiring each of them. Such was the power of the cantor in the mind of the Jewish community.

By no means are these selections comprehensive. But they are representative. The perception of the cantor in literature, folk sayings, and song is as ambivalent as it is in the legal texts. Maddeningly, the cantor often fails to meet the established ideals. But in those rare, magical moments when the cantor succeeds in blending the meaning of the words with the expressiveness of his voice, the mood with the mode, the congregation can be lifted to the heights.

THE CANTOR IN JEWISH HUMOR

A cantor tells his congregation's board of directors that he will have to find work elsewhere; he simply isn't earning enough to support his family. The synagogue's leadership tells him they don't have the money to give him a raise, but they will help him in other ways:

The butcher promises to supply his family with meat and chicken every week.

The baker promises a never-ending supply of bread and cake.

The clothing-store operator promises to clothe his whole family.

The sisterhood president says: "I promise to sleep with you every Monday and Thursday."

The room becomes deathly quiet. Finally, the synagogue president asks the woman why she is making such an offer.

"I asked my husband what we could give to the cantor and he said, 'Screw the cantor.'"

This story told by Rabbi Joseph Telushkin[85] capitalizes on two recurrent themes: the inability—or unwillingness—of synagogues to financially support their religious leaders and the dire financial straits in which cantors often find themselves. But the story also reveals a more ominous theme that lurks beneath the surface, namely the vulnerability of cantors to the predilections of the congregations they serve. Cantors may be revered or reviled independent of their skills or professionalism. It is the naïveté of the sisterhood president that drives the humor of this story: she confuses her husband's insulting remark for a mandate. But it is her husband's attitude that points to the precariousness of the cantor's vocation.

Given the fact that a cantor's position remains insecure, that more than the very few would aspire to the position is problematic. Addressing this issue is the story recounted by Henry Spalding.[86]

A new immigrant made his way to Brooklyn in search of a cousin he had not seen since childhood in the old country. He stopped a man who looked Jewish and, in Yiddish of course, asked: "Sir, I am looking for Cantor Rosenzweig of the Pitkin Avenue Synagogue. Can you give me directions, please?"

85. Telushkin, *Jewish Humor*, 87–88.
86. Spalding, *Encyclopedia of Jewish Humor*, 92.

"Sure, I know the man well," said the passerby. "You are speaking of Cantor Berel Rosenzweig, a chazzen who can't carry the simplest tune. You'll reach the synagogue six blocks ahead, two blocks to the left and a block-and-a-half to the right."

The newcomer thanked him but soon had to stop someone else. Again he asked directions to the Pitkin Avenue Synagogue, explaining his wish to see Cantor Rosenzweig.

"Oh you mean Rosenzweig the crook—the one who has all those phony sales every year. Sure, just turn left at the subway and walk two blocks."

He finally reached the synagogue and, in the lobby, he spied a man who looked as though he might be the long lost cousin.

"Pardon me," he asked politely, "but are you Cantor Rosenzweig?"

"Who, Rosenzweig the miser, who lets his wife and children starve while he buys for himself only the best? No, thank God, I'm not. But that is he, standing over there."

The stranger approached Cantor Rosenzweig, introduced himself and exchanged the usual greeting. At length, the visitor asked curiously; "Tell me, Cantor, why do you devote so much time to the synagogue? Is it the money they pay you?"

"I don't get paid," Rosenzweig said, "Not a penny!"

"Then why do you do it?"

The Cantor inflated his chest proudly. "Why, for the honor, of course."

Like many good stories, this one succeeds on several levels. First, it drips with irony. The cantor who imagines himself an honorable man doing an admirable job in an honorable profession has earned a reputation for being musically incompetent, a cheat, and a miser. Second, it points to the ongoing and centuries-old conflict between cantors and the congregations they serve on what remuneration the cantor merits. In this story, the new immigrant assumes that the cantor must be well compensated to account for his devotion to his calling. Yet the story reveals—incredibly—that the cantor receives no compensation at all. In reality, this would hardly be the case, at least since the eleventh century.[87] But the exaggeration allows the story to convey an element of truth: while a few cantors are paid extremely well, most cantors struggle financially, often forced to take on other jobs. This story turns this harsh reality on its head: a cantor who actually desires to work for nothing. The further irony

---

87. Cf. Al-Fasi, *She'elot U'Teshuvot Ha-RIF*, No. 281.

lies in the fact that the cantor who serves the synagogue for nothing is a scoundrel at home and in business.

The flawed cantor becomes the subject of many popular tales. Here is an example.

> A cantor applies for a position at a synagogue and lists the congregations where he has worked previously. The synagogue's president contacts his counterpart at one of the congregations for a reference. The man writes back: "This cantor is like Abraham, like Moses; indeed, he is like an angel."
>
> The president immediately hires the cantor, but when he comes to the synagogue that Shabbat, catastrophe ensues. The cantor's voice warbles, he is arrogant, and every one is very disappointed.
>
> Monday morning, the president makes a furious call to the man who had written him the letter of recommendation. "How could you dare tell me that he was like Abraham, like Moses, and an angel? He was horrible."
>
> "Everything I said is absolutely true," the man insists. "Abraham couldn't sing, and this cantor can't sing. Moses stuttered (Exod 4:10), and this cantor stutters. And an angel isn't a *mensch*,[88] and this cantor isn't a *mensch*."

This story[89] is a variant of the same story told by Spalding[90] about a rabbi who was compared to Moses, Shakespeare, and God. Like Moses, he could not speak publicly. Like Shakespeare, he knew no Hebrew. Like God, he simply wasn't human. The humor of this story hinges on the misinterpretation of the truthful "recommendation." The story also exposes some of the failings popularly associated with cantors. Not all cantors are musically gifted. And even those who are may continue to sing beyond the time they are physically capable. Worse still is feeling that cantors are self-absorbed egotists who treat their employers with disdain.

Both themes—the cantor with questionable skills and the cantor with an inflated ego—are intertwined in this story told by Spalding:[91]

> Cantor Rosenblatt could not sing a note but his conceit was so ingrained that all the hints and snide remarks about his croaking voice simple did not penetrate.

---

88. Meaning a decent human being, in Yiddish.
89. Telushkin, *Jewish Humor*, 156–57.
90. Spalding, *Encyclopedia of Jewish Humor*, 85.
91. Spalding, *Encyclopedia of Jewish Humor*, 96.

He had just finished singing the service one evening when a stranger approached him. "It is truly a burden, this profession of ours," he sighed.

"Oh, you're a cantor too?"

"Good Lord, no! I'm a butcher."

This story included in Joseph Telushkin's *Jewish Humor* was published with minor variation in 1953 in Nathan Ausubel's *A Treasury of Jewish Folklore*.[92] Even when the cantor's skills remained sharp, Jews could not resist poking fun at the cantor's affectations. Rosten includes this representative little gem:[93]

It is said that when you inform a chazzen of a calamity, he whips a tuning fork out of his pocket, taps it, gets the right key, then cries, "Gevaaaalt!"[94]

The cantor's virtue is also subject to question:

A young doctor had moved out to a small Jewish community to replace a doctor who was retiring. The older doctor suggested that the young one accompany him on his rounds, so the community could become used to a new doctor.

At the first house a woman complained, "I've been a little sick to my stomach."

The older doctor said, "Well. You've probably been overdoing the fresh fruit. Why not cut back on the amount you have been eating and see if that does the trick?"

As they left, the younger man said, "You didn't even examine that woman. How'd you come to the diagnosis so quickly?"

"I didn't have to examine her. You noticed I dropped my stethoscope on the floor in there? When I bent over to pick it up, I noticed a half dozen banana peels in the trash. That was what probably was making her sick."

"Wow," the younger doctor said. "Pretty clever. I think I'll try that at the next house."

Arriving at the next house, they spent several minutes talking with younger woman. She complained that she did not have the energy she once did. "I'm feeling terribly run down lately."

"You've probably been doing too much work for the synagogue," the younger doctor told her. "Perhaps you should cut back a bit and see if that helps."

92. Ausubel, *Treasury of Jewish Folklore*, 390.

93. Rosten, *Joys of Yiddish*, 69, *s.v. chazzen*.

94. An expletive from the German, meaning an act of providence in Yiddish.

As they left, the elder doctor said, "I know that woman well. Your diagnosis is almost certainly correct, but how did you arrive at it?"

"Well, just as you did at the last house, I dropped my stethoscope on the floor and when I bent down to retrieve it, I noticed the cantor under the bed."

Even the cantor's intelligence was held in low esteem. As Rosten[95] notes:

The intellectual status of *chazzonim* is, indeed, derided. "He has the brain of a *chazzen*" is not a compliment.

Rosten cites what he describes as a "folk saying" that claims that "All cantors are fools, but not all fools are cantors."[96] And where Yiddish was spoken, it was popularly held that: "*Chazzonim zenen naronim*"—"All cantors are fools," an acronym formed by the three Hebrew letters for the word "cantor."

But the most disparaging jibe at the intelligence of the cantor appears in *Sarei Ha-Me'ah*, Part 4, Rabbi Yehudah Leib Ha-Kohen Maimon's multivolume history of the Polish rabbinate in the eighteenth century. The author reports an exchange at a wedding ceremony between a guest who had some issues with the cantor of Zamosz, fifty-year-old Shlomo Kashtan, and Rabbi Jacob of Dubno, a man noted for his wit. The guest asked:

"Where do we know from Scripture or rabbinical literature that any given cantor is an imbecile?" Rabbi Jacob responded that the source is in Proverbs, in the Talmud, and also reflected in Jewish custom and practice. Every cantor, Rabbi Jacob went on to explain, stands on the pulpit facing the usual inscription that reads: "I am ever mindful of the Lord's presence" (Ps 16:8), more literally, "I have set the Lord always before me." And everyone knows there is an explicitly clear verse in Proverbs (21:30) that states "There is no wisdom and no understanding before the Lord," implying that he who stands before the Lord—the cantor—is without wisdom or understanding. In the Talmud,[97] we learn that if a person sends an agent to burn down a neighbor's field, he is not responsible unless the agent is a deaf-mute, an imbecile, or a minor. (If the agent is fully and legally compe-

95. Rosten, *Joys of Yiddish*, s.v. "Chazzen."

96. Rosten, *Joys of Yiddish*, 81.

97. *b. B. Kam.* 59b.

tent, it is the agent who is held responsible for the damages.) Analogously, the cantor is an agent of the congregation[98] and if he errs in his chanting, it is a bad sign for the congregation. Since the cantor, by law, can be neither a deaf-mute nor a minor, the only conclusion to be drawn is that he must be an imbecile. Finally, it is common Jewish synagogue practice that the cantor recites Kiddush on Friday night while the sexton recites Havdalah on Saturday night. The Jerusalem Talmud[99] (Berakhot 5:2) explains the difference: "If there is no understanding, how can one say Havdalah?"[100]

Cantor Kashtan heard of this exchange and felt greatly insulted. When the community leaders gathered to consider increasing the salaries of both rabbi and cantor, Cantor Kashtan argued that his age and tenure demanded that he alone receive a raise. The congregation agreed. The amity between the cantor and rabbi turned into enmity. When the rabbi would preach, the cantor would absent himself; and when the cantor would sing, the rabbi would pray elsewhere—a state of affairs not unknown in other synagogues subsequently.

As in any random sampling of a particular professional group, one would expect to count any number of rascals or incompetents. Yet the vitriol reserved for cantors seems especially harsh. No doubt one could find crooked lawyers, bungling doctors, dishonest accountants, greedy businessmen, penurious magnates, and even inept rabbis. And folklorists will note that these, too, are subject to considerable derision. But even with its share of less-than-stellar members, rabbis, as a group, are treated more kindly and respectfully than cantors.

There are four reasons why this is the case. First, while the rabbi might also stretch the patience of the congregation by speaking at length, this was not perceived as a fatal flaw. One story relates how an itinerant preacher was invited by the *gabbai* to speak at his local synagogue. The visiting rabbi inquired: "How much time is allotted for me?" The host said: "Take as long as you like. The clock on the wall is broken." So the preacher

---

98. *b. Ber.* 34b.

99. *y. Ber.* 5:2.

100. In the *Amidah*, recited at the conclusion of the Sabbath, the prayer or separation (*Havdalah*) is placed in the fourth blessing that ends with ". . . He who gives [human beings] knowledge." The reason for this placement is that knowledge or understanding is necessary to make distinctions. *Havdalah* is also recited as a public ritual. That the cantor is not accustomed to recite the public prayer is ascribed to his lack of understanding.

droned on and on. When he finished, the *gabbai* looked perturbed. The preacher, reading consternation in the face of the gabbai, said: "But you said the clock on the wall is broken!" "Yes," responded the gabbai, "but the calendar on the wall is not!" Indeed, rabbis can take liberties with time. But rabbis have no fixed text to recite. It is tacitly understood that the length of a rabbi's address is—or ought to be—proportionate to the complexity of the topic and the importance of the occasion. Cantors, on the other hand, follow the fixed liturgy. Hence, any additions, interpolations, and repetitions were generally perceived as unnecessary delays in the service. To put it somewhat differently, a rabbi who extemporizes is praised for scholarship. A cantor who extemporizes is criticized for insensitivity to the forbearance of the congregation.

Second, the cantor is the most prominent figure in the synagogue. Until the modern period, rabbis rarely preached. The rabbi's role was subtler. Communities relied on the rabbi's learning and insights to resolve matters of Jewish law and practice and to offer advice and counsel. But these functions were generally performed in private. Individuals would come to the rabbi with their questions and the rabbis would respond to them alone. The workings of the rabbinical courts on which rabbis would serve were not open to the public. For most of the community and for most of the time, the rabbi was a figurehead whose importance was undeniable, but whose actions were largely unnoticed. In contrast, the cantor was essentially visible. He stood at the center of the congregation for all to see and hear. He was the voice of the community: speaking to God on their behalf. His emotive chanting and artful musicality could bring the congregation to tears or to ecstasy. As the most prominent figure in the synagogue, it is not surprising, then, that the cantor would be subject to the most scrutiny and the most criticism.

Third, although tradition required that any prayer leader must possess many virtues, the important role performed by the cantor hinged on one skill. The cantor's privileged position was contingent on his voice alone. To the common folk, this inequality did not seem fair or reasonable. After all, a good voice was a natural gift. It could be cultivated and trained; but it could not be acquired, no matter the effort. No measure of hard work could transform a weak or tinny voice into a sweet and mellifluous one. Thus, it seemed that whatever standing the cantor held, it was not based on merit. This rankled the sensibilities of Jews who strained under pressure to eke out a living by working long hours under difficult conditions. Hence, Rosten includes this short exchange.

"Our new *chazzen!*" said one Jew. "What beautiful singing, no?"

"Ehh," scoffed the other. "If I had his voice, I'd sing just as good."

This derisive observation, worded slightly differently, appeared in Nathan Ausubel's *A Treasury of Jewish Folklore.*[101] It exposes the ambivalence the Jewish community felt with regard to the cantor. On the one hand, the voice of the masterful cantor could be inspiring. On the other hand, the skill of the cantor was dismissed as pedestrian. At the same time, there is a measure of jealousy detectable: the cantor's critics would jump at the chance to serve in his position. That jealousy would only intensify and so would the contempt. As Ronald L. Eisenberg notes, "Criticism of hazzanim escalated with their increasing popularity."[102]

The cantor's celebrity lay in his voice, but this asset made the cantor one-dimensional. As long as his voice retained its power and range, the cantor retained his prestige. But when his voice faltered—as wouldinevitably happen with age—his failings would then be exposed. Satirists soon took to considering the possibility. So well known is the story of the cantor in decline that it appears, with minor variations, in three separate anthologies.[103] This is the most recent iteration:

> When the Holy One, Blessed Be He, created the world, He assembled all his creatures and assigned them their allotted life span—forty years to each—as well as their tasks on earth. When it was the horse's turn, that animal asked the Holy One, Blessed Be He, "What will my labor be?"
>
> "Human beings will ride on you," replied the Holy One, Blessed be He.
>
> "If that is what I have been created for," replied the horse, "twenty years are enough."
>
> After the horse came the donkey. He too asked what his task would be. When he heard that he would carry heavy loads on his back he, too, asked to be exempted from twenty years of such toil.
>
> Finally, the cantor entered and asked what his mission would be. The Holy One, Blessed Be He, replied, "Yours will be a clean and easy job—singing melodiously."
>
> "When the cantor heard this he asked that his years be augmented. What did the Holy One, Blessed be He, do? He gave

101. Ausubel, *Treasury of Jewish Folklore*, 390.

102. Eisenberg, *Jewish Traditions*, 348.

103. Ausubel, *Treasury of Jewish Folklore*, 391; Rosten, *Joys of Yiddish*, 71; Ben-Amos, *Folktales of the Jews*, 2:427.

him the twenty years returned by the horse and the twenty years returned by the donkey.

And this is why until the age of forty a cantor sings with the voice of a cantor. But when he passes forty he starts neighing like a horse—and eventually he brays like a donkey!

This story imitates the style of ancient Jewish legends, including the use of "Holy One, Blessed Be He" for God. Putting it in classical, legendary form also lends an air of authenticity to it. In fact, as Dan Ben-Amos notes, this story mirrors other Jewish legends that associate aging with different animals and their respective characteristics. What makes this particular version so interesting is that it describes the job of the cantor as one that is "clean and easy," reflective of the popular view that cantors—unlike other Jews—work short hours and away from the muck and grime of real laborers. In Ausubel's version, God describes the cantor's liturgical contribution as one that will put the congregation "in raptures" thus creating a stronger point of contrast with the aging cantor who can no longer do so. Further, in Ausubel's version, the cantor's life will be "an endless pleasure." In Jewish folklore, few have it as good as the cantor, making the cantor a satirical target.

It is, however, the cantor's vocal ability that will always be debated. Ausubel[104] includes a story about a cantor's carping critics.

The congregation advertised for a cantor. A candidate appeared and on the following Sabbath he held forth.

When the congregation met later to discuss his qualifications the membership was split wide open on the issue.

"He croaks like a frog!" contended one group.

"He sings with feeling!" countered the others.

They argued so long and excitedly about the matter that the rabbi, who all along had held aloof from the controversy, was drawn in as mediator.

"My sons," began the rabbi, in a soothing voice. "What is all this about? Our holy Torah requires a cantor to be pious, a fairly good scholar, mature in age, of praiseworthy character, and lastly—to have a melodious voice. Just let us examine the qualifications of this candidate. Are we all agreed that he's pious, a fairly good scholar, mature in age, and that he has a praiseworthy character?"

"Yes, Rabbi!" answered the congregation.

104. Ausubel, *Treasury of Jewish Folklore*, 388.

"In that case, what is all the fuss about?" asked the rabbi. "The only difference of opinion is whether he has a good voice or not, and surely you won't let a little matter like that deprive the man of a job!"

This story is based on a recurrent theme in Jewish folklore: the rabbi as the wise mediator. It also features a listing of most of the criteria Jewish law requires of a prayer leader. The humor lies in its surprise. Both the candidate's supporters and detractors have made his voice the focus of the conflict. The rabbi, however, dismisses that factor as trivial. Ironically, the rabbi's view coheres with the norms of Jewish law that places greater emphasis on a prayer leader's nonmusical abilities. The popular view is quite otherwise, hence the surprise. But in the rabbi minimizing the weight given to the cantor-candidate's voice, the story actually demonstrates the opposite. It is the quality of the cantor's voice that will always be debated. That the rabbi is an advocate of the auditioning cantor is a bonus feature, and also a surprise.

The one-dimensionality of the cantor made him a musical specialist. Consider the story told by Ausubel[105] and repeated in Spalding[106] without the Yiddish jargon.

> The cantor and the treasurer of the synagogue had been carrying on a bitter feud for many months, but it reached a climax one day when the cantor publicly denounced the treasurer as a crook who had been appropriating the synagogue's funds for his own use.
>
> Understandably enraged, the treasurer complained to the rabbi who immediately sent for the slanderer.
>
> "You have made a serious charge against an honest man," the rabbi said coldly. "You know as well as I that the accusation is untrue. I must insist that you make a public apology in the synagogue this coming Saturday. Nor are you going to mince any words about it, either. You will say 'I made a false charge and I apologize.'"
>
> "All right, so I'll say it," the cantor grumbled.
>
> "Let me hear you say it right now,"
>
> "I made a false charge and I apologize," the cantor mumbled almost inaudibly.
>
> "That's no good!" the rabbi stormed. "You are to enunciate your words clearly and loudly enough for all to hear.

105. Ausubel, *Treasury of Jewish Folklore*, 390.

106. Spalding, *Encyclopedia of Jewish Humor*, 96.

> "Now just a minute, Rabbi," the cantor said resentfully. "I
> don't tell you how to interpret the Torah, so don't you instruct a
> cantor in matters of tone and voice!"

Synagogue conflicts are not rare so the setting of this story is entirely believable. Here again, the rabbi serves as a mediator: this time
with the cantor as one of the disputants. The cantor does not challenge
the rabbi's power to compel him to apologize. What he challenges is the
rabbi's presumption to demand it be offered in a particular tone. The cantor alone is the expert in matters of voice: at least according to the cantor.
The folklorist interpreted the self-declared musical preeminence of the
cantor as an expression of egotism and snobbery. Thus, one riddle that
made the rounds in New York City in the middle of the twentieth century
was designed to put the cantor in his place:

> What is the difference between a cantor and an opera singer?
> The opera singer clears his voice with "Mi, mi, mi, mi." The can-
> tor clears his voice going: "Kha-kha-kha, p'too-ie."

Contrasting the boorishness of the cantor with the refinement of
the opera singer was a jibe against the cantors who believed that they too
should be counted with Robert Merrill, Richard Tucker, and Jan Peerce
who, in addition to serving as cantors, were esteemed tenors in New
York's Metropolitan Opera Company. What galled the folk was the cantor
with middling skill who behaved as though he was an opera star, replete
with the performer's ego.

The deflation of the cantor's ego is the objective in this oft-repeated
exchange between the boastful cantor and a doyenne of the congregation:

> "I will have you know, madam," said the cantor contemptuously,
> "that my voice is insured with Lloyd's of London for a million
> dollars!"
> "Really? What did you do with the money?"

Not only does this popular story expose the exaggerated self-impor-
tance of some cantors, it reinforces the singular emphasis on the cantor's
voice as well as the criticism to which it is subject.

With the impression that the cantor's job is easy and that, after all,
the quality of the cantor's voice will always be debatable, it was a career
choice that attracted both the unqualified and the unscrupulous:

> A man tries out for a job as a cantor. When he comes home from
> the service, his wife asks him how it went.

"Terrible. The *shammes* [synagogue sexton or ritual direc-
tor] said my voice was monotonous: nobody liked the way I
sang."

"Ah, what do you pay attention to him for?" the wife says.
"Everybody knows the *shammes* just repeats what he hears."[107]

The humor of this story—told by many but appearing in print in
Joseph Telushkin's *Jewish Humor*—lies in the failed attempt of the audi-
tioner's wife to offer some consolation to her husband. In the synagogue
hierarchy, the *shammes* (sexton) is situated near the bottom of the list
of professional staff members. But in her attempt to be dismissive, the
woman reveals that the *shammes's* opinion is actually reflective of the
congregation's. What this anecdote highlights is that while many cantors
are trained professionals, with many today holding academic degrees,
others attempt to enter the field with little competence and no credentials.

Satirists had a low opinion of the unscrupulous who exploited the
ignorance of the Jewish community. The following story, originally published in 1965 by Dov Noy, was republished in three versions by Dan
Ben-Amos,[108] based on a Romanian report:

One clear summer day, a Polish Jew came to a town in Germany looking for a way to make some money. He saw that the
townsfolk were all *amaratzim*—unlettered ignoramuses when
it came to Hebrew and religious matters. What did he do? He
pounced on his prey and informed the Jews that the next day
was Yom Kippur. The Jews were in a panic—where would they
find themselves a cantor?

Hearing this, the Polish Jew immediately offered—for he
was a professional cantor—to stay and conduct the services if
they paid him a handsome sum.

The local Jews were delighted and agreed to his terms. The
next day they celebrated Yom Kippur.

During the services, however, another Polish Jew, a certain
Hayyim who hailed from the same town as the cantor, happened
to be in the synagogue. What did the cantor do? When he saw
Hayyim enter, he continued the service without interruption,
singing the same melody but changing the Hebrew words:

"Greetings, Reb Hayyim!
I told them today is Yom Kippur.
Half is mine and half is yours:

107. Telushkin, *Jewish Humor*, 157.
108. Ben-Amos, *Folktales of the Jews*, 437.

O Holy One!"

The joke is on the community that, because of its ignorance, was led into believing the next day was Yom Kippur. Of course, this in itself is ridiculous. As ignorant as the members of any Jewish community may be, it is impossible to imagine any community being unaware of the scheduling of the holiest day of the Jewish year. But by straining the limits of credulity, the satirist demonstrates just how easy a mark they would be to a confidence man.

Yet while they may not know when Yom Kippur falls, they do know they need a cantor. Interestingly, a rabbi does not figure in the story. The transmitters of this story, and perhaps the listeners as well, understood that Jewish law prefers the leadership of a cantor over the leadership of a rabbi.[109] When the visitor arrives it becomes clear to the "cantor" that his subterfuge would be exposed. Thinking quickly, he offers to evenly split the handsome fee he finagled the community into paying him while disguising his plan in Hebrew words that sounded like a prayer to the members of this ignorant congregation. This further impugns the Jewish knowledge of German Jewish townsfolk and results in laughter at their expense. Concomitantly, it suggests that where ignorance abides, cantors will thrive. And all that was really required was to sound convincing.

The fourth reason that the cantor was made the special target of satirists was the perceived shift from cantor as leader of sacred prayer to cantor as performer. Israel Abrahams assigns the transformation to as early as the Middle Ages:

> The Hazan became less a reader than a singer, less a singer than a spirited declaimer. He gave to his emotions an expression which can only be described as dramatic; he wept or was glad as the prayers called for it.[110]

Abraham Millgram adds:

> the adulation of admiring listeners prompted many a hazan to forget his primary function and to see himself as a virtuoso. Instead of striving to arouse in the congregation feelings of piety, the hazan has often striven to entertain his appreciative audience.[111]

109. Karo, *Shulhan Arukh*, OH 53:24; that is unless the rabbi is an acknowledged scholar.

110. Abrahams, *Jewish Life*, 277.

111. Millgram, *Jewish Worship*, 526. Incidentally, Rabbi Abraham Price, revered

Worse still:

> Some cantors began to violate good musical taste. They indulged in excessive vocal gymnastics and even corrupted the sense of the prayers for the sake of demonstrating their vocal agility. At times they employed incongruous tunes. A kind of musical pilpul of technical intricacy became the goal of hazanut, and emotionalism of a ludicrous nature often climaxed the hazan's performance.[112]

As a result:

> The more the service was turned into a professional concert, the less the congregation identified itself with the hazan as a shaliah tzibbur.[113]

Humorists and satirists sought to rebuke the cantor who had gone too far, thus restoring the cantor's role in the service to the traditional ideal.

Although the cantor was held out for particular criticism, the importance of the cantor was undeniable. Humorists put the cantor on the same plateau as the rabbi, sometimes at the expense of an even more lightly regarded functionary: the *shammes*.[114] The well-worn story that appears in several unattributed versions tells of the solemn approach of rabbi, cantor, and *shammes* to the Holy Ark on the Day of Atonement:

> To show his humility, the rabbi cries out: "O Lord, I am nothing!"
> The cantor, not to be outdone, cries out: "O Lord, I am nothing!"
> The *shammes* come next and he, too, cries out: "O Lord, I am nothing!"
> The cantor looks at the *shammes* disdainfully, then turns to the rabbi and says: "Look who thinks he is nothing!"

---

dean of Orthodox rabbis in postwar Toronto, leveled the same charge against rabbis at the end of his collection of sermons published in 1945. He observed with disdain that North American rabbis were increasingly becoming entertainers, summoning up laughter or tears, but at the cost of less and less Torah content.

112. Millgram, *Jewish Worship*, 526.

113. Millgram, *Jewish Worship*, 526.

114. A Yiddish word from the Hebrew root "to serve," the *shammes* was the synagogue sexton, also known as beadle, and currently known as ritual director. He was assigned all manner of support roles.

To be sure, in this story, it is the cantor who self-servingly seeks to put himself on par with the rabbi, but so did many congregations, as the following unattributed story indicates:

> Terrorists invade a synagogue and take the rabbi, cantor, and president hostage. The terrorists intend to kill them all but to demonstrate their compassion they offer all three one last request.
>
> The rabbi says: "I have been working on this sermon for so many years and before I die I would like the opportunity to preach it."
>
> The cantor says: "I have composed a piece of liturgical music that is long and demanding. I would like to sing it."
>
> The synagogue president says: "Shoot me first."

This story resonates with many congregants who bemoan the burden they bear in being forced to listen to clergy with mediocre skills and lackluster ability. But that the rabbi and cantor were equally reviled is a testament to their comparable status.

What emerges from this brief and by no means comprehensive analysis of the cantor as a subject of humor is that as much as cantors were the targets of jokesters, their very humiliation was evidence of their esteemed standing. While this initially may seem preposterous, it is supported by scholarship.

Among the regnant theories of humor is that of incongruity.[115] Philosopher John Morreall,[116] for instance, maintains that incongruity—and the ensuing humor—results from the recognition of the absurd clash between conflicting ideas or experiences. In the case of the cantor, the jokes that have been passed down and repeated with amusement speak to the distance between the ideal and the actual; between the cantor as mediator of Jewish prayer, the link between human beings and God, the expert who fulfills the obligations of the untutored, and the cantor as a pretender with overwhelming ego and underwhelming talent or character. And in highlighting the incongruity, each humorous story induces Jews to make a cognitive shift and a psychological reorientation that affirms the ideal.

Hence, while cantor jokes reveal the duality of attitudes toward the cantor reflected in Jewish law and literature—at times defending the

---

115. Cf. D.H. Monro, *Argument of Laughter*. Among the champions of this theory of humor were Frances Hutcheson and Arthur Schopenhauer.

116. Morreall, "New Theory of Laughter."

cantor and at times deriding—the intention of Jewish humorists was to reassert the standards demanded of cantors and hold the occupiers of that esteemed and essential position accountable. Renewed respect would ineluctably result.

3

The Cantor: Retrospect and Prospect

In 1957, Rabbi Abraham Joshua Heschel, Professor of Ethics and Mysticism at the Jewish Theological Seminary of America and author of several influential books on theology, was invited to deliver a paper to the Cantor's Assembly, the nascent international organization of cantors serving in conservative synagogues, at the assembly's tenth annual convention held in the Catskill Mountains. At the time of his speaking, the Cantor's Institute, as it was then called—the training academy for new cantors at the Jewish Theological Seminary—was five years old. Graduates of the school, along with other qualified cantors accepted as members of the assembly, were to fill the positions open in the expanding number of synagogues built in the American postwar building boom. In his address, titled in its printed form, "The Vocation of the Cantor," Heschel opted to provoke rather than compliment his audience.

To be sure, he sympathized with his listeners, admitting that: "One must realize the difficulties of the Cantor. The call to prayer often falls against an iron wall. The congregation is not always ready to worship. The Cantor has to pierce the armor of indifference . . ."[1] But Heschel did not let his sympathy shade his criticism. He added:

> The tragedy of the synagogue is in the depersonalization of prayer. *Hazzanuth* has become a skill, a technical performance, an impersonal affair. As a result the sounds that come out of the *hazzan* evoke no participation. They enter the ears; they do

1. Heschel, *Insecurity of Freedom*, 244.

not touch the hearts. The right Hebrew word for Cantor is *baʾal tefillah*, master of prayer. The mission of the Cantor is to lead in prayer. He does not stand before the ark as an artist in isolation, trying to demonstrate his skill or to display vocal feats. He stands before the Ark not as an individual but with a Congregation. He must identify himself with the Congregation. His task is to represent as well as to inspire a community. Within the synagogue music is not an end to itself but a means of religious experience. Its function is to help us to live through a moment of confrontation with the presence of God; to expose ourselves to Him in praise, in self-scrutiny and in hope.[2]

Heschel did not mince words. He accused members of the very audience he addressed of forgetting their mission, of concentrating on being technically excellent rather than being inspirational. Shortly thereafter he again indicted his audience for their collective egotism: "[Music] often voices man's highest reverence, but often brings to expression frightful arrogance."[3] And even more bluntly, he said: "The Cantor who prefers to display his voice rather than to convey the words and to set forth the spirit of the words, will not bring the congregation closer to prayer."[4]

Heschel sounded an alarm. Synagogues—although few recognized the sad state of affairs during this time of expanding memberships and burgeoning buildings—are in fragile spiritual shape. And one of the principal culprits is the cantor. Heschel was relentless: "One of the main causes of the decay in prayer in the synagogue is the loss of *nussah*, the loss of chant; and surely the disengagement of cantorial music from *nussah* has been most harmful."[5] And even more pointedly, he warned: "The decline of *hazzanuth* will continue as long as we fail to realize that reverence and faith are as important as talent and technique, and that the music must not lose its relationship to the spirit of the words."[6]

Heschel offered more than condemnation. He offered a solution. He called it "a liturgical revival."[7] The program for liturgical revival should include a renewed effort to understand the words of the prayer book both by cantors and their congregants. It requires a careful and considered

2. Heschel, *Insecurity of Freedom*, 244.
3. Heschel, *Insecurity of Freedom*, 246.
4. Heschel, *Insecurity of Freedom*, 247.
5. Heschel, *Insecurity of Freedom*, 246.
6. Heschel, *Insecurity of Freedom*, 247.
7. Heschel, *Insecurity of Freedom*, 247.

effort to match the music with the words. "All we have are words in the liturgy and reverence in our hearts," says Heschel, "But even these two are apart from each other. It is the task of music to bring them together."[8] And it is the task of the cantor to find the proper music. Most important of all, it requires cantors to understand deeply that "his audience is God."[9]

Heschel confirms much of the criticism that has been directed against cantors for almost two millennia, criticism that ranges from ignorance to arrogance. But what is of particular note is his observation that the cantorial arts were in decline even as some of the world's most renowned cantors were still attracting hundreds, if not thousands, to concerts and to their synagogues.

The theme of *hazzanut* in decline recurs. It is repeated with increasing intensity. In 1973, Rabbi Harold Schulweis condemned as "metallic"[10] the synagogue service and advocated a restructuring of the synagogue, creating smaller, congenial groupings called *havurot*. The decentralization of the synagogue was partly motivated by the recognition that for most Jews prayer is alien. The restructuring of the synagogue entailed a rethinking of the role of ritual professionals, including the cantor and the rabbi.

Twenty five years after Heschel's critique, one of the notable chroniclers of cantors and their music, Akiva Zimmerman, responded to an interviewer's question saying:

> Chazanuth in general is declining, mainly because there is no more challenge to the young and talented Chazan. He feels no necessity or need to continue to study, to develop his musicality, and to inspire his congregants, because there is no demand for it. In those congregations where they engage Chazanim, either as part-time or just for the High Festivals, they would not make any demands on the young Chazan. As long as he has a pleasant voice and knows how to lead the Congregation in prayer it is sufficient for them, and I think this applies to every country.[11]

What seems like a defense of cantors (the congregation is to blame for not demanding more) is really a further indictment. Cantors are not incapable or untalented, argues Zimmerman; they are merely lazy and

---

8. Heschel, *Insecurity of Freedom*, 250.

9. Heschel, *Insecurity of Freedom*, 247.

10. Schulweis, "Restructuring the Synagogue," 13.

11. Delibe, "Cantors' Review," para. 20.

indifferent. Further, by 1982, it was clear that the congregational land-
scape was changing. Full-time cantors were disappearing, replaced by
part-timers.

Four years later, in an interview with the *Chicago Tribune*,[12] Samuel
Rosenbaum, then Executive Vice President of the Cantors' Assembly,
conceded that forty-five to sixty cantorial positions were going unfilled.
It is also the case that many synagogues were content to allow untrained
laymen to lead prayer services in whole or part. By 2008, the decline of
the cantor was exacerbated by the economy. As reported by the Jewish
Telegraphic Agency,[13] budgetary constraints and diminishing membership had compelled many synagogues to leave the position of cantor
unfilled. And faced with a choice between hiring a rabbi or a cantor,
other synagogues had opted for a rabbi and replaced the cantor with a
"cantorial-soloist" or layperson.

In 2010, partly as a cost-saving measure and partly a casualty of its
"re-envisioning program," the Jewish Theological Seminary of America
decided to eliminate the position of dean of the Miller Cantorial School.
Indeed, the "re-envisioning" was impelled by the decline in enrollment.
In the four years between 2008 and 2012, the number of students enrolled
in the Conservative Movement's cantorial program dropped by almost 50
percent, from thirty-eight to twenty students.[14] Only three graduates of
the H. L. Miller School of Sacred Music of the Jewish Theological Seminary of America were invested as cantors in 2016, and six in 2017. The
Reform Movement showed a parallel decline in the same period. Students attending the Debbie Friedman School of Sacred Music dropped
from forty-three to thirty-six students.[15] Accelerating the decline in the
cantorial arts is the fact that many more synagogue attendees are He-
braically illiterate. As a result, cantors have found a need to include more
niggunim,[16] wordless melodies, thus becoming the architects of their
own demise. Ironically, the inability of congregants to recite the proper

12. "Judaism's Call for More Cantors Draws Only a Whispered Response," *Chicago Tribune*, June 27, 1986.

13. October 3, 2008.

14. As evidenced by the names of graduates posted on the internet.

15. All figures come from *The Jewish Week*, "Cantors Changing Tune To Stay
Relevant," November 1, 2012.

16. *The Jewish Week*, "Cantors Changing Tune To Stay Relevant," November 1,
2012..

prayers—the initial impetus for establishing the position of cantor—is now the reason for disestablishing the very same position.

The decline of the cantor was all but predictable. Postwar suburban synagogues built huge school wings, but small sanctuaries. And as Lawrence Hoffman noted, "floor plans tell the tale."[17] While Jewish education was a priority, Jewish prayer was not. And even in those synagogues that included large and ornate sanctuaries, it was clear early on that the seats would go unfilled. The 1970 National Jewish Population Survey revealed that 55 percent of American Jews attended synagogue prayer services fewer than four times annually. As prayer became increasingly ignored, the cantor became increasingly irrelevant.

Far fewer cantors serve in Orthodox synagogues, but not for the same reasons. Despite the protestations of some who view the cantor as an enhancement of prayer and a guarantor of decorousness,[18] most Orthodox synagogues are content to rotate *davening* among the many capable worshipers, including those whose *yeshiva* experiences did not include any exposure to a cantor. Some Orthodox synagogues, no doubt, are reflective of the opinion of the Alter Rebbe of Chabad-Lubavitch, who dispensed with the position altogether.

Going forward, there is even more reason to worry about the future of the cantorate. Writing in 2005,[19] American historian Professor Jack Wertheimer identified a number of factors that further compromise the cantor's function and standing. Among these factors are the experimentation with new kinds of music and the reconfiguration of the role of the cantor accordingly;[20] the trend toward customized prayer books[21] making knowledge of both the liturgy and the *nussah* less important; replacing the traditional cantorial repertoire with popular music often imported from summer camps or from the Carlebach songbook;[22] the transformation of

17. Hoffman, "From Common Cold," 10.

18. Cantor David Nemtzov writes: "The tradition of having a cantor and choir in the synagogue dates back centuries, and to this day, those synagogues display a sense of dignity as well as better decorum" (Letter to the *Canadian Jewish News*, July 30, 2015). He calls the dearth of cantors in Orthodox synagogues in large cities like Toronto "pathetic."

19. Wertheimer, "American Synagogue." Though his research focuses on American synagogues, the same largely applies to Canadian synagogues as well.

20. Wertheimer, "American Synagogue," 29.

21. Wertheimer, "American Synagogue," 31.

22. Wertheimer, "American Synagogue," 35. Cf. Kligman, "Contemporary Jewish Music in America."

the cantor from a classically trained musician to a simple song leader;[23] and the balancing of competing congregational constituencies resulting in far less time for *hazzanut*.[24] Further, among the common themes for the twenty-first-century synagogue, Wertheimer sees an emphasis on greater congregational participation[25] and communal singing[26]—what some have called "the democratization of prayer"—which can only limit the function of the cantor, particularly when the shortening of the time for prayer services is the rule.

But pessimism need not be the consequence. If the ferocity and persistence of criticism are indicators, cantors have been "in decline" from the inception of the position. Philosopher and historian Simon Rawidowicz (d. 1957) once chided pessimists who latched on to the predictions of doom for Jews and Judaism, dismissing their view as "the myth of the ever-dying people."[27] The same might be applied to those who predict the demise of the office of cantor and the death of *hazzanut*. It is the myth of the "ever-dying cantor." The cantorate is not in the midst of elimination, but of transformation.

To be sure, there is some evidence that the traditional cantorial function might enjoy a renaissance. In 2006, a full house of 4,000 fans filled New York's Metropolitan Opera House to hear Cantor Yitzchak Helfgott, accompanied by sixty-four members of the New York Philharmonic Orchestra, in a rousing concert. More than 1,000 disappointed customers remained on the waiting list.[28] Pro Musica Judaica, an organization launched in 2008 and sponsored by Charles and Robyn Krauthammer, is dedicated to recovering the rich tradition of Jewish liturgical music. In addition to a series of concerts held at the Kennedy Center in Washington, D.C., a successful and well-attended concert in New York's historic Eldridge Street Shul, now essentially a museum, took place in 2012. Rabbi Allan Nadler, Professor of Jewish Studies at McGill University in Montreal, argues[29] that concerts like these augur well for the future

23. Wertheimer, "American Synagogue," 35.

24. Wertheimer, "American Synagogue," 37.

25. Wertheimer, "American Synagogue," 76.

26. Wertheimer, "American Synagogue," 74.

27. Rawidowicz, *Israel*, 51.

28. Gabriel Sanders, "After Years of Decline, Cantorial Music Gets a Second Act," *The Jewish Daily Forward*, December 8, 2006.

29. "Not Dead Yet: The Remarkable Renaissance of Cantorial Music," *Jewish Ideas Daily*, December 25, 2012.

of *hazzanut* and *hazzanim*. Whereas the pool for *hazzanim* in the past had been central European communities, the revival is centered in Israel and, perhaps surprisingly, in the Hasidic world. And interest is strong in both these sectors. Others argue that the trending "return to tradition" can only help revive interest in the cantorial arts.[30]

Whether the renewed interest in *hazzanut* can be sustained (assuming it is sustainable) is a legitimate question, but one that misses the point. If anything, the role and the function of the cantor, as evidenced by the sources, have been remarkably adaptive. The cantor evolved from a functionary serving to fulfill the Jewish legal obligation of prayer into a mediator bridging the gap between the earthly and the heavenly realms. Cantors changed from strictly following a fixed liturgy that pleased the rabbis to musical extemporizing that pleased the congregation. And while the introduction of *piyyut* was a controversial cantorial innovation, the resistance of the rabbis was eventually limited to point of placement rather than a matter of complete exclusion. Some cantors recognized the inclusion of children in the service centuries before American congregations became obsessed with juvenile participation. Other cantors imported tunes from popular songs to the chagrin of some rabbis, but with the intent of enlivening the service. In each of theses cases, cantors were at the forefront of liturgical experimentation. Riv-Ellen Prell has called the synagogue "the testing ground" for shaping Judaism.[31] Cantors have been at the forefront of determining the parameters the testing would take.

Given the history of cantorial transformation, there is good reason to believe it is still a work in progress rather than an institution that has run its course. The position of cantor has changed, evolved, transmogrified (as the title *hazzan* itself has) to suit the needs of the Jewish people. So it should continue. Rather than think and talk of decline, we should be thinking metamorphosis. Cantors are now being trained to oversee the congregational school, teach adult education classes, perform pastoral duties, work in administration, blow shofar, and read Torah. In other words, revert back to the original concept of *hazzan ha-kenesset*. It is a case of back to the future.

Rabbi Dana Evan Kaplan reacted to the decision of the Reform Movement to ordain cantors by telling *The Jewish Week*: "I would argue that they don't need a rabbi if a cantor can do everything rabbis can do.

30. Gabriel Sanders, "After Years of Decline, Cantorial Music Gets a Second Act," *The Jewish Daily Forward*, December 8, 2006.

31. Prell, "Communities of Choice and Memory," 271.

They can sing and run the music. With the emphasis on spirituality, you don't need a great scholar . . . I would see the cantor as more important to the future of American Judaism. I hate to say it, but cantors can make people feel good."[32] And with apologies to Carl W. Buehner, people may forget what cantors pray, but they will never forget how cantors made them feel.

---

32. Chernikoff, "Cantors Changing Their Tune," 5.

Bibliography

Abrahams, Israel. *Jewish Life in the Middle Ages*. New York: Atheneum, 1973.

Al-Ashbili, Yom Tov. *She'elot U'Teshuvot RITVA*. Edited by Yosef Kafah. Jerusalem: published by the author, 1959.

Alharizi, Judah. *The Book of Tahkemoni: Jewish Tales from Medieval Spain*. Translated by David Simha Segal. Portland: Littman, 2003.

Alon, Gedalyahu. *The Jews in Their Land in the Talmudic Age*. Jerusalem: Magnes, 1980.

Ausubel, Nathan, *A Treasury of Jewish Folklore: Stories, Traditions, Legends, Humor, Wisdom, and Folk Songs of the Jewish People*. New York: Crown, 1953.

Ben Abraham, Zedekiah. *Shibbolei Ha-Leket Ha-Shalem*. Edited by Solomon Buber. Jerusalem: Pe'er Ha-Torah, 1977.

Ben-Amos, Dan. *Folktales of the Jews*. 3 vols. Philadelphia: Jewish Publication Society, 2007.

ben Asher, Jacob. *Arba'ah Turim*. 7 Vols. New York: Grossman, n.d.

Berlin, Adele, and Marc Zvi Brettler. *The Jewish Study Bible*. New York: Oxford, 2004.

Breslov, Nahman. *Likutey MoHaRaN*. Jerusalem: Breslove Research Institute, 1995.

Brody, Robert. *The Geonim and the Shaping of Medieval Culture*. New Haven: Yale University Press, 1998.

Buber, Martin. *Tales of the Hasidim*. New York: Schocken, 1947.

Burkholder, J. Peter, et al. *A History of Western Music*. 9th ed. New York: Norton, 2014.

Caplan, Kimmy. "In God We Trust: Salaries and Income of American Orthodox Rabbis, 1881–1924." *American Jewish History* 86.1 (1998) 77–106.

Chazan, Robert, and Raphael Marc Lee. *Modern Jewish History: A Source Reader*. New York: Schocken, 1977.

Chernikoff, Helen. "Cantors Changing Their Tune." *The Jewish Week*. November 1, 2012. https://jewishweek.timesofisrael.com/cantors-changing-tune-to-stay-relevant/.

Cordovero, Moses. *The Palm Tree of Deborah*. Trnslated by Louis Jacobs. New York: Sepher-Hermon, 1974.

Dan, Joseph. "The Emergence of Mystical Prayer." In *Studies in Jewish Mysticism*, edited by Joseph Dan and Frank Talmage, 85–120. Cambridge, MA: AJS, 1982.

Dan, Joseph, and Frank Talmage, eds. *Studies in Jewish Mysticism*. Cambridge, MA: AJS, 1982.

Danby, Herbert. *The Mishnah*. London: Oxford University Press, 1974.

De Castro, Adolfo, and Edward D. G. M. Kirwan. *The History of Jews in Spain: From the Time of Their Settlement in That Country till the Commencement of the Present Century*. Westport, CT: Geenwood, 1851.

Delibe, Elie, ed. "Is Chazanut in Decline?" *The Cantors' Review* (Sept 1982). https://geoffreyshisler.com/the-cantors-review/is-chazanut-in-decline/

Donin, Hayim Halevi. *To Pray as a Jew*. New York: Basic, 1980.

Eisenberg, Ronald L. *Jewish Traditions: A Jewish Publication Society Guide*. Philadelphia: JPS, 2004.

Epstein, Isidore. *The "Responsa" of Rabbi Solomon ben Adreth of Barcelona (1235–1310)*. New York: Ktav, 1968.

Feldman, Louis H. "Diaspora Synagogues." In *Sacred Realm: The Emergence of the Synagogue in the Ancient World*, edited by Steven Fine, 48–66. New York: Yeshiva University Museum, 1996.

Fine, Lawrence. *Safed Spirituality*. New York: Paulist, 1984.

Finkelstein, Louis. "The Origin of the Synagogue." *Proceedings of the American Academy for Jewish Research* 30 (1928) 49–59.

———. *Sifre*. New York: JTSA, 1969.

Fishkoff, Sue. "As Rural Congregations Get Smaller, They Make Due Without Cantors, Rabbis." *Jewish Journal*, September 8, 2005. https://jewishjournal.com/culture/religion/membership/11872/.

Flam, Gila. "Music." In *Encyclopedia Judaica, Vol. 14*, edited by Fred Skolnik, 636–701. 2nd ed. 22 vols. New York: Gale, 2007.

Fleischer, Ezra, "Towards a Clarification of the Expression 'Poreis 'al Shema.'" *Tarbiz* 41 (1972) 133–44.

Foerster, Gideon. "Synagogue Art and Architecture." In *The Synagogue in Late Antiquity: Conference: Papers*, edited by Lee I. Levine, 139–46. Philadelphia: American Schools of Oriental Research, 1987.

Fox, Marvin. *Interpreting Maimonides: Studies in Methodology, Metaphysics and Moral Philosophy*. Chicago: University of Chicago Press, 1990.

Fox, Samuel J. *Hell in Jewish Literature*. Northbrook, IL: Whitehall, 1972.

Frideman, Jonathan L. "Know Before Whom You Stand." *Journal for the Renewal of Religion and Theology* 4.9 (2008) 1–5.

Ginzberg, Louis. *Legends of the Jews*. 7 vols. Philadelphia: Jewish Publication Society of America, 1968.

Goldin, Hyman. *Code of Jewish Law*. New York: Hebrew, 1961.

Golinkin, David, ed. *Proceedings of the Committee on Jewish Law and Standards of the Conservative Movement 1927–1970*. 3 vols. Jerusalem: Rabbinical Assembly, 1997.

———, ed. *The Responsa of Professor Louis Ginzberg*. New York: JTSA, 1996.

Greenberg, Blu. "Woman as Messenger of the Congregation." *Journal of Synagogue Music* 17.1 (1987) 9–16.

Gumbiner, Abraham. *Magen Avraham on Shulhan Arukh*. Dyhemfurth: published by the author, 1692.

Hafstein, V. T. "The Politics of Origins." *Journal of American Folklore* 117.465 (Summer 2004) 300–15.

Haldon, John F. *Byzantium in the Seventh Century the Transformation of a Culture*. Cambridge: Cambridge University Press, 2003.

Harris, William V. *Ancient Literacy*. Cambridge, MA: Harvard University Press, 1989.

Heller, Charles. *What to Listen for in Jewish Music*. Toronto: Ecanthus, 2006.

Heschel, Abraham Joshua. *The Insecurity of Freedom*. New York: Schocken, 1972.

———. *Maimonides*. New York: Farrar, Straus, Giroux, 1982.

Heskes, Irene. "Miriam's Sisters: Jewish Women and Liturgical Music." *Notes* 48.4 (June 1992) 1193–1202.

Hoffman, Lawrence. "From Common Cold to Common Healing." *CCAR Journal* 41 (Spring 1944) 1–30.

Howe, Irving. *World of Our Fathers: The Journey of the East European Jews to America and the Life They Found and Made*. New York: Touchstone, 1976.

Idelsohn, Abraham Zevi. *Jewish Music in Its Historical Development*. New York: Schocken, 1967.

Jastrow, Marcus. *A Dictionary of the Targumim, the Talmud Babli and Yerushalmi, and the Midrashic Literature*. New York: Judaica, 1971.

Jedlicki, M. Z. "German Settlement and the Teutonic Order." In *The Cambridge History or Poland*, edited by William F. Reddaway et al., 125–47. Cambridge: Cambridge University Press, 1950

Josephus, Flavius. "Against Apion." In *The Works of Josephus*, translated by William A. M. Whiston, 773–812. Peabody, MA: Hendrickson, 1987.

Kadushin, Max. *Worship and Ethics: A Study in Rabbinic Judaism*. Evanston, IL: Northwestern University Press, 1964.

Kaplan, Aryeh. *Until the Mashiach: The Life of Rabbi Nachman's Biography*. Edited by Dovid Shapiro. Jerusalem: Breslov Research Institute, 1985.

Kellerman, Harry. *Saturday the Rabbi Went Hungry*. New York: Crown, 1966.

Klein, Isaac. *A Guide to Jewish Religious Practice*. New York: Jewish Theological Seminary of America, 1979.

Kligman, Mark. "Contemporary Jewish Music in America." *American Jewish Yearbook* 101 (2001) 115–25.

Kumove, Shirley, and Frank Newfeld. *Words Like Arrows: A Collection of Yiddish Folk Sayings*. New York: Warner, 1986.

Landman, Leo. *The Cantor: An Historic Perspective*. New York: Yeshiva University Press, 1972.

Levine, Lee I. "The Second Temple Synagogue: The Formative Years." In *The Synagogue in Late Antiquity: Conference: Papers*, edited by Lee I. Levine, 7–31. Philadelphia: American Schools of Oriental Research, 1987.

Lieberman, Saul. *Hellenism and Jewish Palestine*. New York: Jewish Theological Seminary of America, 1962.

———. *Tosefta Kifshuta*. Jerusalem: Jewish Theological Seminary of America, 1992.

Lyman, Darryl. *Great Jews in Music*. New York: Jonathan David, 1986.

Marcus, Jacob Rader. *The Jew in the Medieval World: A Source Book: 315–1791*. New York: Atheneum, 1969.

Medwed, Karen G. Reiss. "Walking Humbly with God." In *The Observant Life: The Wisdom of Conservative Judaism for Contemporary Jews*, edited by Martin Samuel Cohen and Michael Katz, 5–60. New York: Aviv, 2012.

Metzker, Isaac. *A Bintel Brief: Sixty Years of Letters from the Lower East Side to the Jewish Daily Forward*. New York: Schocken, 1990.

Meyers, Eric M. "Current Galilean Synagogue Studies." *The Synagogue in Late Antiquity: Conference: Papers*, edited by Lee I. Levine, 139–46. Philadelphia: American Schools of Oriental Research, 1987.

Millgram, Abraham Ezra. *Jewish Worship*. Philadelphia: Jewish Publication Society of America, 1971.

Monro, D. H. *Argument of Laughter*. Notre Dame, IN: University of Notre Dame Press, 1963.

Morreall, John. "A New Theory of Laughter." In *Philosophy of Laughter and Humor*, edited by John Moreall, 38–59. Albany, NY: State University of New York Press, 1987.

Neusner, Jacob. *The Talmud of the Land of Israel.* 35 vols. Chicago: University of Chicago Press, 1988.

Noy, Dov. *A Tale for Each Month . . . 12 Selected and Annotated IFA Folktales.* Haifa: Ethnological Museum and Folklore Archives, 1965.

Patterson, Vincent. "The Cantor: From Soloist to Song Leader Leader." *Pastoral Music Magazine* 2.4 (Apr-May 1978) 23–25.

Peretz, Isaac Leib. "Ne'ilah in Gehenna." In *A Treasury of Yiddish Stories*, edited by Irving Howe and Eliezer Greenberg, translated by A. M. Klein, 213–19. New York: Viking, 1968.

Posner, Raphael, and Israel Ta-Shema. *The Hebrew Book: An Historical Survey.* Jerusalem: Keter, 1975.

Prell, Riv-Ellen. "Communities of Choice and Memory: Conservative Synagogues in the Late Twentieth Century." In *Jews in the Center: Conservative Synagogues and their Members*, edited by Jack Wertheimer, 269–325. New Brunswick, NJ: Rutgers University Press, 2000.

Rawidowicz, Simon. *Israel: The Ever-Dying People, and Other Essays.* Edited by Benjamin C. I. Ravid. Rutherford, NJ: Fairleigh Dickinson University Press, 1986.

Reddaway, William F., et al., eds. *The Cambridge History of Poland.* 2 vols. Cambridge: Cambriedge University Press, 1950.

Rosten, Leo. *Hooray for Yiddish!* New York: Simon and Schuster, 1982.

———. *The Joys of Yiddish.* Rev. ed. New York: Crown, 2001.

Rubens, Alfred. *A History of Jewish Costume.* New York: Crown, 1973.

Ryback, Solomon F.. "Minkowski's Eighteen Takkanot for the Cantorate." *Journal of Synagogue Music* 6 (1983–1984) 24–30.

Safrai, Shmuel, ed. *The Literature of the Sages.* Philadelphia: Fortress, 1987.

Scholem, Gershom. *Major Trends in Jewish Mysticism.* New York: Schocken, 1941.

Schulweis, Harold. "Restructuring the Synagogue." *Conservative Judaism* 27.4 (Summer 1973) 1–9.

Schwartz, Howard. *Tree of Souls.* Oxford: Oxford University Press, 2004.

Segal, David Simha. *The Book of Tahkemoni: Jewish Tales From Medieval Spain.* Oxford: Littman, 2003.

Shinan, Avigdor. "Synagogues in the Land of Israel: The Literature of the Ancient Synagogue and Synagogue Archaeology." In *Sacred Realm: The Emergence of the Synagogue in the Ancient World*, edited by Steven Fine, 130–52. New York: Yeshiva University Museum, 1996.

Sigal, Phillip. "Responsum on the Status of Women: With Special Attention to the Questions of Shaliah Tzibbur, Edut, and Gittin." In *Proceedings of the Committee on Jewish Law and Standards of the Conservative Movement: 1980-1985.* New York: Rabbinical Assembly, 1988.

Shir Ha-Shirim Rabbah. *Midrash Rabbah.* Edited by Moshe Aryeh Mirkin. 9 vols. Tel Aviv: Yavneh, 1956–64.

Singer, Isidore, et al., eds. *The Jewish Encyclopedia.* 12 vols. New York: Funk and Wagnalls, 1901–1906.

Sky, Hyman. "Development of the Office of the Hazzan Through the Talmudic Period." PhD diss., Dropsie University, 1977.

Slobin, Mark. *Chosen Voices: The Story of the American Cantorate.* Urbana, IL: University of Illinois Press, 2002.

Spalding, Henry. *Encyclopedia of Jewish Humor: From Biblical Times to the Modern Age.* Middle Village, NY: Jonathan David, 1969.

Sperling, Harry, et al., trans. *The Zohar.* 5 vols. London: Soncion, 1970.

Spitzer, Shlomo, ed. *Sefer MaHaRIL*. Jerusalem: Machon Yerushalayim, 1989.

Strunk, Oliver, et al. *Source Readings in Music History*. New York: Norton, 1998.

Telushkin, Joseph. *Jewish Humor: What the Best Jewish Jokes Say About the Jews*. New York: William and Morrow, 1992.

Townsend, John. *The Study of Judaism*. New York: ADL, 1972.

Trachtenberg, Joshua. *Jewish Magic and Superstition*. New York: Behrman, 1939.

Twersky, Isidore. *Introduction to the Code of Maimonides*. New Haven: Yale, 1980.

Wertheimer, Jack. "The American Synagogue: Recent Issues and Trends." *American Jewish Yearbook* 105 (2005) 3–83.

Wiernick, Peter. *History of the Jews in America*. New York: Jewish History, 1931.

Yaffe, Mordekhai. *Levush*. Jerusalem: Zikhron Aharon, 2000.

Yahalom, Joseph. "Piyyut as Poetry." In *The Synagogue in Late Antiquity*, edited by Lee I. Levine, 111–26. Philadelphia: ASOR, 1987.

HEBREW WORKS

Abba Mari, Isaac. *Sefer Ha-Ittur*. New York: published by the author, 1979.

Abudraham, David. *Abudraham Ha-Shalem*. Jerusaem: Usha, 1963.

Adret, Solomon. *She'elot U'Teshuvot Ha-RaShBA*. Edited by Zvi Saul Book et al. Jerusalem: Tiferet Ha-Torah Institute, 1990.

Al-Fasi, Isaac. *She'elot U'Teshuvot Ha-RIF*. Jerusalem, 1974.

———. *She'elot U'Teshuvot Rabbenu Yitzhak*. Edited by Zev Wolf Leiter. Pittsburgh: Rambam, 1954.

Alfasi, Yitzhak. *Ha-Rav Mi-Kotzk*. Jerusalem: Mossad Ha-Rav Kook, 2013.

Al-Fasi, Yitzhak. *Sefer Ha-Halakhot*. Warsaw: published by the author, 1859.

Alon, Gedalyahu. *Toldot Ha-Yehudim B'Erez Yosrael B'Tekufat Ha-Mishnah v'Ha-Talmud*. N.p.: Hakibbutz Hameuchad, 1975.

Alshikh, Moshe. *Rav Peninim*. Venice: printed by the author, 1601.

Asher, Rabbenu. *She'elot U'Teshuvot Ha-ROSh*. Teshuvot: Jerusalem, 1971.

Assaf, Simchah. *Ha-Onshin Aharei Hatimat Ha-Talmud*. Jerusalem: printed by the author, 1922.

Bachrach, Yair. *She'elot U'Teshuvot Havat Yair*. Jerusalem: printed by the author, 1973.

Bar Sheshet, Yitzhak. *She'elot U'Teshuvot Ha-RIBaSh*. Jerusalem: printed by the author, 1964.

Ben Hayim, Nissim, ed. *Teshuvot Ha-Geonim, Sha'are Tzedek*. Salonika: printed by the author, 1792.

Ben Moshe, Yitzhak. *Or Zaru'a*. Zhitomir, Ukraine: published by the author, 1862.

ben Yehiel, Asher. *She'lot U'Teshuvot Rabbenu Asher*. Jerusalem: Teshuvot, 1971.

Bonfil, Reuven. *HaRabbanut B'Italia B'Tekufat HaRenaissance*. Jerusalem: Schechter Institute, 2005.

Bonfil, Robert. *The Rabbinate in Renaissance Italy*. Jerusalem: Magnes, Schocken, and Schechter, 2005.

Borensztain, Abraham. *She'elot U'Teshuvot Avnai Nezer*. New York: Friedman, 1965.

Breslov, Nahman. *Likutey MoHaRaN*. Jerusalem: Breslov Research Institute, 1995.

Bruna, Yisrael. *She'elot U'Teshuvot Rabbi Yisrael Bruna*. Jerusalem: printed by the author, 1967.

Buber, Solomon. *Pesiqta D'Rav Kahana*. Lyck, Poland: Mekize Nirdamin, 1868.

Cohen, Boaz. *Kuntras Ha-Teshubot.* Westmead, UK: Gregg International, 1970.

Colon, Yosef. *She'elot U'Teshuvot, MaHaRIK.* Warsaw: published by the author, 1884.

Conforte, David. *Korei Ha-Dorot.* Venice: published by the author, 1746.

Di Modena, Leon. *Bet Yehudah.* Zolkiew, Ukraine: published by the author, 1695.

Druck, Zalman. *Sefer Sha'arei Halakhah.* s.l.: published by the author, 1992.

Duran, Shlomo. *She'elot U'Teshuvot Ha-RaShBaSh.* Edited by Moshe Sobel. Jerusalem: Or Ha-Mizrah, 1998.

Duran, Simon. *She'elot U'Teshuvot Ha-TaShBaZ.* Lemberg, Ukraine: printed by the author, 1891.

Emanuel, Simhah, ed. *Teshuvot Ha-Ge'onim Ha-Hadashot.* Jerusalem: Ofeq Institute, 1995.

Epstein, Yehiel Mikhel. *Arukh Ha-Shulhan.* 8 vols. New York: Frideman, n.d.

Falk, Joshua. *Bet Yisrael (Perisha and Derisha).* New York: Grossman, n.d.

Felder, Gedaliah. *Yesodei Yeshurun.* 2 Vols. Jerusalem: Otzar Ha-Poskim, 1977.

Frankel, David. *Korban Ha-Edah on Jerusalem Talmud.* New York: Otzar Seforim, 1968.

Ganzfried, Shlomo. *Kitzur Shulhan Arukh.* New York: Hebrew, 1961.

Geshuri, Meir Shimon. "Rabbi Ya'akov Prager: The Musician of Alexander." In *Kerem Ha-Hasidut,* edited by David Hayyim Zilberschlag, 153–56. Jerusalem: Zekher Naftali, n.d.

———. "Zlilei Neginah B'veit Alexander." In *Kerem Ha-Hasidut,* edited by David Hayyim Zilberschlag, 145–56. Jerusalem: Zekher Naftali, 1987.

Ha-Hasid, Judah. *Sefer Hasidim.* Edited by Re'uven Margaliot. Jerusalem: Mossad Ha-Rav Kook, 1973.

Ha-Lahmi, David Weisbord. *Hakhmei Yisrael.* 4 vols. B'nei Brak: Mishor, 2001.

Ha-Rofeh, Zedekiah. *Shibbolei Ha-Leket Ha-Shalem.* Edited by Solomon Buber. Jerusalem, 1976.

Heyman, Aaron. *Toldot Tanaim v'Amoraim.* 3 Vols. Jerusalem: Keriah Ne'emanah, 1964.

Hoffman, David Zvi. *Melamed L'Ho-il.* New York: Frankel, 1954.

Hurwitz, Shimon, ed. *Mahzor Vitry.* 2 vols. Nürenberg: Bulka, 1923.

Ibn Migash, Joseph. *Teshuvot Rabbi Yosef ibn Migash.* Jerusalem: M. L. Frumkin, 1974.

Kagan,Yisrael Meir. *Mishnah Berurah.* 6 vols. Tel Aviv: Mercaz L'Hinukh Torani, 1975.

Karelitz, Avraham Yeshaya. *Hazon Ish.* Bnai Brak, Israel: Grainiman, 1951.

Karo, Yosef. *Shulhan Arukh.* New York: Pollack Brothers, 1959.

Katznellenbogen, Meir. *She'elot U'Teshuvot MaHaRaM Mi-Padua.* Edited by Asher Ziv. New York: Yeshivah University Press, 1995.

Klein, Menashe. *Sefer Mishneh Halakhot.* New York: Mishneh Halakhot Institute, 1992.

Landau, Jacob Baruch. *Ha-Agur Ha-Shalem.* Edited by M. Pe'er Herschler. Jerusalem: Moznaim, 1960.

Leib, Hanokh ben Judah. *Rsehit Bikkurim.* Frankfurt: published by the author, 1708.

Levi, Eliezer. *Yesodot Ha-Tefilllah.* Tel Aviv: Abraham Zioni, 1967.

Levin, Benjamin Menashe. *Otzar Ha-Ge'onim.* 13 vols. Jerusalem: Hebrew University Press, 1928–1944.

Liady, Shneur Zalman. *She'elot U'Teshuvot Ha-Rav.* K'far Chabad: Eshel, 2004.

Lieberman, Saul. *Tosefta Kifshuta.* New York: Jewish Theological Seminary, 1992.

Loew, Yehudah Leib. *Ba'er Ha-Goleh.* Prague: published by the author, 1598.

Luria, Solomon. *She'elot U'Teshuvot MaHaRShaL.* Jerusalem: Y. Kohen, 1969.

Maimon, Moses. *Commentary on Mishnah.* Naples: published by the author, 1492.

———. *Teshuvot Ha-RaMBaM*. Edited by Jehoshua Blau. Jerusalem: M'kitzei Nirdamim, 1958.

Maimon, Yehudah Leib HaKohen. *Sarei HaMe'ah*. 3 vols. Tel Aviv: Achiasaf, 1970.

Mandelbaum, B., ed. *Pesiqta D'Rav Kahana*. New York: JTSA, 1962.

Margaliot, Mordechai. *Encyclopedia L'Toldot Gedolei Yisrael*. 4 vols. Tel Aviv: Joshua Chachik, n.d.

Melamed, Ezra Z. *Pirke Minhag v'Halakhah*. Jerusalem: Kiryat Sefer, 1959.

Metzger, Yonah. *She'elot U'Teshuvot Miyam Ha-Halakhah*. Tel Aviv: self-published, 1993.

Meyuchas, Moshe Mordechai. *Teshuvot Ha-Ge'onim Sha'arei Tzedek*. Jerusalem: printed by the author, 1966.

Minz, Moses. *She'elot U'Teshuvot MaHaRaM Minz*. Edited by Yonatan Domb, Jerusalem: Machon Yerushalyim, 1991.

Modena, Yehudah Aryeh. *Ziknei Yehudah*. Edited by Penina Naveh. Jerusalem: Bialik Institute, 1956.

Moellin, Jacob. *Sefer MaHaRIL*. Edited by Shlomo Spitzer. Jerusalem: Mif'al Torat Hakhmei Ashkenaz, 1989.

Reischer, Ya'akov. *Shevut Ya'akov*. Jerusalem: published by the author, 1972.

Rothenberg, Meir. *Teshuvot, P'sakim, U'Minhagim*. 3 vols. Edited by Kahana Y. Z. Kahana. Jerusalem: Mossad HaRav Kook, 1957.

Schick, Moshe. *She'elot U'Teshuvot MaHaRaM Schick*. 2 vols. Jerusalem: published by the author, 1972.

Schreiber, Moshe. *She'elot U'Teshuvot Hatam Sofer*. 3 vols. New York: Grossman, 1958.

Shimoni, Yalkut, ed. *Dov Hyman*. Jerusalem: Mosad Ha-Rav Kook, 2009.

Sifra D'vai Rav. Jerusalem: Sifra, 1959.

Sirkis, Yo'el. *Bayyit Hadash*. Krakow: published by the author, 1633.

Sobel, Moshe. *She'elot U'Teshuvot RaShBaZ*. Jerusalem: Machon Yerushalayim, 1998.

Solnik, Benjamin Aaron. *Sefer Mas'at Binyamin*. Metz: published by the author, 1776.

———. *Mas'at Binyamin*. Cracow: published by the author, 1633.

Sperber, Daniel. *Minhagei Yisrael*. Jerusalem: Mossad HaRav Kook, 1995.

Sperling, Avraham Yizhak. *Sefer Ta'mei Ha-Minhagim*. Lwow, Poland: published by the author, 1896.

Steinhart, Yosef. *She'elot U'Teshuvot Zikhron Yosef*. Padua, Italy: published by the author, 1773.

Sternbuch, Moshe. *She'elot U'Teshuvot Teshuvot V'Hanhagot Ha-Shalem*. 5 vols. Jerusalem: published by the author, 1992–2009.

Suslin, Alexander. *Sefer Ha-Agudah*. Krakow: published by the author, 1571.

Ta-Shma, Israel. "On the Beginning of the Piyyut." *Tarbiz* 53.2 (1984) 285–88.

Uziel, Benzion Mei Hai. *Mishpatei Uziel*. 2nd ed. 4 vols. Tel Aviv: published by the author, 1947–1964.

Weiss, Yitzhak Hirsch. *Dor Dor v'Dorshav*. 2 vols. New York: Platt and Minkus, 1924.

Yaffe, Mordekhai. *Sifrei Ha-Levushim*. Rev. ed. 7 vols. Jerusalem: Ohel Rabbenu Yonosn Ublima, 2004.

Yisraeli, Shaul. *She'elot U'Teshuvot B'mareh Ha-Bazak*. Jerusalem: WZO, 2000.

Zahalon, Yom Tov. *She'elot U'Teshuvot MaHaRYTaZ*. Jerusalem: Machon Yerushalayim, 1979.

Zimra, David. *She'elot U'Teshuvot Ha-RaDBaZ*. 2 vols. New York: Otzar Ha-Sefarim, 1967.

Zundel, Hanokh, ed. *Midrash Tanhuma*. Jerusalem: Lewison-Epstein, 1973.

General Index

Scripture Index

CPSIA information can be obtained
at www.ICGtesting.com
Printed in the USA
LVHW051116050323
740982LV00001B/130

9 781532 658303